# The Loneliest Campaign

Other Books by Irwin Ross

STRATEGY FOR LIBERALS

THE IMAGE MERCHANTS

IRWIN ROSS

# The Loneliest Campaign

## THE TRUMAN VICTORY OF 1948

GREENWOOD PRESS, PUBLISHERS
WESTPORT, CONNECTICUT

**Library of Congress Cataloging in Publication Data**

Ross, Irwin.
 The loneliest campaign.

 Reprint of the ed. published by the New American
Library, New York.
 Includes bibliographical references and index.
 1. Presidents--United States--Election--1948.
2. Truman, Harry S., Pres. U. S., 1884-1972.
I. Title.
[E815.R6 1976] 329'.023'730918 75-22761
ISBN 0-8371-8353-7

Originally published in 1968 by The New American Library,
New York

Reprinted with the permission of The New American Library, Inc.

Reprinted in 1977 by Greenwood Press, Inc.

Library of Congress Catalog Card Number 75-22761

ISBN 0-8371-8353-7

Printed in the United States of America

FOR JULIETTE
AND
GEORGE ABELOFF

# Acknowledgments

In researching this book, I was able to tap the recollections of many of the participants in the events described. I conducted extended (and in some cases serial) interviews with Arthur Barnett, William L. Batt, Jr., Stewart Beach, David E. Bell, Elliott V. Bell, Andrew J. Biemiller, Kenneth Birkhead, R. Burdell Bixby, Charles D. Breitel, Herbert Brownell, Albert Z. Carr, Oscar L. Chapman, Clark M. Clifford, Donald S. Dawson, Paul Douglas, Thomas E. Dewey, George M. Elsey, Adrian Fisher, James C. Hagerty, Leonard W. Hall, Charles A. Halleck, Hubert H. Humphrey, Edwin F. Jaeckle, Harold E. Keller, Evron Kirkpatrick, Paul E. Lockwood, W. McNeil Lowry, the late J. Howard McGrath, Charles S. Murphy, David M. Noyes, Merlyn S. Pitzele, Lee Pressman, Joseph L. Rauh, Jr., Alex Rose, Hugh D. Scott, John F. Shelley, John R. Steelman, David Stowe, J. Strom Thurmond, Rexford G. Tugwell, and Henry Zon. Inasmuch as personal meetings were not possible, I interviewed Charles L. Brannan, James Roosevelt and Samuel I. Rosenman over the telephone.

I had two helpful sessions with Governor Dewey and one with Senator J. Strom Thurmond. President Truman was not available for an interview. Henry A. Wallace was already suffering from his fatal illness when I began my researches. I am most grateful to all the individuals who consented to be interviewed; for those on the losing side in 1948, the memories evoked could not always have been too pleasurable. In most instances, my informants have been cited in the text or notes. In only a few cases, sources did not wish to be identified, and I have also indicated, in the notes, where such reluctance was expressed.

I am particularly indebted to Clark Clifford and George Elsey, who opened their personal files to me. Philip C. Brooks and his staff at the Truman Library in Independence, Missouri, were very helpful in leading me through the archival residue of the campaign; the library has the files and papers of most of Truman's aides and confidants of 1948. Three journalists who covered the campaign —Richard H. Rovere, Robert G. Spivack and James A. Wechsler —gave me the benefit of their personal memories of the events they chronicled. I gained a number of insights into the technical aspects of analyzing the 1948 results from conversations with Louis Harris and Richard M. Scammon. Louis Harris also read the manuscript and was exceedingly generous in making available the services of one of his staff members, Victor A. Soland, who prepared a valuable analysis of the farm vote of 1948.

I wish to express my gratitude, as well, to Patricia Brooke Rummel, for the efficiency with which she handled a variety of research assignments; to Edward T. Chase, for perceptive editorial counsel and an unfailing enthusiasm which at times became contagious; and to Daniel Seligman, Henry T. Volkening and James Wechsler for their painstaking and astute evaluation of the manuscript before it went to the printer.

I.R.

# Contents

# The Loneliest Campaign

## CHAPTER 1

# The Loneliest Campaign

Just about everyone believed that Truman was doomed in 1948. On October 28, the President came to New York City for two days of energetic campaigning. At dusk, his motorcade arrived for a rally at Sara Delano Roosevelt Park on Manhattan's Lower East Side, an impoverished and traditionally Democratic neighborhood. A crowd was awaiting him.

Truman sprang out of his car with his characteristic jauntiness, but at least one member of his entourage was reluctant to join him. Ed Flynn, "boss" of the Bronx and former Democratic national chairman, remained in his car seat. Donald S. Dawson, one of the President's aides, had to lock arms with Flynn and literally pull him out of the car and up onto the platform. "I thought it was important for Flynn to be seen on the platform with the President," Dawson has recalled.[1] Truman clearly needed all the local support he could get. But Flynn, a man who played politics to win, had an equally understandable desire not to be seen with a sure loser.

A few days earlier, in Chicago, Paul Douglas was riding in a car with Adlai Stevenson, on their way out to the stadium where Truman was to speak. Douglas was then a professor at the University of Chicago, making his first campaign for the Senate; Stevenson was the Democratic candidate for governor. Their car passed through the west side of town some time before Truman's motorcade was due; the streets were already packed four and five deep with silent spectators. The crowds were later to cheer enthusiastically when Truman appeared, but Douglas only witnessed the solemn, almost funereal hush—so different from the noisy mobs which had awaited Roosevelt in 1940. Moved by the contrast, Douglas remarked to Stevenson, "They have come out today to see the death of a dream that they cherish." [2] The dream, of course, was that of Roosevelt's New Deal, soon to be effaced by a bland new era in American politics that would bear the name of Thomas E. Dewey.

Long before the campaign began, the certainty of Dewey's victory was almost universally accepted. On the eve of the Republican convention in June, the *New York Times'* James A. Hagerty, dean of American political writers, reported "the general conviction that the nominee of the convention will become the next President of the U.S." [3] Prior to the Democratic convention in July, Joseph and Stewart Alsop wrote that "if Truman is nominated, he will be forced to wage the loneliest campaign in recent history." [4] After the convention opened, Walter Lippmann commented that "Mr. Truman's insistence that he be nominated, though he has been repudiated by the active elements of his party . . . is remarkable as showing how the pomp and power of the Presidency can turn humility into stubborn pride." [5]

After the campaign opened in September, many correspondents noted the warmth and friendliness of the crowds which Truman attracted, but saw no reason to revise their view that he was engaged in a hopeless and quixotic effort. In one of the memorable lines of 1948, Richard H. Rovere wrote in *The New Yorker* that the American people seemed willing to give Truman "just about anything he wants except the Presidency." [6] Governor Dewey shared the same judgment. He went about the country confidently delivering a serial paean to "unity" and carefully avoiding any mention of his opponent's name. "The governor of New York," Sidney Shallett aptly observed in the *Saturday Evening Post,* "talks not like a man who wants to be President, but like a man who already is President in everything but name, and who merely is awaiting the inaugural date before taking over." [7]

For months, the three national polling organizations—Gallup, Roper, Crossley—periodically reported that Dewey was leading Truman by a wide margin. As early as September 9, Elmo Roper announced that he was no longer going to publish a poll on the Presidential race. "Thomas E. Dewey," he declared, "is almost as good as elected . . . That being so, I can think of nothing duller or more intellectually barren than acting like a sports announcer who feels he must pretend he is witnessing a neck and neck race . . ." [8] Roper's judgment impressed the experts because of his own past performance: in 1936—the year scientific polling started in Presidential campaigns—his estimate of Roosevelt's popular vote was off by only 1.1 percent; by 1944, Roper's margin of error had been reduced to .3 percent.

The evidence of the polls seemed to be confirmed by an analysis of what had happened to the old Democratic coalition. Franklin D. Roosevelt's long tenancy in the White House had been basically grounded on the traditional Democratic control of the Solid South, plus a firm hold on the urban voters in the North who generally swung the electoral vote in the most populous states. Truman, by contrast, was harassed by both a right-wing revolt in the South and a left-wing revolt in the North and West. With the States' Rights party in the field, the Solid South had cracked beyond chance of immediate repair; Truman was clearly going to lose the electoral votes of at least four southern states—and perhaps more. In the North, he faced a similar breakaway from the newly created Progressive party of Henry Wallace, whose appeal was to the militantly liberal urban voters who had always favored F.D.R. No one gave Wallace a chance of winning the electoral vote of a single state; on the other hand, he was likely to attract enough votes from Truman in New York, Pennsylvania, Illinois, Michigan, Ohio, and California to allow Dewey to take some or all of those states on a minority poll. In addition, Dewey was the favorite to win the traditionally Republican farm belt of the Midwest, where he had done well against Roosevelt in 1944. It thus seemed impossible for Truman to put together a winning combination of electoral votes.

The psychological atmosphere of the campaign was also demoralizing to Democratic partisans. The Republicans were clearly on an upward spiral, having won control of the House and Senate in 1946. Such a midterm victory by the opposition party had traditionally foreshadowed a Presidential triumph at the next election. The Republicans were well financed, blessed with overwhelming press support, and stimulated by the certainty of a victory long overdue. The Democrats suffered from a malaise that could be traced back to that bleak day in April 1945 when F.D.R. had died. Truman's problem as a candidate, quite apart from the odds against him, was that he inspired disparagement even on the part of citizens who planned to vote for him out of party loyalty, fear of the Republicans, or a simple sense of *faute de mieux*. Measured against the towering memories of F.D.R., he had always been a puny figure. There was no commanding presence about him and when he read a speech, in his flat, staccato manner, the only emotion he seemed sure to arouse was ennui. The common tag of derision applied to Truman was "ex-haberdasher," as if there was something disreputable as well as ridiculous in having once sold gents' furnishings.

As Truman's campaign progressed, periodic expressions of confidence did come, to be sure, from Senator J. Howard McGrath, the Democratic national chairman, but such statements were part of the ritual expected of a national chairman. The President never wavered in his public display of confidence; his bravado won him a measure of admiration, as well as a good deal of ridicule, but it persuaded no one. His staff notably failed to share his confidence— a fact not lost on the reporters traveling on the Truman campaign train.

The outcome seemed so certain that many journals printed Truman's political obituary even before the votes were cast. On the eve of the election, *Life* declared that "the U.S. was about to ditch Truman and take Dewey for reasons that involved the brain as well as the emotions." [9] *Life* wound up its eight-page story on the campaign with a handsome full-page picture of Governor and Mrs. Dewey, captioned, "The next President travels by ferry boat over the broad waters of San Francisco Bay." [10]

Scoring what it no doubt regarded as a coup, the *Kiplinger Magazine* put its November issue to press with a bold-face cover entitled "What DEWEY will do—32-page feature complete in this issue." On election night, November 2, long before all the votes were counted, the Chicago *Tribune* published an early edition with the banner headline "DEWEY DEFEATS TRUMAN." Eagerness to beat the competition also led to a number of morning-after appraisals penned too rashly the night before. Thus, Drew Pearson's widely syndicated column startled his readers, on November 3, with its opening assertion: "I surveyed the close-knit group around Tom Dewey, who will take over the White House 86 days from now." [11] The piece went on to discuss Dewey's cabinet choices.

That same morning, the Alsop brothers published a sober essay which began, "The first post-election question is how the government can get through the next ten weeks. . . . Events will not wait patiently until Thomas E. Dewey officially replaces Harry S. Truman. Particularly in the fields of foreign and defense policy, somebody somewhere in Washington must have authority to give answers that will still be valid after Jan. 20." The Alsop brothers' solution was to have Dewey's State and Defense Department appointees immediately go on the government payroll as "special assistants" in order to work out a smooth transition of power.[12]

Also troubled by the problem of the interregnum, the Detroit *Free Press* presented a bolder solution: Secretary of State George C. Marshall should resign and Truman should appoint John Foster Dulles, Dewey's candidate for the job, as his successor. "That would restore confidence in our foreign policy abroad and at home," the *Free Press* asserted. "True, that is asking a good deal of Mr. Truman. Yet these are times which, with all our unity and patriotism, will ask a great deal more of millions of other Americans." The *Free Press* also bestowed a few pleasantries on our "lame duck" President—"a game little fellow, who never sought the Presidency and was lost in it, but who went down fighting with all he had. . . ." The *Free Press* reassured its readers that Mr. Truman faced no dismal future: "There's first, the prospect of a $25,000 pension as a former President. Then there are all the radio contracts and the magazine articles and books which he can look forward to and which will net him a handsome income—close, they say, to a million. The path for him doesn't lead from the White House to the poor house." [13]

It merely led right back to the White House. Although the outcome was not certain until the morning after the election, Truman's victory was overwhelming. He carried 28 states with 303 electoral votes to Dewey's 16 states with 189 electoral votes. Truman's popular vote was even more impressive—a margin of more than 2 million over Dewey, despite the fact that both the Progressive and States Rights' candidates each polled over 1.1 million votes, which would normally have gone to the Democratic candidate. As expected, Truman lost four states in the formerly Solid South. What was remarkable, however, was that he managed to win without the large blocks of electoral votes of such normally Democratic states as New York, New Jersey, Pennsylvania and Michigan.

It was the most astonishing political upset in modern times. How it occurred, how Truman managed to win out over the defeatism in his own party and the exuberant confidence of his adversaries, how he confounded the experts, embarrassed the pollsters, and at one stroke transformed the political atmosphere will all be examined in considerable detail in the pages that follow.

On the morrow of the election, the dramatic quality of Truman's victory was endlessly celebrated. The drama has hardly lessened, but with the passage of time the historic significance of 1948 emerges more clearly. To start with, the election proved that the Democratic party had become the nation's majority party. It became apparent that Democratic victories in the four preceding Presidential elections were not merely the result of adventitious circumstances, such as the impact of the great depression and the magnetic personality of Roosevelt. Instead, there had been a profound alteration in the political loyalties of the great mass of Americans, a shift of allegiance from the Republican to the Democratic party. Truman's decisive victory in the popular vote, despite the many disadvantages he labored under, confirmed the fact that the nation's center of political gravity had shifted several degrees to the left.

Growing awareness that the Democratic party had become the majority party led to unexpected consequences for the Republicans. The first consequence was the emergence of the movement to nominate Eisenhower in 1952; there is a logical line of progression between the Truman upset and Eisenhower's successive victories in 1952 and 1956, as we shall have occasion to demonstrate. A similar connection exists between the events of 1948 and the Goldwater boom which began in 1961, reached fruition with his nomination in July 1964, and ended four months later in disaster. The Goldwater adventure was perhaps the most paradoxical consequence of 1948.

The 1948 election was of historic significance in a variety of other ways. It was the first time the Democrats won the Presidency despite the crackup of the Solid South; Kennedy in 1960 and Johnson in 1964 were later to repeat the feat. The southern defection occurred, of course, because in 1948 the issue of civil rights for the first time figured prominently in a Presidential election. It was Roosevelt who had broken the traditional Republican hold on the Negro vote, but his appeal had more to do with economic issues and his general aura of human brotherhood than with concrete legislative proposals to eliminate racial discrimination. Truman, with his civil rights program, introduced a new issue into Presidential politics whose potency was proven by an outpouring of Negro support which was of considerable importance in a number of states where the popular vote was close.

In 1948, as well, the labor movement became a more significant factor than it had ever been before in a Presidential election. It is true that in 1944, when the CIO's Political Action Committee was organized, the Republicans blew up a huge propaganda storm over labor's role. While the labor effort was helpful in 1944, it was of much greater importance in 1948, when Democratic party organization was weak and defeatist; in many parts of the country the only strong local organization was provided by the labor unions. Labor, of course, had no greater faith in Truman's chances of election than did the party leadership, but it was eager to elect liberal Democrats to the Senate and House of Representatives; its strenuous effort on the part of local candidates inevitably helped the national ticket.

And, finally, 1948 was the year when a whole new generation of political leaders first achieved national prominence. Hubert H. Humphrey, Jr., of Minnesota, after leading the dramatic civil rights fight at the Democratic convention, went on to win his first term as U.S. senator. In Illinois, Adlai Stevenson was elected governor and Paul Douglas U.S. senator; they had both been underdog candidates and they both achieved overwhelming victories.

In Michigan, G. Mennen Williams, a young man whose trademark was a green bow tie, was elected governor on the Democratic ticket; he was to serve in that office until 1961, longer than any other man in Michigan's history. In Connecticut, Democrat Chester Bowles was unexpectedly elected governor. Tennessee sent Estes Kefauver to the Senate, after a hard-fought campaign against the candidate of "Boss" Ed Crump of Memphis. And, although

## CHAPTER 2

# Backdrop
# for 1948

Seventeen years after the great victory of 1948, Clark M. Clifford was enjoying a mellow moment of reminiscence in his Washington law office. "The greatest ambition Harry Truman had was to get elected in his own right," Clifford said. "Every President who comes in as Vice-President has this feeling. Truman felt it especially because he had been so criticized and deprecated." Clifford could speak with the authority of an intimate adviser who had perhaps been more responsible than any other individual, apart from Truman, for Truman's victory.

In part, Clifford said, Truman's eagerness for vindication resulted from the jolting rebuke he suffered in the congressional elections of 1946, nineteen months after he succeeded Roosevelt as President. The Republicans won an overwhelming victory, taking control of both houses of Congress—the first time that had occurred since Hoover had been elected President in 1928. In the Senate, they won a majority of 51 to 45 seats and in the House of Representatives, 246 to 188. "It was a bitter disappointment to Truman," Clifford recalled. "He had asked the American people for a vote of confidence and he got a vote of no confidence." [1] The election seemed to herald the end of the New Deal, the end of Truman, and the resurgence of a militant Republican spirit which had been little more than an impotent whimper during the years of Roosevelt's ascendancy.

So demoralized was the Democratic party that one of its well-regarded senators, J. William Fulbright of Arkansas, went so far as to propose that Truman resign, so that a Republican could take over as President and thereby avoid a deadlock between a Democratic executive and a Republican legislature.[2] Fulbright's plan had a breathtaking simplicity about it. At that time, the Secretary of

State was next in line of succession when there was no Vice-President. Fulbright suggested that Truman appoint Senator Arthur Vandenberg, the leading Republican spokesman on foreign affairs, as Secretary of State, then step down and have Vandenberg succeed him. "My suggestion is not a reflection on anyone's integrity, patriotism or anything else," Senator  Fulbright explained. "It would merely correct an obvious defect in our present system which has resulted when the President is a member of one party and the majority of Congress another." [3]

While Fulbright's eccentric plan won few converts, many responsible citizens would have regarded Truman's departure as no great loss. Disparagement of Truman had become something of a national sport that over the next two years was not to be limited to his ideological opponents; hostility among liberals could be even more bitter because it had been partly provoked by disillusion, partly by nostalgia for Roosevelt, the great lost leader. "To err is Truman" became a popular aphorism. Several versions were heard of the joke that Truman had been late to a meeting because he had awakened that morning somewhat stiff-jointed and had difficulty putting his foot in his mouth. By 1948 a more indulgent crack, in allusion to his keyboard skill, was "Don't shoot the piano player, boys. He's doing the best he can."

On the morrow of Roosevelt's death, in April 1945, there had been great sympathy for Truman. His limitations were lost on no one, least of all on himself, but his humility made him an appealing figure. On April 13, the day after he was sworn into office, he had said to a group of reporters, "Boys, if you ever pray, pray for me now. I don't know whether you fellows ever had a load of hay fall on you, but when they told me yesterday what had happened, I felt like the moon, the stars, and all the planets had fallen on me." People not only sympathized but could identify with Truman as few had sought to identify with the patrician Roosevelt. There was nothing outsize about the new President. He was of medium height, medium weight, an ordinary-looking man with a ready smile and the dapper jauntiness of a country boy who had learned to wear pointed shoes but still preferred a western-style hat. He wore eyeglasses—conventional ones, not pince-nez, as

F.D.R. did. And he spoke in the flat accents of the Midwest, with no echo of fancy eastern prep schools.

To be sure, there was a quality of unpretentious drama about Truman's life story, if only because he had so swiftly been lifted from obscurity by the unpredictable processes of Vice-Presidential selection and the accident of Presidential death. Few men have risen so far powered by so meager a thrust of early ambition. Harry S. Truman was born on May 8, 1884, in the village of Lamar, Missouri. His father was a farmer and mule trader. Harry never got beyond high school, owing to a financial disaster that befell his father, and worked as a timekeeper on a construction project and a bank clerk before returning to the family farm at the age of twenty-two. He stayed there ten years, courting a girl he had known since grade school, Bess Wallace, who lived twenty miles away in Independence. Farmer Truman was passionately fond of playing the piano and reading history; otherwise his interests were conventional—his motorcar, his Masonic lodge, the weekly drill sessions of the National Guard unit. The World War came along and dislodged him from his comfortable rut. Placed in charge of an artillery battery in France in July 1918, Captain Truman discovered that he could command men and he also showed a degree of courage under fire which he had no prior reason to believe he possessed.

He came out of the war with a new sense of self-confidence, promptly married Bess Wallace, and invested his life savings in a Kansas City haberdashery which he and his partner, an army buddy named Eddie Jacobson, were certain would make them a fortune. The year was 1919, Truman was thirty-five, and the country was enjoying boom times. Then depression struck and in 1922 the store closed its doors.

Truman turned to politics, under the sponsorship of the powerful Pendergast organization which ultimately controlled Kansas City and all of Jackson County. The Pendergasts needed a candidate for one of the three posts of county judge, a misnomer for an administrative office concerned with such matters as the upkeep of county roads and buildings. The choice fell on Truman, for he had a considerable following among veterans and an extensive network of relatives around Jackson County. He won a hard-fought primary, then took the general election with ease—and found himself with a $3,000-a-year job and a new career. Defeated two years later—the only electoral defeat in his career—he made a comeback in 1926, when he was elected presiding judge and served in that post eight years, gaining a reputation as a conscientious official and, above all, an honest one—a rare distinction, in that part of the world, in a job that involved disbursing large sums of money for construction projects.

Truman was but a small cog in the Pendergast machine; he was later to say that Tom Pendergast had never asked him to do a dishonest deed, but for years Truman's reputation was to suffer from guilt by association—an unfailingly loyal association—with one of the most corrupt political gangs in the country. In 1934, through an improbable stroke of luck, Truman obtained a senatorial nomination. Once again Pendergast needed a candidate to make a tough race; his first three choices rejected the offer, and in the end he turned to Judge Truman to be the sacrificial runner. Truman was eager for the chance, campaigned vigorously, and won.

In Washington, he was for a long time an undistinguished figure; derided as "the Senator from Pendergast," he voted the straight New Deal line, tended to the needs of his constituents, and was held at arm's length by the White House; F.D.R. had a fastidious nose for the Pendergast aroma. By the time Truman came up for reelection in 1940, Tom Pendergast was in jail (for not paying income tax on a huge bribe), his machine was in ruins, and Truman was on his own. With meager funds, and a hastily improvised organization of a few old friends, he won the primary by little more than 7,000 votes; it was the triumph of the underdog and a foretaste of 1948. In the general election, he improved on his performance, winning by some 50,000.

It was in his second term that Truman made his mark as a senator. His instrument was a special committee to investigate the national defense program, an ad-hoc body which he persuaded the Senate to establish early in 1941. The Truman Committee, as it came to be known, developed into a kind of congressional conscience and auditor of the entire war production program, crusading against mismanagement, unnecessary production bottlenecks, bureaucratic waste of all kinds; by the time Truman resigned as chairman, in August 1944, it had issued thirty-two reports and saved the taxpayers some fifteen billion dollars, according to Truman's estimate,[4] which few observers were willing to dispute.

The committee's exertions gave Truman the sort of reputation which can lead to lifetime tenancy of a Senate seat; he had come a long way, by May of 1944, when he was sixty years old. Then chance again intervened. A southern revolt had developed against Vice-President Henry Wallace, who was regarded as too militantly liberal; the big city bosses in the North were certain that he would hurt the ticket in the fall; and the aged and ailing President was persuaded to accept a new running mate for the autumn election. After a long series of intricate manuevers, Truman, an avowed noncandidate, emerged as the convention's choice. As a Vice-Presidential candidate, he was an excellent selection, for he had an impeccable New Deal record, he was acceptable both to the South and to organized labor, he was something of a hero of the home front war effort, and he had no enemies. Few people had any reason to believe that he would one day sit in the White House. To millions of Americans, Roosevelt seemed larger than life and indestructible; he was a father surrogate; he would always be President.

As it turned out, Roosevelt served less than three months of his fourth term before he was felled by a cerebral hemorrhage. Initially, while the nation mourned F.D.R., Truman enjoyed a honeymoon with the Congress as with the country. Disenchantment, when it came, was gradual and it was both personal and political. As President, Truman seemed hopelessly miscast, lacking even the dignity associated with his office. A typical display of his style occurred at a state convention of the American Legion in Caruthersville, Missouri, in October 1945. Truman jovially disported himself about the hotel lobby and along the streets as if he were still running for county judge. He signed autographs by the score, gave an exuberant piano concert in the hotel dining room, clambered aboard a "40 and 8" locomotive in the Legion parade, attended the horse races at the county fair, and played a lot of poker—just as he had in the old days. "Mr. Truman did everything except have himself shot from the mouth of a cannon," wrote Edward T. Folliard in the *Washington Post*.[5]

Truman's personality delighted some people, dismayed others, but what fundamentally affected attitudes was the way he faltered and fumbled under a weight of responsibility for which neither experience nor personal endowment seemed to have prepared him. New Dealers were especially dismayed by his erratic ideological course. His rhetoric was suitably liberal on occasion, only to be belied by what were regarded as unnecessary concessions to conservative pressure. Liberals attacked him for undermining price controls, for making a mess of the veterans' housing program, and for such eccentric gestures as trying to draft the railway strikers into the army. His conservative appointments were deplored, as was the departure of many New Deal figures.

To many people, Truman's ineptitude was exemplified by his handling of the railway strike in May 1946. After months of deadlocked negotiations, a nationwide strike was called by the Brotherhood of Locomotive Engineers and the Brotherhood of Railroad Trainmen. A crisis atmosphere quickly developed, for the coal mines were also on strike at the time, causing factory shutdowns and a curtailment of electric power in some areas, and the country had recently been harassed by a massive strike wave in steel, autos, communications, and other industries. Faced with a similar crisis in 1963, the Kennedy administration headed off a railway strike by getting Congress to legislate compulsory arbitration, in itself a drastic and unprecedented solution. Truman went much further. In a dramatic appearance before a joint session of Congress, he demanded the right to draft strikers into the army whenever the national safety was imperiled. After he began his speech, Truman was handed a slip of paper saying that the strike was settled. He made the announcement, but stuck to his legislative proposal. The House of Representatives voted for it overwhelmingly, but in the Senate the bill was blocked by Robert A. Taft, the leader of the Republican conservatives. The incident may well have been Truman's rashest and most inglorious act as President; it enraged his labor supporters and left many disinterested citizens with pronounced doubts about his judgment.

Those doubts were further reinforced a few months later by the odd circumstances surrounding the departure of Henry A. Wallace from Truman's Cabinet. After Wallace had been cast aside in

1944, Roosevelt had made him Secretary of Commerce as a kind of consolation prize. Truman retained him in the office. Wallace was soon off on a foreign policy gambit of his own. While the administration was taking an increasingly firm line toward the Soviet Union—on the grounds that our wartime ally had broken many commitments about the postwar order—Wallace favored a policy of accommodation, lest peace be endangered. He was clearly headed on a collision course with the administration, but Truman seemed unaware of it.

On September 12, Wallace was to address a political rally in New York's Madison Square Garden. Two days before, he called upon the President with a copy of his speech. Wallace had some critical words about the Soviet Union, but he also inveighed against American policy being unduly influenced by Great Britain, spoke tolerantly about Russia's increasing influence in Eastern Europe, where he thought the United States had no business interfering, and argued that "the tougher we get with Russia, the tougher they will get with us." [6]

Truman clearly gave the speech his approval. That was evident at his press conference on the afternoon of September 12. Reporters had obtained advance texts of Wallace's address; one of them asked Truman whether it represented the policy of his administration. "That is correct," said Truman, later adding, "I approved the whole speech." Another correspondent pressed Truman as to whether Wallace's speech indicated "a departure" from Secretary of State Byrnes' policy toward Russia. Truman denied it. "They are exactly in line," he said

The contrary was of course the case. Wallace's speech caused a furor in the United States and abroad. Newspapers reported it as marking a major shift in American policy toward Russia; Secretary of State James F. Byrnes, in Paris attending a conference of foreign ministers, felt he had been both embarrassed and betrayed.[7] Senator Vandenberg, a member of the U.S. delegation, stated bluntly that "we can only cooperate with one Secretary of State at a time." [8]

Truman had blundered badly. He could hardly avow his error; instead, two days after the speech, he issued a clarifying statement. He explained that he had not meant to convey the thought that he had approved the contents of Wallace's speech. Rather, he had merely wanted to indicate that "I approved the right of the Secretary of Commerce to deliver the speech." And he added that there had been "no change in the established foreign policy" of the government.[9] Reporters were not allowed to question Truman about his clarification; it could hardly have sustained textual analysis.

Soon afterward, Wallace announced that he "stood" on his New York speech and that he would be heard from again on foreign policy. At that point, Byrnes wired Truman that if he could not keep his Secretary of Commerce from speaking on foreign affairs, his Secretary of State would have to resign.[10] Within a few days, Truman asked for Wallace's resignation. Even Wallace's detractors regarded him as a victim—and Truman as a fool.

As the 1946 congressional elections approached, Truman had been in office for only nineteen months, but already his administration seemed dispirited and directionless. He had presided over the final victory in the greatest war the country had ever fought, but the mood of exultation and hope had long since faded. People were irritated and bewildered by rising prices, labor strife, shortages of consumer goods of all sorts. Returning veterans had difficulty finding a place to live; the purchase of a new car was often an impossible task, unless one was willing to pay an under-the-table bonus; in many places it was even difficult to come by razor blades and nylon stockings. The frustrations of daily living were easy to attribute to confusion and mismanagement in Washington; the Republicans summed up a national mood and provided a focus for resentment with a brilliant political slogan, "Had enough?" By the time the elections came, the Democratic debacle seemed foreordained.

Thereafter, to almost everybody's surprise, Truman's fortunes began to improve. A few weeks after the elections, he found himself in a dramatic encounter with John L. Lewis, the powerful leader of the United Mine Workers. The previous spring the government had taken over the bituminous coal mines, under its continuing wartime power, and signed a contract that favored the union after Lewis had called off a nationwide strike. In the autumn, however, Lewis suddenly announced that he was going to break the contract on November 20 and indicated that unless he got a better deal, coal would not be mined, under the traditional "no contract, no work" policy of the union. At this juncture, Truman's advisers were divided; some favored appeasing Lewis, others advocated a firm line.[11] Truman took a firm line. The government went into federal court and obtained an injunction prohibiting the strike. Lewis defied the court and was soon held in contempt; the union was fined a record $3,500,000 and Lewis, $10,000. Before the union appeal could be argued, the White House announced that the President would go on radio to urge the miners to disregard their leader and return to work. It was a courageous act, and a gamble: no one knew whether the prestige of the Presidency would outweigh Lewis' hold on the loyalty of his men. A few hours before Truman was to make his speech, Lewis called a press conference and called off the strike.

The episode began an upswing in Truman's popularity that was to continue throughout 1947. The new air of resolution and authority which he had invoked in facing down Lewis was now to be manifested in foreign affairs. Late in February 1947, the British informed the United States that they could no longer afford to aid the Greek government, then engaged in a desperate civil war with Communist guerrillas. If the United States did not immediately take up the burden, the country might soon fall to the Communists. At the same time, Turkey, an anti-Communist bastion on the perimeter of the Soviet Union, was in serious economic trouble. Within a matter of weeks, the Truman administration proposed to Congress a $400 million program for military and economic aid for Greece and Turkey and enunciated a policy which became known as the "Truman Doctrine"—generous American support for nations everywhere which were resisting Communist pressure. Congress followed Truman's lead.

Later in the year, after the new Secretary of State, George C. Marshall, made his famous speech at Harvard, the administration launched the Marshall Plan—a program of massive financial assistance, over a period of years, to repair the physical plants and revive the economies of European countries still crippled by the war. The Marshall Plan was the most generous and imaginative venture in our postwar diplomacy, spurring the European nations to a vast cooperative effort for recovery; over a four-year period the United States was to spend $12.5 billion in aid and lay the basis for the longest era of prosperity in modern European history.

These new ventures in foreign policy, like the showdown with Lewis, displayed Truman for the first time in full command of the powers of his office. While his detractors were by no means silenced, Truman was beginning to win back large groups of disaffected voters. By July 1947, Dr. George Gallup found that 55 percent of the public now favored the Democrats in a Presidential election—a startling shift of sentiment from December 1946, a month after the congressional elections, when only 47 percent would have voted for a Democratic Presidential candidate. Gallup spoke of the Democrats having executed "a major political feat." [12]

By mid-1947, as well, the Truman administration's posture in domestic affairs came into clearer focus. The key event was Truman's vigorous veto of the Taft-Hartley Act, which was no "slave labor law," as the unions were claiming, but which did impose significant restrictions on the exercise of labor's power in collective bargaining. There was of course a large element of irony in Truman's emergence as the champion of the labor movement, little more than a year after he had demanded power to put the railroad strikers into the army. The veto message was also ineffective, inasmuch as Congress passed the law again with more than a two-thirds majority, but Truman's action restored his standing with the unions and made it likely that they would support him in the Presidential election the following year.

The Taft-Hartley veto was an important victory for Truman's liberal advisers. During the previous year or so, a polarization had occurred in the Truman circle, with John W. Snyder, a lifelong friend who was now Secretary of the Treasury, emerging as the leader of the conservatives and Clark Clifford, the President's Special Counsel, becoming leader of the liberal group.[13] Truman, a man of humane instincts but few firm convictions on the great substantive issues of national policy, was at the center of an incessant tug of war; he let himself be pulled first in one direction, then in the other, depending on the varying pressures, at any moment, of expediency, friendship, and what the last admirer with whom he spoke assumed to be the national interest.

The conservatives in Truman's circle included most of his Cabinet appointees and many of his old Senate cronies. The liberal group consisted largely of second-rung government officials whose names were little known to the general public. At the end of 1946, a number of them began to meet regularly each week for dinner at the Wardman Park apartment of Oscar R. Ewing, the director of the Federal Security Agency. Apart from Ewing, members of the informal caucus were Clifford; Leon Keyserling, then a member and later chairman of the Council of Economic Advisers; C. Girard Davidson, Assistant Secretary of the Interior; David A. Morse, Assistant Secretary of Labor; and Charles S. Murphy, one of Truman's administrative assistants.[14]

The group operated as a self-appointed strategy board dealing with domestic issues. Its members' aim was to come to a meeting of minds on specific items of policy, such as the Taft-Hartley veto, and then persuade the President to adopt their thinking. "We were up against tough competition," Clifford has recalled. "Most of the Cabinet and congressional leaders were urging Mr. Truman to go slow, to veer a little closer to the conservative line. They held the image of Bob Taft before him like a bogeyman. We were pushing him the other way, urging him to boldness and to strike out for new, high ground . . . it was two forces fighting for the mind of the President, that's really what it was. It was completely unpublicized, and I don't think Mr. Truman ever realized it was going on. But it was an unceasing struggle . . . and it got to the point where no quarter was asked and none given." [15]

The Clifford group eventually won, for a variety of reasons: the course they advocated appealed to Truman's combative instincts and to his underlying liberal sympathies; it made a good deal of political sense if the administration was to have any hope of winning the 1948 election; and it had a persuasive advocate in the person of Clark McAdams Clifford.

Clifford's emergence as leader of the liberals—one of those accidents in which American political history abounds—deserves some attention at this point.[16] Clifford was no zealot and to most outside observers he seemed a typically bland, homogenized product of the American success factory. He was tall, leanly built, with the wavy blond hair and precision-ground good looks of a movie actor. He had a silken voice, a dazzling smile, and the courtly manners of a less hurried time; nothing ever seemed to ruffle him. He had spent almost his entire life in St. Louis, Missouri, where he had graduated from the Washington University School of Law at the age of twenty-one, and thereafter developed a successful law practice. A Democrat by inheritance, he had once helped manage a congressional campaign, but had never been prominently involved in politics. In his quiet way, however, he was a committed New Dealer, the greatest influence on his political thinking having been the liberal views of his uncle, Clark McAdams, who had been in charge of the editorial page of the St. Louis *Post-Dispatch*.

The war unexpectedly led to Clifford's political career. Joining the Navy as a lieutenant junior grade in 1944, he had a desk job and would have slipped back unnoticed into civilian life, a year or so later, had not a former law client of his, James K. Vardaman, Jr., been appointed naval aide to President Truman. Soon afterward Truman decided to include old friend Vardaman in the entourage which he was taking to the July conference in Potsdam, Germany, where he was to meet with Churchill and Stalin. Vardaman decided he needed someone to mind his shop in Washington and so he had Clifford appointed assistant naval aide.

Clifford, then thirty-nine, arrived at the White House to discover that an assistant naval aide had little to do; to fill in his time he took to helping the President's Special Counsel, Judge Samuel I. Rosenman. Early in 1946, Rosenman left the White House and Truman appointed Vardaman a member of the Federal Reserve Board; Clifford succeeded Vardaman as naval aide and for several months also handled the duties of the Special Counsel's office. In June Truman suggested that it was time Clifford got out of uniform and formally named him Special Counsel.

From the outset, Clifford had hit it off well with Truman; they came from the same part of the country and spoke the same language, though in manner the elegant Clifford and the homespun President seemed miles apart. As Special Counsel, Clifford was responsible for preparing Truman's state papers, public speeches, and a good many private memoranda. It was a job which put him at the fulcrum of power, for the man who writes a President's words inevitably has much to do with determining policy. Clifford was also a master of the art of personal ingratiation and, though an amateur, he was a shrewd political strategist. He, more than anyone else, had persuaded Truman to take on John L. Lewis.[17] By mid-1947, he had become Truman's most influential adviser.[18]

It was one of the ironies—perhaps one of the public relations triumphs—of the 1948 Democratic campaign that it generally gave the impression of being an improvised, desperate effort of an embattled President fighting single-handedly against overwhelming odds. There was no doubt about the desperation of the Democratic campaign, but it was not improvised. Careful planning preceded every step, with the general lines of strategy being articulated as early as the autumn of 1947.

The basic blueprint was contained in a lengthy memorandum on "the politics of 1948," for which Clifford began to gather intelligence and sift ideas in the summer of 1947. The President was all for the project and suggested a variety of individuals to be consulted.[19] When Clifford began his soundings, Truman was hardly the underdog that he became the following year. As already mentioned, his popularity had begun to rise; no one had any reason to predict a revolt in the South and Henry Wallace had not yet declared his candidacy. On the other hand, none of the people around Truman suffered from an excess of optimism. The 1946 debacle was too fresh in memory, the Republicans had many able candidates—Dewey, Stassen, Taft, and Warren being the most prominent—and Henry Wallace, while not an avowed candidate, was certainly a threat.

During 1947, Wallace had been traveling around the country, collecting large audiences for his denunciations of Truman's foreign and domestic policies; many disaffected Democrats had rallied to his cause and he had behind him the not inconsiderable apparatus of the Communist party and the support of those unions in the CIO which the Communists controlled. Many of Wallace's followers were urging him to run for President in 1948 and he freely scattered hints that he might lead the first major third-party effort since Robert La Follette ran in 1924. A Wallace candidacy was understandably a nightmare to the Truman strategists; many of them refused to believe that in the end he would take the leap.

In mid-November, Clifford presented Truman with a 43-page

double-spaced memorandum on legal-size paper.[20] It was a remarkable political document—bold and unambiguous in its analysis of present trends, surprisingly accurate in treating of the future, courageous and not a little cynical in proposing a vigorous course of action for the President in the twelve months leading up to the election.

The memorandum predicted that Thomas E. Dewey would be the Republican candidate, though the contest for the nomination had barely gotten under way; that Henry Wallace would run on a third-party ticket; that President Truman could win even with the loss of the populous states of the East, so long as he held the support of the South and of the West and recaptured the labor vote which F.D.R. had always commanded. Events eventually confirmed each of these judgments

Clifford was wrong in one prediction: that there would be no break in the South, no matter what program the President presented. "As always, the South can be considered safely Democratic," he wrote. "And in formulating national policy, it can be safely ignored."

He argued that "If the Democrats carry the solid South and also those Western states carried in 1944, they will have 216 of the required 266 electoral votes. And if the Democratic party is powerful enough to capture the West, it will almost certainly pick up enough of the doubtful Middlewestern and Eastern states to get 50 more votes . . . We could lose New York, Pennsylvania, Illinois, New Jersey, Ohio, Massachusetts—all the 'big' states and still win." While Clifford was mistaken in assuming no southern breakaway—the Dixiecrat rebellion in the end lost Truman 39 electoral votes—he was quite correct in stressing the importance of winning the West and in arguing that a victory there presupposed sufficient strength to win some Midwestern states; in the end Truman took Idaho, Iowa, Minnesota, Missouri, Wisconsin—as well as Ohio and Illinois.

Clifford went on to provide a shrewd analysis of the various special interest groups which the Democrats had to attract Only the farmer "was presently favorably inclined towards the Truman administration"—a judgment which continued to be correct throughout 1948, but which the Republicans somehow failed to appreciate. The farmer's crops were good, Clifford pointed out; he was protected by parity and would be aided by the Marshall Plan. Should he be inclined to defect in 1948, nothing more could be done by way of "political or economic favors" to win back his support. The implication was that only rhetoric could be employed —an exercise in which Truman was never deficient throughout the campaign.

The labor vote was a great imponderable. Clifford flatly asserted that Truman "cannot win without the *active* support of organized labor. It is dangerous to assume that labor now has nowhere else to go in 1948. *Labor can stay home.*" Labor had been "inspired" to vote for Roosevelt, but had largely abstained in the 1946 congressional elections. "The labor group has always been politically inactive during prosperity," Clifford wrote. "The effort to get out the labor vote will thus have to be even more strenuous than in 1944." Much would also have to be done to attract independent liberals, who were not important numerically but exerted a considerable leavening effect on public opinion. "The liberal and progressive leaders are not overly enthusiastic about the administration," Clifford commented with tolerable understatement.

He warned that the Republicans would make a strong appeal for the Negro vote, which had been Democratic since 1932, and foresaw that the Negroes might hold the balance of power in states like New York, Illinois, Pennsylvania, Ohio, and Michigan. "The Negro voter has become a cynical, hard-boiled trader," Clifford suggested, and the Republicans were likely to appeal to his self-interest by offering an anti-poll-tax bill and Fair Employment Practices legislation in the next Congress. Clearly, the Democrats would have to outbid the Republicans in order to hold the Negroes. Truman's civil rights message in February 1948 followed logically from this premise.

Clifford's appraisal of the Catholic vote, which had begun to defect from the Democrats in 1944, turned out to be prophetic: "The controlling element in this group . . . is the distrust and fear of communism. . . . The attitude of the President and the administration toward communism should exert a definite appeal . . ."

Turning to the issues in the campaign, Clifford saw "considerable political advantage to the administration in the battle with the

Kremlin." Relations with Russia would probably continue to dete-
riorate and, as in all times of crisis, the average citizen would tend
to rally to his President. As for Republican attacks on the administration's foreign policy, "President Truman is comparatively invul-
nerable to attack because of his brilliant appointment of General
Marshall who has convinced the public that as Secretary of State he
is nonpartisan and above politics." On the other hand, the Republicans would probably intensify their efforts to make an issue of
Communist infiltration in government. In this area, however, "The
President adroitly stole their thunder by initiating his own government employee loyalty investigation procedure."

In the domestic field, Clifford saw high prices and the housing
shortage as the most pressing issues to the average citizen. He
urged that the President call upon the next session of Congress to
enact a maximum anti-inflation program, including mandatory
price controls, an ambitious housing program, and tax revisions
favoring lower-income groups. The President would offer his program in full awareness that the Republicans would reject it and
thus be politically vulnerable. Clifford's strategy could hardly have
been more forthright or candidly phrased (this was, after all, a
private memorandum): ". . . the Administration should select
the issues upon which there will be conflict with the majority in
Congress. It can assume it will get no major part of its own program approved. Its tactics must, therefore, be entirely different
than if there were any real point to bargaining and compromise. Its
recommendations—in the State of the Union message and elsewhere—must be tailored for the voter, not the Congressman; they
must display a label which reads 'no compromises.' "

This strategy was designed not only to embarrass the Republicans but to steal Henry Wallace's thunder, for if Wallace drew
enough votes, especially in the West, he would defeat Truman.
Clifford pointed out that in 1924 the third-party candidate, Robert
La Follette, polled more votes than the Democratic candidate in
eleven western states. To undercut Wallace's appeal, Clifford urged
that at the psychologically correct moment the Communist inspiration behind Wallace's campaign should be denounced by "prominent liberals and progressives—*and no one else.*" But denunciation

would not be enough; Truman had to move to the left in order to attract Wallace's followers. An ambitious program of economic measures and civil rights reforms was only part of the strategy which Clifford proposed, for he was worried by Wallace's calling the roll of the many Wall Street figures in the Truman administration—such men as Averell Harriman, Robert Lovett, James Forrestal and William Draper. Clifford saw Wallace appealing "to the atavistic fears of all progressives—the fear of 'Wall Street.'" Clifford urged the President to make "some top level appointments from the ranks of the progressives—in foreign as well as domestic affairs." It was important to make the effort, he argued, even if some of the appointees should not be confirmed by the Senate.

The memorandum deplored the decay of the Democratic party organization, urged that a new chairman be soon appointed to rebuild the party, and that a small working committee be established to coordinate the political program of the administration, provide monthly estimates of the political situation, and begin the drafting of memoranda for the 1948 platform and major campaign speeches. Clifford also stressed the need for close liaison with the labor movement and with independent liberals. In these sections Clifford's memorandum became a fascinating manual on the practical arts of politics at the Presidential level. He urged President Truman personally to cultivate labor leaders, who of late had rarely been seen in the White House. "It is easy for the incumbent of the White House to forget the 'magic' of his office," Clifford explained. But he cautioned that in such private colloquies the President ask advice on "matters in general," for "it is dangerous to ask a labor leader for advice on a *specific* matter and then ignore that advice."

Clifford spent a good deal of space on the problem of refurbishing what he called the President's "portrait" ("image," as a public relations term, had not yet come into general use). He pointed out that most people get their impressions of a President from his activities as Chief of State, but that Truman had been notably reticent in this area, with the consequence that he was largely thought of as a politician. Clifford made a number of proposals whereby the President might correct this distorted view. One of them was to exploit the social resources of the White House, by inviting one or two "nonpolitical personages" for lunch each week; the newspapers would inevitably give these encounters great publicity. Henry Ford II, who was receiving an excellent press as the young head of the Ford Motor Company, was an obvious candidate; Clifford saw considerable popular appeal in "this picture of the American President and the Young Business Man together."

Equally impressive would be a lunch with Albert Einstein, with the President explaining at his next press conference "that they talked, in general, about the *peacetime* uses of atomic energy and its potentialities for our civilization. He can then casually mention that he has been spending some of his leisure time getting caught up with atomic energy"—which would doubtless have acted as a corrective to the common impression that Truman spent much of his leisure time at the poker table. Another way to display his more reflective side to the public would be for the President to suggest to the newsmen "that it would do them no harm at all to read such and such a book (as long as he picks the right one) which he has just read." His staff would have presumably provided the President with an appropriate list.

Clifford also suggested that Truman repeat the nonpolitical "inspection tours" which Roosevelt employed in the 1940 campaign. The problem was that a President could not campaign openly until after the party conventions, yet there was urgent need for him to carry his case to the voters long before the late summer of 1948. F.D.R.'s inspection tours had been marvelously effective. "No matter how much the opposition and the press pointed out the political overtones of those trips," Clifford wrote, "the people paid little attention because what they saw was the Head of State performing his duties." The people were to show a similarly tolerant attitude toward President Truman on his "nonpolitical" coast-to-coast train tour the following June.

Truman read the document carefully and discussed it at length with Clifford. He was in general agreement with the analysis and proposed strategy, although he had little sympathy for the public relations gimmickry to sell the President to the American people. He was not about to turn the White House over to labor leaders with whom he felt little personal rapport or to invite Albert Einstein or Henry Ford to lunch or to nominate prominent liberals to high office in the knowledge that the Senate would knock them down. He found these gestures too obviously synthetic and out of character. On the other hand, the concept of a bold, uncompromising political offensive appealed to him.[21] He subsequently agreed that it would start with the State of the Union message on January 7.

# CHAPTER 3
# Scramble for the Republican Nomination

In November 1947, Clark Clifford's memorandum named Thomas E. Dewey as Truman's Republican opponent—an assertion that would have been a great comfort to the New York governor, had he known of it and been willing to believe it, during the anxious, fatiguing months when he was campaigning for the nomination. What Clifford so confidently set down on paper was more than a shrewd guess, but it was by no means an inevitable consummation. At the time, Dewey was the leading aspirant for the nomination, but he was hardly so far in the lead that he could not be overtaken.

Dewey's early ascendancy was due to a variety of factors. He was titular leader of the party, having been its Presidential candidate in 1944. His defeat in that election—by 3,600,000 votes, Roosevelt's smallest plurality in four elections—was no personal disaster, for he had run against a popular wartime commander-in-chief. The campaign had the advantage of making him the best-known Republican in the country, although he later suffered in some quarters from being considered a bit shopworn; his detractors loved to echo the remark attributed to Alice Roosevelt Longworth, "You can't make a soufflé rise twice."

After 1944, Dewey's standing in the party had been enhanced by his remarkable victory in the 1946 gubernatorial election; his majority of nearly 700,000 votes was the largest in New York's history. The case for Dewey was further strengthened by the surprising recovery in President Truman's popularity during 1947. If Truman was no longer a pushover, the argument went, the Republicans needed the most vigorous available campaigner and one who

29

could appeal to the progressive urban voter who would normally favor the Democrats. Dewey was preeminently that man, for he was liberal, dynamic and young. Unhappily for Dewey, the argument cut both ways: after the turn of the year, when Truman's popularity declined again, Dewey's candidacy no longer seemed so essential.

From the outset, Dewey had vigorous competition. Unlike the situation four years before, in 1948 the Republican nomination for President was clearly no mere honorific distinction but a presumptive claim on power. No matter how Truman's popularity fluctuated on the pollsters' charts, most Republicans believed that the Republican triumph in 1946 had heralded the end of the long era of Democratic supremacy. Many men wanted the Republican nomination: Senator Robert A. Taft, the leading Republican in the Senate whose tireless advocacy of orthodox doctrine was to win him the title of "Mr. Republican"; Harold E. Stassen, the former boy-governor of Minnesota, who had announced his availability as far back as December 1946 and who had been energetically cultivating delegates ever since; the genial Earl Warren, California's popular governor who in 1946 had won both the Republican and Democratic nominations for governor. All three were openly in the race by the end of 1947, although Warren had stated that his duties in California precluded him from campaigning actively. Then there were the "dark horses," of varying degrees of obscurity but all touted endlessly in the newspapers: General Dwight D. Eisenhower, soon to retire as Chief of Staff, a man of immense popularity whose aloofness from politics only seemed to enhance his political appeal; General Douglas MacArthur, the hero of the Pacific war and our proconsul in Japan, a man of legendary grandeur whose personal sense of destiny rivaled that of Charles De Gaulle; Senator Arthur H. Vandenberg, the chairman of the Senate Foreign Relations Committee whose reluctance to be considered for the Presidency only stimulated the ardor of his supporters; and Representative Joseph W. Martin, Jr., the Speaker of the House of Representatives, a man whose pallid public personality made Calvin Coolidge's seem iridescent by comparison and whose inclusion in the list indicated how contagious Presidential aspirations can be in a year when victory seems preordained. Of the four dark horses, the two generals were viewed by their supporters as men whose irresistible public appeal could stampede the party managers were they to campaign openly; Vandenberg and Martin, on the other hand, were regarded as plausible compromise candidates if the convention should find itself deadlocked.

Of the principal candidates, Dewey was the last to announce his availability. When the announcement came—on January 15, 1948 —it was made not by the Governor but by his press secretary, James C. Hagerty, the son of the *New York Times'* political writer, and it was in keeping with a tradition favored by many candidates that they were not pursuing the nomination but were agreeable to having it thrust on them. Hagerty remarked that a group of "friends" had entered Dewey's name in the Oregon primary, which was to be held in May, and went on to declare, "As the Governor has frequently said, he is fully engaged with the work of the legislative session and cannot actively seek the nomination of his party for President, but if nominated he would accept."

The ritualistic disavowal of Presidential aspirations was especially ironical on Dewey's part, for he had been pressing his candidacy since 1939, when he was but thirty-seven years old. Unlike Truman, Dewey never suffered from a meager endowment of ambition: he had made his mark early in life as a crusading district attorney and he rapidly pyramided one political success atop another until it seemed reasonable to reach for the grandest prize of all.

Dewey's achievement was the more impressive, given the handicaps of his personality. More than most politicians, he displayed an enormous gap between his private and his public manner. To friends and colleagues, he was warm and gracious, considerate of others' views, never too proud to ask questions and thereby display ignorance. He could tell a joke and was not dismayed by an off-color story. In public, however, he tended to freeze up, either out of diffidence or too stern a sense of the dignity of office. The smile would seem forced, the occasional glad-handing gesture awkward. In 1948, an old acquaintance was quoted as saying, "Till he gets to the door, Tom may be cracking jokes and laughing like a schoolboy, but the moment he enters the room he ceases to be Tom Dewey and becomes what he thinks the Governor of New York State ought to be." [1]

Dewey even had the misfortune to be derided for his appearance. His moustache lent a certain primness to his features and there was a quality of dapper stiffness about his bearing that led people to repeat the well-worn jest that he looked like the groom atop a wedding cake. His advisers were dismayed that photographs often showed him looking too short, though he was of average height (5 feet 8 inches); the impression may have come from the fact that his head was somewhat large for his body—or it may have been deliberately caused by photographers who shot him from unflattering angles. It is certainly true that Dewey suffered from a measure of disesteem among the working press, perhaps partly inspired by political hostility but primarily caused by his aloofness and occasional brusqueness.

Dewey rubbed a number of people the wrong way, for he had little patience for the diplomatic jollities in which most politicians excel. His problem, according to his old friend Elliott V. Bell, was that he "tensed up" during a political campaign, like a prize fighter before a match.[2] His manner inspired a whole series of acerbic quips which were gleefully and endlessly repeated in the press. "You have to know Mr. Dewey very well in order to dislike him" was attributed to Mrs. Kenneth Simpson, the wife of the one-time Republican leader of New York County. Another famous line was "I don't know which is the chillier experience—to have Tom ignore you or shake your hand."

Envy, of course, may well have accounted for much of the derogation heaped on Dewey, for he had indeed come a long way in a short time. A small-town product of the Midwest, he had been born in Owosso, Michigan, on March 24, 1902. His father ran the local newspaper. Young Tom took his undergraduate training at the University of Michigan, went on to Columbia University to study law; he was a sober-minded, diligent student, conventional in all ways except for an ambition, abandoned early in life, to be a concert singer.

He spent his apprentice years in a New York law firm; when he was twenty-eight, he worked on a case with the well-known trial lawyer, George Z. Medalie, who was greatly impressed with Dewey's capacity. Soon afterward, when Medalie was appointed U.S. attorney for the Southern District of New York, he named Dewey as his chief assistant. Dewey performed so zealously that, in 1935, Democratic Governor Herbert Lehman designated him as special prosecutor to lead a drive against racketeering in New York City. Dewey assembled a staff of brilliant young lawyers who were soon roiling the underworld, dispatching the thugs to jail and making headlines. Within a matter of months "racket buster" Dewey was a popular hero; in 1937, he was overwhelmingly elected district attorney of New York County.

Never one to lose momentum, the next year Dewey ran for governor. He was defeated by the immensely popular Lehman, but by a majority of only 64,000—which represented at least a moral victory. By 1939 Dewey was thinking of himself as a possible Republican candidate for President. He got together a group of "brain trusters," headed by the erudite Elliott V. Bell, then a financial writer on the *New York Times,* to provide him with the necessary background in national and international affairs; he realized that as a district attorney his angle of vision was far too narrow. His candidacy in 1940 attracted a fair amount of support, but in the end could not prevail against Wendell Willkie's bandwagon. At Dewey's age, the failure was hardly crushing. Two years later, after Lehman retired, Dewey was elected governor of New York. Now he was clearly set on a Presidential course.

In 1944, Dewey did not have to bestir himself to get the nomination. Willkie was once again eager to run, but he had offended most of the leaders of the party, who needed a strong candidate to stop him. Dewey seemed the best choice and, despite a flurry of activity on behalf of Stassen, MacArthur, and Governor John Bricker of Ohio, sentiment was overwhelming for Dewey long before the convention began. Thus Dewey was not only able to avoid the exertions of campaigning in Presidential primaries, but he was even spared the necessity of announcing his candidacy. He was nominated on the first ballot.

In 1944, however, there is reason to suspect that Dewey was at least ambivalent in his attitude toward the nomination; Paul E. Lockwood, his long-time secretary, is not alone in believing that Dewey did not want the wartime nomination, but felt that if he refused it, out of a transparent desire to avoid a likely defeat, he would so distress party leaders that he would foreclose any chance to be nominated in 1948.[3]

In Dewey's circle, the 1944 defeat seemed only to confirm a

pattern that could be traced throughout his career: he tended to lose on the first round and win on the second. Thus, he had failed to convict Jimmy Hines, the corrupt Tammany district leader, at his first trial, only to succeed at the second; similarly with his attempts to become governor in 1938 and to win the Presidential nomination in 1940. According to this design, the loss in 1944 foreshadowed victory in 1948.

Four additional years as governor had added to his credentials. He had given New York a brisk, businesslike government, having recruited a staff of excellent administrators; Dewey liked to say that his job was to persuade $50,000-a-year men to accept $10,-000-a-year state jobs. He had retained the liberal reforms of the Lehman administration and pushed ahead in some areas, such as increasing unemployment and disability benefits and extending their coverage. He had enhanced his appeal to liberal voters and to Negroes when New York passed the first state law prohibiting racial and religious discrimination in employment. Conservatives were naturally impressed by substantial reductions in both personal income and business taxes. During the war, he had accumulated a $623 million reserve in the state treasury for postwar reconstruction. And he had kept the labor peace with one of the best state mediation boards in the nation. It was an impressive record.

As 1948 approached, Dewey initially tried the tactics he had used four years before. Throughout 1947, he withheld any announcement of his candidacy. He was frequently criticized for his cautious refusal to speak out on national and international issues. In November, he finally broke his silence with a widely publicized address criticizing the "serious economic and diplomatic blunders" of the Truman administration and proposing economic aid to China, then still controlled by the Nationalists, as part of the Marshall Plan program.[4]

Dewey's reticence about his Presidential aspirations led no one to believe that he was uninterested. Politicians knew that since 1944, Dewey's strategists, notably Herbert Brownell and J. Russel Sprague, had diligently kept in touch with party leaders from around the country. When an important out-of-state politician came to New York, Dewey was usually available for lunch and his minions would thoughtfully provide such hospitality as tickets to hit Broadway shows. Dewey himself did some judicious politicking in 1947, notably on a "nonpolitical" vacation trip to Sapulpa, Oklahoma, Mrs. Dewey's home town. There he received politicians from Oklahoma, Texas, and Arkansas ("I've talked with the next President," announced an exuberant Arkansas Republican) and then continued his soundings in Kansas, Missouri and Salt Lake City, where he attended the annual Governors' Conference. In Kansas City he even set up shop in the penthouse suite of the Muehlebach Hotel, normally Harry Truman's headquarters, which local Democrats regarded as a gesture of *lèse-majesté*.[5] But throughout, Dewey rebuffed journalistic prompting that he announce his candidacy.

By the time the announcement finally came, it was clear that Hagerty's statement that Dewey could not "actively seek" the nomination hardly represented a realistic appraisal of the situation. The year 1948 was not 1944 and, if Dewey did not seek the nomination, he was certain not to get it; on the other hand, no one had reason to anticipate how strenuously he would have to seek it.

Throughout 1947 and the early part of 1948, Senator Robert A. Taft was regarded as Dewey's major opponent. Taft had known the White House as a young man, when his father was the twenty-seventh President; like the Adamses, his was one of those rare political families whose members could seriously fantasize about a proprietary claim to the Presidency. His more realistic claim was that he represented that great weight of conservative sentiment in the Republican party which basically differentiated it from the Democratic party. He was the effective though not the nominal leader of the Senate Republicans and derived considerable prestige from his co-authorship of the Taft-Hartley Act, the first legislative restraint imposed on the trade unions since the Democrats had come to power. Taft had strong support in the Congress and among professional party managers around the country. His greatest handicap was that many party leaders, who privately agreed with his views, thought that he might be too conservative to win. Taft had made his first vain effort to get the nomination in 1940, when he was a freshman senator. In 1944, when the nomination hardly seemed worth scrambling for, he threw his support to his fellow Ohioan, John Bricker, whose prospects had never looked better than hopeless. Like Dewey, Taft regarded 1948 as his year.

In many ways, Taft was a paradoxical figure as a politician. He was very knowledgeable, he had a keen lawyer's mind and considerable intellectual curiosity, but there was something of the mustiness of the law library about him. He was totally devoid of personal color and rhetorical flair; he was too dignified to be folksy and too unpretentious to cultivate an artful patrician style, which could also be immensely popular, as F.D.R. proved. With his thin-lipped smile, old-fashioned steel spectacles, and his half-bald head plastered by strips of lank hair, he looked like a faintly disapproving schoolmaster.

For a successful politician—state representative and senator, two-term member of the United States Senate—his methods were also unusual. Taft was candid to the point of bluntness. When he approached an issue, he did not circle warily around it, sniffing its hazards, calculating the advantage of a bold assault as against a discreet retreat covered by a verbal smoke screen. He spoke his mind. In September 1947, he was asked for his solution to the problem of high food prices. "We should eat less," he suggested.[6] In 1946 he denounced the verdict of the Nuremberg tribunal which had ordered the execution of the former Nazi leaders. "The hanging," said Taft, "will be a blot on the American record which we shall long regret."[7] He was promptly and unfairly accused of being pro-Fascist, when he was merely voicing his dismay at retroactive law imposed by victors.

When he lacked an opinion, he was equally willing to ventilate his uncertainties. Surveying the farm problem, back in 1940, he remarked, "I know the country has got to do something for the farmers; I don't think what the New Deal has done is practical, but I'm not yet sure what to do myself."[8] Few other Presidential aspirants would have made that confession.

Taft's candor often brought him a bad press, but seemed only to consolidate his hold on his bedrock conservative supporters whose political attitudes were rooted in prewar isolationism and passionate hostility to the New Deal; they always responded gleefully to his cantankerousness and his continual nay-saying. By 1948, however, Taft was no longer as conservative as many of his supporters. He readily conceded that he had changed his mind on some issues; for example, he now favored federal aid in the areas of health, housing, and education and had introduced legislation in all these fields. He had an excellent record on civil liberties. He had opposed Truman's plan to draft strikers, back in 1946, because he had regarded it as a dangerous suppression of personal freedom. Taft's occasional deviations from orthodoxy did not dismay his admirers, for they were more impressed by his record of nearly a decade of unremitting opposition to the leftward course of history.

It was one of the many ironies of 1948 that Harold Stassen's candidacy was initially not taken very seriously by his opponents. No one disputed that Stassen had popular appeal, but he lacked any substantial following among the professionals who controlled the state organizations. They regarded him as something of a maverick, a young man (only forty-one in 1948) who was running much too fast, a purely self-propelled candidate who could hardly claim that he was responding to widespread demand that he serve the nation in its highest office. Stassen also lacked the kind of base normally regarded as necessary to launch a campaign for the nomination—the governorship of a large state or a commanding position in the Congress, either of which guaranteed considerable national publicity.

Though he had not held office for several years, Stassen had an impressive political background. He had been governor of Minnesota when he was thirty-one. Twice reelected, he had resigned in 1942 to enter the Navy, where he had seen a good deal of action. Toward the end of the war, Roosevelt had given his career an unexpected boost by appointing him a delegate to the founding conference of the United Nations. Out of uniform early in 1946, Stassen did not return to state politics. Instead he decided to run for President and began almost immediately, although he did not formally announce his candidacy until December.

A large, hulking man, 6 feet 3 inches tall, Stassen was moon-faced and balding, but still ruggedly handsome; he had a warm smile and he smiled easily. A friendly concern was the quality he most readily communicated to voters; he brought the massive handshaking ritual to Presidential politics while Estes Kefauver and Lyndon Johnson were still operating on the state level. One reporter, clocking Stassen after a meeting, discovered that he had clasped the hands of one thousand people in twenty minutes.[9]

Since he was neither a governor nor a senator, he had to start earlier and run harder than anyone else. Throughout 1946 and 1947, his problem was to keep his name before the public. Stassen sped over the lecture circuit, wrote widely for the magazines, took a well-publicized tour throughout Europe, the high point of which was an interview with Joseph Stalin; Stassen assured Stalin that there would be no depression in the United States. By August 1947, according to a calculation by *Time,* Stassen had covered 40 states and appeared before 250 audiences—everything from garden clubs to university commencements; his lectures were not only promoting his candidacy but bringing him between $500 and $1,000 in fees for each appearance.[10]

Wherever he went Stassen presented the same sales talk—a strong plea for international cooperation through the United Nations, lively expressions of confidence in the productive potentialities of the free enterprise system, and a request for support in his efforts to humanize and liberalize the Republican party. He was appealing to the same constituency that Dewey claimed as his own. But Stassen was taking off from a dead start; he was to be the challenger until midway in the primary campaign, when he suddenly surprised everyone.

Liberal Republicans had a third choice in Governor Earl Warren of California. He might well have become a front-runner, but from the outset he indicated a curious ambivalence toward the nomination: he had announced his candidacy on November 13, 1947, but consistently refused to campaign. He set up no organization, raised no money, solicited no delegates outside California. His self-restraint relegated Warren to the role of a potential compromise choice, but he was taken seriously.

He had excellent credentials, not the least of which was that he had no enemies; in 1948 it would have been impossible to visualize him a dozen years later as the embattled Chief Justice of the United States, being assailed by bigots who wanted to impeach him. Warren was a big, hearty, vigorous man with immense resources of personal warmth which charmed both politicians and voters;

with his attractive wife and six spirited children, he also had the most photogenic family in American politics. He was a lifelong Republican with an irresistible appeal to Democrats in a state where the Democrats far outnumbered Republicans; elected by a large majority in 1942, he had been reelected without opposition four years later after he won both the Democratic and Republican primaries.

Warren's administration had been marked by a fiscal soundness that reassured conservatives and a degree of innovating zeal that delighted liberals: he had revamped the public health program, reformed the prison system, built a lot of new roads, hospitals, child-care centers, and schools. The only fight that he lost was over a system of statewide medical insurance that was far in advance of his time; the doctors' lobby beat him on the issue, but the defeat only enhanced Warren's appeal to progressive-minded citizens. Over all his works he cast a genial aura of nonpartisanship; his was the kind of independent Republicanism that evoked memories of George Norris and the elder La Follette. There was every reason to believe that it would be attractive far beyond California.

The number of candidates in the field, each with more than an illusory hope of victory, enhanced the importance of the Presidential primaries which were to begin, as they do every four years, in New Hampshire in March. Primaries play a peculiar role in the complex process of nominating a President. In terms of the numbers of delegates involved, they are of minor significance; in 1948, the delegate votes in New Hampshire, Wisconsin, Nebraska, Ohio and Oregon only totaled 115, whereas 548 votes were required for victory at the convention. The importance of the primaries lies rather in their role as trial runs, and in the psychological impact of victory or defeat. They are a testing ground for popular appeal, an indication whether a candidate with an impressive vote-getting record in his home territory is equally attractive in other states.

It is often claimed that the primaries are not representative of voter sentiments, for the turnout is often small. Nonetheless, the party managers as well as the press closely follow primary results; successive victories may build up a bandwagon psychology whereas a sharp defeat can puncture the most persuasive claims to preferment. In 1948, everybody remembered how the Willkie campaign had collapsed four years before when he ran poorly in the Wisconsin primary. Willkie's role as titular leader of the party, his national stature, the enormous publicity that he engendered availed him nothing; everything depended on primary victories, inasmuch as the party leadership in most states had turned against him. Thus, when a relative handful of voters in Wisconsin rejected him, he had to withdraw from the race.

When one candidate is substantially ahead, he can safely ignore the primaries. Thus Dewey did not campaign in Wisconsin in 1944, but won anyway. Had he lost to Willkie in that primary, his setback would have been a minor one, given his long lead. In 1948, however, it was to Dewey's advantage to test his strength in the primaries. By the time he announced his candidacy, his early lead seemed to be slipping. Truman was looking more vulnerable, largely because of the announcement of Henry Wallace's third-party candidacy in December, and thus Dewey could no longer be presented as the one man who could defeat Truman; even in New York State he was no longer essential. Moreover, Stassen was receiving a good deal of favorable publicity with dramatic charges that various associates of Truman had been illegally profiting from commodity speculation. In July 1947 the Gallup poll had showed that 50 percent of Republican voters favored Dewey; [11] he still led the list in January, but his strength was now reduced to 33 percent.[12] A series of primary victories therefore offered Dewey an opportunity to reassert his preeminence. On the other hand, if he held aloof from the primaries, Stassen or Taft might increase their strength to the point where a convention deadlock was likely.

Stassen's strategy, of course, clearly called for exploiting the primaries to the full. From the outset, he had adopted an aggressive posture, continually challenging Dewey to debate the issues. The primaries gave him an opportunity to prove that his rhetoric moved the voters as well as the headline writers; it was the standard strategy of the underdog aggressively seeking to become the top dog. Primary victories would not assure his nomination, but he would lose all his momentum if he avoided the confrontation.

Taft might have opted for the same strategy as Dewey's. On the other hand, unless he felt certain of winning the primaries, the game was not lost for him if he avoided the preliminary contests and quietly sought delegates in states which did not hold primaries. The worst that could happen, from his point of view, was that Dewey would further increase his lead, though still falling short of enough delegates for a first-ballot victory at the convention. On the other hand, an uninhibited contest between Dewey and Stassen might result in a standoff—which would only enhance Taft's chances. Thus Taft stayed out of the primaries in New Hampshire, Wisconsin, and Oregon; he fought in Ohio to hold his own state, and in Nebraska, where he had no alternative.

Delegates favoring Dewey, Stassen, and General Eisenhower were entered in the New Hampshire primary, which was to be held March 9. On January 23, Eisenhower eliminated himself from the primary in a strongly worded letter to Leonard Finder, publisher of the Manchester *Union-Leader*. "I am not available for and could not accept nomination to high political office," wrote Eisenhower, who was shortly due to take up his duties as president of Columbia University. With an unintentional irony that was only apparent four years later, he added that "the necessary and wise subordination of the military to civil power will best be sustained . . . when life-long professional soldiers . . . abstain from seeking high political office." Eisenhower's declination was gratefully received by all the Republican contestants, for he was already exhibiting the immense popularity which was to lead to his easy victory four years later.

The New Hampshire primary itself was an undramatic affair. Dewey had the backing of Governor Charles M. Dale and most of the state's leading Republicans; Dale lent the support of his state-wide organization, which had the manpower to conduct a house-to-house canvass in most areas.[13] During the campaign, Dewey did not get closer to New Hampshire than Boston, where he made a major address; he had last been in New Hampshire on a "nonpolitical" visit in November. Stassen sought to compensate for the weakness of his organization by two visits to the state in January and February. When the results were in, Dewey had won six out of the eight delegates; while Stassen had only two, he could take a measure of comfort from the fact that he had outdistanced Dewey in those communities which he had personally visited.

The next primary was in Wisconsin on April 6—and this turned out to be a great surprise. Wisconsin's primary is always important, for the state is large, with both a substantial industrial and farm population; its heterogeneity and size provide a far better test of a candidate's drawing power than does tiny New Hampshire. In 1948, Wisconsin provided additional interest: it was to be the first exposure to the voters of the candidacy of the formidable Douglas MacArthur. MacArthur, from his headquarters in Tokyo, had long been an inscrutable presence looming over the campaign. His views on domestic issues were unknown, but both his record and his personality inspired adulation, which was generously fueled by the Hearst press and the Chicago *Tribune*.

In mid-March, the General finally declared his availability in a statement in which he rumbled, "In this hour of momentous importance . . . I can say, and with due humility, that I would be recreant to all my concepts of good citizenship were I to shirk . . . accepting any public duty to which I might be called by the American people." The other nonshirkers in the primary were Dewey and Stassen.

It was an odd campaign. Inasmuch as he was on active duty, MacArthur was barred from campaigning; he issued no further public statements and never set foot in the state. Indeed, he had not been in the country for eleven years. He was acclaimed, however, as Wisconsin's favorite son, for he had once gone to high school in Milwaukee and had received a Wisconsin appointment to West Point. His cause was pushed by a MacArthur for President Committee, among whose prominent adherents were Fred R. Zimmerman, Wisconsin's secretary of state, and Philip La Follette, former governor and son of the famous senator. The MacArthurites comprised an odd united front of Taft Republicans and former Progressives who had gone into the Republican party in the '40's; cynics suggested that Phil La Follette had enlisted in the cause in order to regain a position of prominence in party affairs.[14] They had a grass roots organization, plenty of money, backing from various veterans' leaders, and the tireless support of the Hearst newspapers in Milwaukee and Chicago.

Early in April, Dewey came into the state for two days of energetic campaigning. As for Stassen, he cultivated Wisconsin with the assiduity of a Fuller Brush man canvassing a high-rise apartment house. He made ten visits, crisscrossing the state in a Greyhound bus that had typewriter tables for newsmen, a mimeograph machine and a public address system; he worked from sunup to midnight jollying the voters at factory gates, country crossroads, and urban mass meetings. He also had a question period at the end of each of his speeches—a popular gimmick that established great rapport with his audience. When it was over, he would post himself at the exit of the hall to shake hands. His detractors derided his tactics as "amateurish," more appropriate for a candidate for sheriff than for President; he was actually establishing a precedent in Wisconsin that even so dissimilar a candidate as John F. Kennedy felt compelled to adopt, twelve years later.[15] Nor was Stassen's a one-man effort; he had the support of the state organization led by Tom Coleman and his list of delegates was headed by Senator Joseph R. McCarthy, who had unseated Robert M. La Follette, Jr., in the Republican primary two years before. McCarthy was an important booster, a popular young politician of vigorous though imprecise views; he was two years short of becoming a McCarthyite.

Despite Dewey and Stassen's energetic campaigning, most observers gave MacArthur a substantial lead. "M'ARTHUR VICTORY DUE IN WISCONSIN" read the *New York Times* headline on March 29; the paper's survey showed that the General would take at least 14 of the 27 delegates. On the eve of the election, betting favored MacArthur at odds as high as 5 to 1. So certain was MacArthur's victory that the relevant question, for Dewey's and Stassen's supporters, became who was to finish second. Senator McCarthy was quoted as saying, "I don't think the Presidential hopes of any of the candidates could survive running a bad third." That included Stassen, he added.[16]

The results astounded everyone. Stassen won 19 delegates, MacArthur 8, Dewey none. Dewey had run as badly as Willkie in 1944.

Wisconsin finished the MacArthur boom. Stassen suddenly jumped to the front rank. As the *Herald-Tribune* put it in an editorial, "The former three-time Minnesota Governor is no longer a dark horse. All at once Mr. Stassen has emerged from the fringe of interesting possibility. From now on he is in the first division of contenders for the Republican Presidential nomination. . . ."[17] Dewey's right-wing critics in the party were particularly unkind.

Representative Clare Hoffman of Michigan suggested that "Dewey might consider second place on the Stassen ticket." Former Representative Hamilton Fish of New York proposed that the Governor withdraw from the campaign, as Willkie had in 1944. "Dewey's nonveteran feet of clay collapsed when he tried to keep up with real war veterans such as Stassen and MacArthur . . . ," Fish commented. A more objective observer, James A. Farley, F.D.R.'s former political manager, thought the Wisconsin results "could be fatal" for Dewey. Inasmuch as Farley still could not visualize Stassen getting the nomination, he concluded that Wisconsin had benefited Taft—and Vandenberg even more so, in the event of a Dewey-Taft deadlock at the convention.[18] More and more talk was being heard of Vandenberg as a possible compromise choice.

It was left to Senator J. Howard McGrath, chairman of the Democratic National Committee, to strike a prophetic note. Remarking about how wrong the journalistic predictions had been about Wisconsin, he drew a reassuring moral for his dispirited party. "The results in Wisconsin proved the fallacy of the political judgment of the principal sources of public information," said McGrath. "This leads me to the conclusion that to insure the election of the Democratic ticket in November we need only have the commentators united in predicting defeat." [19] No one took McGrath seriously.

Dewey sought to mitigate the effects of his defeat by telling reporters, "Now we have lost one primary and won one primary," referring to his New Hampshire victory, and by pointing out that on the day of the Wisconsin poll, he had picked up ninety delegates in New York—"more than four times the number any other candidate has acquired." [20] But New York was no triumph; everyone knew that Dewey controlled the delegation.

The day after his Wisconsin debacle, Dewey and a press party flew from Albany to Nebraska in a chartered airplane. The primary there, scheduled for April 13, was being heralded as even more significant than Wisconsin's, for all the candidates, declared and undeclared, were on the ballot—Stassen, Dewey, Taft, Warren, Vandenberg, MacArthur and Martin. A peculiarity in Nebraska's law allowed a candidate's name to be placed on the ballot not only without his permission but even against his expressed wishes; once on the ballot there was no way to withdraw. Raymond A.

McConnell, Jr., a newspaper editor in Lincoln, originated the idea of giving the voters a choice of all the candidates and formed a committee to collect the necessary signatures. He agreed not to include Eisenhower, in view of his emphatic withdrawal from the New Hampshire primary. But McConnell insisted on presenting Vandenberg's name to the voters despite the latter's objections, inasmuch as the Senator would not flatly promise to decline the nomination if it were offered by the convention.[21]

The free-for-all brought a large press contingent into the state for the final week of the campaign. Dewey arrived for a two-day tour, in which he was to cover 467 miles and make eleven speeches; he then extended his trip for another day. Taft, who had planned to enter no primaries but Ohio, where he was the favorite son, devoted four days to touring the state. Stassen also returned for the windup, though he had already been in and out of the state over a two-year period. In a speech in Omaha, he argued that the most important difference between him and Dewey was over his proposal to outlaw the Communist party—a note he was insistently to sound in the weeks ahead. All the other candidates refused to campaign.

There was a record turnout of over 185,000 voters. When the returns were in, Stassen led with more than 43 percent of the poll —a remarkable showing given the large field of candidates. Stassen received some 79,000 votes, 16,000 more than Dewey; Taft's vote was only 21,000; Vandenberg's, 9,000.

Stassen was now clearly the man to head off. "The Dewey and Taft forces are already more enfeebled than they appear," Joseph Alsop wrote a few days later in his syndicated column. "If Stassen's onward march continues through the next primaries, a very great number of Republican professionals, herding delegates with the peevish ferocity of aging collie dogs, are going to be needed to stop the Minnesota former Governor at Philadelphia." [22] Twelve days after the Nebraska primary, the Gallup poll showed that Stassen had for the first time displaced Dewey as the favorite candidate of Republican voters; 31 percent declared for Stassen to 29 percent for Dewey. By May 14, Stassen's lead had lengthened to 37 percent and Dewey had only 24 percent.[23]

Late in April, Stassen won more headlines when he bested

Dewey in a write-in campaign in the Pennsylvania primary. None of the candidates had formally entered the primary, and hence there were no names on the Republican ballot. Almost on the eve of the balloting a Stassen organization was set up to conduct a write-in campaign; Dewey and Taft made no effort to counter the move. The results were not binding on the state's 73 delegates, but Stassen had the satisfaction of polling 74,000 votes to Dewey's 69,000 and Taft's 15,000.

The Stassen bandwagon stumbled for the first time in Ohio, which held its primary on May 4. Stassen's decision to invade Taft's home state had been variously regarded as courageous, fool-hardy, and ill-mannered, for there had long been an unwritten rule in Presidential politics that a candidate's status as "favorite son" should not be threatened by outsiders. Prudence as well as good manners sustained the rule, for a candidate was usually strongest in his own state; moreover, candidates had a reciprocal interest in keeping out of each other's territory: the number of campaigns they had to wage was thereby reduced. In 1948, this meant no primary contests in Dewey's New York, Warren's California, Stassen's Minnesota and Taft's Ohio—until Stassen decided to break the rule. (Wisconsin was regarded as a special case, for MacArthur was not an active politician and his links to the state were tenuous.)

Stassen's decision to invade Ohio was in keeping with the unorthodox and aggressive tactics he had employed ever since he had announced for the Presidency back in December 1946. Ohio was a large gamble, but there was logic behind it. If Stassen could beat Taft in his own backyard, he would begin to look irresistible even to politicians who passionately disliked him. Stassen hedged his bet, however. Fifty-three delegates were to be selected, but Stassen only contested 23 seats; he concentrated his efforts in the industrial centers of the state and ran only one statewide candidate against 9 for Taft. Stassen was thus in the odd position of seemingly demanding a bold confrontation with Taft—and then backing off from it by picking and choosing his spots where his support was greatest.

Taft campaigned vigorously; his seasoned organization was more than a match for the Stassen enthusiasts. The results were something of a standoff. Of the 23 contested seats, Taft won 14, Stassen 9; Stassen also lost his one statewide race. Both men thereupon claimed victory, Taft because he had held Stassen to a modest gain and Stassen on the ground that nine of his men had triumphed in a "clear-cut" fashion "against combined and extreme opposition." [24] Their optimism was unpersuasive. As James Reston commented in the *New York Times,* "one more 'victory' like this one would be the undoing of both candidates." [25] Stassen had suffered because he had failed to achieve a dramatic victory, Taft because he had not decisively repelled the invader.

With Ohio out of the way, attention shifted to Oregon, where the last of the 1948 Presidential primaries was to be held. Oregon clearly was the crucial test. A direct confrontation between Dewey and Stassen, it was Dewey's last chance to recoup his losses in Wisconsin and Nebraska. If he failed once again, it would be impossible to claim that he held any great attraction for voters outside New York, and he would enter the convention trailing an aroma of defeat. As for Stassen, a victory in Oregon would establish him as front-runner for the nomination, whereas a defeat would efface most of the impact of his prior victories. Momentum is the essential ingredient in creating a bandwagon psychology.

Oregon was to vote on May 21. Polls taken in April by the Portland *Oregonian* and the *Oregon Journal,* the state's largest newspapers, gave Stassen a handsome lead; bookies were offering odds of 5 to 3 in his favor.[26] At a meeting in Dewey's apartment in New York's Roosevelt Hotel, the Governor voiced his anxiety about Oregon to Herbert Brownell and Paul Lockwood.[27] A Dewey organization had been set up under Ralph D. Moores, a well-regarded Oregon politician, but communication between Portland and New York was none too effective. Lockwood was delegated to go to Oregon to survey the situation. He flew into Portland on a Sunday morning and was met by Moores, who took him to Dewey headquarters on the third floor of a downtown office building. Lockwood was appalled that there was no street level office and even more distressed that Moores had set up no statewide organization but merely had a list of contacts in various communities. After he telephoned Brownell to voice his dismay, Lockwood found himself assigned the task of running the Dewey campaign in Oregon; he was cautioned, however, to stay in the background. He had five weeks before the polling date.

Lockwood took a three-room suite in the Multnomah Hotel, hired a stenographer, and started from scratch. It was something of a carpetbagging operation, with Dewey's eastern supporters providing a lot of assistance. Harold E. Talbott, a wealthy New York businessman, who was later to become Eisenhower's Secretary of the Air Force, headed the financial drive; he raised a good deal of money in New York, then came to Oregon to make the rounds of local supporters. Harlow K. Curtice, then head of the Buick division of General Motors, was persuaded to get on the telephone in Detroit and ring up his dealers around the state to spread the word that Dewey was the man to support. Winthrop Aldrich, chairman of the board of the Chase National Bank and a longtime Dewey supporter, was pressed into service to proselytize Oregon bankers. ("Local bankers talk to people every day," Lockwood points out. "When someone would ask, 'What do you hear?' they would say, 'It looks like Dewey.' This is very important.")

Lacking time to build a statewide organization, Lockwood collected mailing lists of state societies of all sorts, was soon deluging doctors, chiropractors, automobile dealers, lumbermen with Dewey's views on causes closest to their pocketbooks. He had recordings made of a 1947 Dewey speech against socialized medicine and sent it to every county medical society; pamphlets on the same subject were prepared for doctors' waiting rooms. "In that way," says Lockwood, "I got every goddamn doctor in the state out for Dewey."

Dewey arrived to campaign three weeks before the polling date. In Wisconsin and Nebraska, Dewey's managers had derided Stassen's crossroads campaigning; now they were frankly imitating him. Accompanied by two staffmen and a platoon of reporters, Dewey traversed the state in a chartered bus, speaking wherever he could gather an audience, handshaking his way up and down Main Streets, distributing autographs by the bushel, and participating in the idiotic local rituals demanded of Presidential aspirants.

He was photographed in a ten-gallon hat and in an Indian headdress previously worn by Queen Marie of Rumania when she had visited the state in the 1920's. At Coos Bay, he allowed himself to be captured by the Coos Bay pirates, underwent a mock trial, had his arm pricked so that he could sign his membership scroll with his own blood. At Grant's Pass, a raucous group of local "cavemen," naked except for tattered furs, ambushed his party by prearrangement. Dewey, dapperly dressed and looking a little bewildered, paraded around with the cavemen, providing one of the memorable photographs of 1948. Considerably more relaxed than he had been in the 1944 campaign (some people began to talk of a "new Dewey"), he was agreeable to everything but a suggestion that he ride a western horse. "I haven't ridden in a couple of years," he explained, "and I'm afraid I'd be stiff and sore for the rest of the campaign."

In three weeks, Dewey covered nearly two thousand miles, addressed 100,000 people; he often campaigned sixteen hours a day and at one point suffered an attack of laryngitis that kept him out of action for two days. He covered considerable ground verbally as well as geographically. He vigorously advocated foreign aid, but proposed that the administration act "like hardheaded Americans instead of softheaded saps," using the leverage of American dollars to help create a United States of Europe. He favored the "formulation of a dynamic, long-term farm and food program." He denounced plans to tax cooperatives, provided a ten-point program for the development of the natural resources of the West. And, increasingly, he took Harold Stassen to task for his proposal to outlaw the Communist party. "I am unalterably, wholeheartedly and unswervingly against any scheme to write laws outlawing people because of their religious, political, social, or economic ideas," he declared.[28]

Alarmed at Dewey's drive, Stassen returned to Oregon several days earlier than he had planned. Though he had previously made two extensive swings around the state, Stassen now devoted the final nine days of the campaign to a whirlwind bus tour that covered 2,465 miles.[29] He lacked the funds, however, to match Dewey's barrage of newspaper, billboard, and radio ads which Stassen's advisers estimated cost about $140,000. Just before the close of the campaign, Stassen charged that Dewey had poured some $250,000 into the campaign and had made a deal with Taft to defeat him in the primary. Dewey angrily denied the accusations. "Our expenditures are but a tiny fraction of the ridiculous sum he mentions," said Dewey. "The frantic efforts to associate me with the views or actions of other Republican candidates for President is false. And Mr. Stassen knows it." [30]

The bad temper of the candidates also showed itself in small incidents. One day, Dewey was to make a brief appearance in Cascade Locks. Stassen arrived ahead of time and was genially distributing autographs when the Dewey bus came into sight. There was a small crowd on hand, as well as newsreel cameramen who had been altered to the expected encounter. But Dewey was not amused. At his orders, his bus picked up speed and whipped past the expectant crowd. The crowd booed and the mayor of Cascade Falls ripped off his Dewey button. [31]

One of the surprises of the Oregon campaign was that the question of outlawing the Communist party eventually emerged as the most contentious issue. In the spring of 1948, the nation had not yet experienced the preoccupation with Communist subversion which was to become one of the dominant political themes of the 1950's. The Hiss and Remington cases did not develop until midsummer; the first arrests of Communist party leaders on charges of violating the Smith Act did not occur until August. Domestic Communism, however, was already an issue early in 1948. The tensions of the Cold War inevitably aroused anxiety about domestic security. Two years before, the unmasking of a Soviet spy ring in Canada had prompted speculation of similar activities in the United States. In 1947, concern about the activities of Communists in government had led to President Truman's executive order setting up a program to investigate the loyalty and security of federal employees. In 1948, moreover, there was still a sizable Communist movement in the United States to inspire fears of subversion.

Stassen first raised the Communist issue by urging that the party be outlawed. Dewey took the opposite tack, arguing that the illegalizing of a political party or of a set of ideas was a dangerous invasion of civil liberty; only subversive acts should be prosecuted. "You can't shoot ideas with a gun," Dewey declared. [32] He reverted to the theme with increasing frequency, invariably getting a favorable audience response; the temper of the times, or of Oregon, was such that a stock invocation of the libertarian pieties was gratifyingly popular.

Midway in the Oregon campaign, Dewey finally agreed to debate

Stassen. Stassen had been challenging him for months, but Dewey had always avoided a confrontation. Lengthy negotiations now ensued as to the conditions of the debate. Stassen wanted to debate all issues before a live audience in a large arena, perhaps a ball park; Dewey's negotiators derided the proposal as a circus stunt, which would subject their candidate to unseemly heckling and perhaps booing; privately, they were even more concerned that Stassen, a taller and bulkier man than Dewey, would seem to dwarf him physically.[33] In the end, Stassen gave way on all points, out of an excess of eagerness or self-confidence. The debate was to be on radio, before a small studio audience, largely limited to journalists; the sole issue to be debated was whether the Communist party should be outlawed; there were to be no questions from the audience. Most importantly, Dewey would have the final rebuttal.

By the time the debate occurred on May 17, four days before the polling date, it had generated almost as much interest as the first Kennedy-Nixon debate in the 1960 campaign. The excitement was by no means spuriously created, for this was to be the first debate over nationwide radio between two Presidential candidates; nine hundred radio stations were to carry it live. On the outcome might hinge both the primary and the nomination.

More than sixty reporters and photographers were in attendance at station KEX in Portland. Apart from the main event, the press chronicled the peripheral encounters with that minute attention to historic detail that is usually reserved for champion prizefights. Dewey and three associates entered the studio first, then came Stassen with four colleagues, including Senator McCarthy. The exchange was hardly memorable. "Good evening, Tom," said Stassen. "We've certainly stirred up a lot of interest." Dewey laughed and replied, "We sure did." Groping for another pleasantry, Stassen remarked, "We've both seen a lot of Oregon." Dewey replied, "We sure have." [34]

The debate ran for an hour—two opening presentations of 20 minutes, followed by 8½-minute rebuttals.[35] Speaking first, Stassen argued that the Communist parties in all countries were directed by the Kremlin and constituted subversive "fifth columns" seeking to overthrow democratic governments and replace them by Soviet puppets. It was thus simple prudence, and no invasion of constitutional freedoms, to pass a law which "would make illegal organized conspiracy of fifth columns." This was Stassen's familiar argument. He then took off on a new tack by endorsing the Mundt-Nixon bill, pending before Congress, which would deny passports to Communists, illegalize conspiracy to establish a foreign-controlled totalitarian dictatorship in the United States, and compel Communist organizations to register and list their members. In Stassen's view, the new legislation would effectively outlaw the Communist party; it was just the sort of thing he had in mind all along. He was sure that Governor Dewey's disagreement was "sincere," but nonetheless accused him of a "soft policy toward communism."

When Dewey's turn came, he discarded his prepared speech and launched into an impromptu assault on Stassen's position. He accused Stassen of distorting the intent of the Mundt-Nixon bill in order to sustain an untenable argument. Copiously quoting from Congressman Mundt and from the committee report on the bill, Dewey maintained that the legislation was not intended to outlaw the Communist party. Rather, it was designed to illegalize subversive acts and, through its registration provisions, to force the party into the open. Dewey charged that Stassen, by embracing the bill, was surrendering on his initial proposal to suppress the Communist party.

In arguing this case, Dewey was well primed with source material. Sitting at a small table beside him were Elliott Bell and a young assistant named Robert Ray, both of whom would hand him bound volumes of congressional hearings. Bell, who had arrived by plane from New York that morning, had anticipated that Stassen might deal with the Mundt-Nixon bill and had spent the day boning up on the congressional hearings and marking passages. Dewey, always a quick study, was able to absorb the new material as rapidly as it was handed to him and improvise his arguments as he went along.[36]

While the Mundt-Nixon issue enabled Dewey to score the most effective debating point of the evening, the irony was that the passage of time later proved Dewey wrong: when similar registration provisions became law in the McCarran Act of 1950, their effect was to force the Communist party further underground. Dewey was on much stronger ground when he eloquently portrayed the dangers of outlawing ideas or associations per se. "This outlawing idea is not new," he argued. "It is as old as government. For thousands of years despots have shot, imprisoned, and exiled their people and their governments have always fallen into the dust." He favored "keeping the Communist party everlastingly out in the open so we can defeat it and all it stands for." When the encounter was over, Dewey had clearly emerged the victor.

It was impossible to know to what extent the debate affected the outcome of the primary, but on May 21 Dewey polled 53 percent of the more than 217,000 votes cast, winning all twelve delegates. The Oregon primary rehabilitated Dewey's candidacy and finished Stassen's.

# CHAPTER 4
# Truman
# Begins Early

Harry Truman's State of the Union speech, delivered before Congress at 1:30 P.M. on January 7, 1948, marked the opening of a reelection campaign that was to last for ten months. The speech of course made no mention of the coming election, for direct political references would be as inappropriate in a State of the Union message as in the British monarch's Speech from the Throne which opens each new session of Parliament. The lack of explicit partisanship is indeed the great advantage of the performance, from the President's point of view, for he is allowed to engage in a significant political act while enveloping himself in the ceremonial dignity of a state occasion. Both the Senate and House of Representatives are in attendance in the House chamber, as well as members of the Cabinet and ranking foreign diplomats. The throng invariably gives the President a standing ovation when he appears, although when Truman walked in two Republican legislators refused to get to their feet. The press reports the speech in full detail, usually placing it in the prime position on page one. In Truman's time, it was also broadcast over nationwide radio; in later years, live television was added. Thus for one long moment in history, at the beginning of each year, the President of the United States has the stage to himself, with the whole world listening.

Back in August 1947, when Clark Clifford was preparing his memorandum on strategy, his young assistant, George M. Elsey, first proposed that the State of the Union speech announce the political program on which the President would campaign. It was Elsey's view that the speech "must be controversial as hell, must state the issues of the election, must draw the line sharply between Republicans and Democrats. The Democratic platform will stem from

55

it, and the election will be fought on the issues it presents." [1]
Clifford agreed with Elsey and sold the proposal to the President.

Brevity, as well as boldness, was the goal Elsey and Clifford had
in mind when they wrote the message; they wanted a speech short
enough for Truman to deliver with ease and for the radio audience
to absorb without discomfort.[2] It had to be simply, not to say
baldly, written, for oratorical flourishes were beyond Truman's capacity. In the end, the speech was only 5,000 words long and,
while it is hardly a memorable political document, it achieved its
aim of providing the President with an audacious and venturesome
set of campaign themes.

In keeping with the occasion, however, the speech was formally
couched in terms of an assessment of the nation's progress over the
previous decade and a forecast of the public policy requirements in
the decade to come. "Our first goal," Truman announced, "is to
secure fully the essential human rights of our citizens," which
meant "effective federal action" to curb racial and religious discrimination. He promised a special message to Congress on the
subject. "To protect and develop our human resources"—which he
called the country's second goal—he proposed several ambitious
measures: federal aid to education; increases in unemployment
compensation, old age and survivors' benefits and their extension
to millions of people not presently covered; and a nationwide system of medical insurance which the American Medical Association
was subsequently to denounce as "socialized medicine." A long-
range housing program was equally essential, but until the severe
housing shortage could be overcome, rent control had to be extended and strengthened.

The conservation of natural resources was presented as the third
goal of national policy, with Truman calling for an expanded reclamation program, more multiple-purpose dams, and more integrated
development schemes on the model of the Tennessee Valley Authority. Fourth on his list came the need "to lift the standard of
living for all our people . . ." For farmers, he advocated continued
price supports, the encouragement of cooperatives, the extension of
rural electrification. Wage earners would be helped by raising the
minimum wage from 40 to 75 cents an hour. He also saw the need
for business to invest "at least $50 billion" to expand productive

facilities over the next few years, but made no specific recommendations to encourage that outlay.

Turning next to foreign affairs, Truman defined the fifth goal as the achievement of world peace based, as always in Presidential addresses, "on principles of freedom and justice and the equality of all nations." Full support was pledged to the United Nations. The President urged Congress to appropriate $6.8 billion for the first fifteen months of the Marshall Plan. He again asked legislation to allow "many thousands of displaced persons," living in refugee camps overseas, to enter the United States.

Winding up his speech, Truman devoted himself to the problem of inflation—the "one major problem which affects all our goals" —which the Clifford memorandum had also stressed two months before. The President put the matter crisply: "Food costs too much. Housing has reached fantastic price levels. Schools and hospitals are in financial distress. . . . Worst of all, inflation holds the threat of another depression . . ." In the sixteen months prior to October 1947, retail prices had gone up 23 percent; in the three months since October, they had increased at an annual rate of 10 percent. Once again, Truman called for the passage of his ten-point anti-inflation program which he had presented to a special session of Congress just two months before and which Congress had largely scorned, passing only three comparatively minor measures.

This time Truman did not bother to repeat his ten points; instead he had a surprise—a legislative proposal that was an artful public relations contrivance. Since inflation caused such hardship to people of modest means, he advocated a "cost of living credit" that would allow each taxpayer to deduct $40 for himself and for each dependent from his final tax bill; thus a married man with two children would save $160 in federal income tax. Federal revenues would thereby be reduced by $3.2 billion; Truman wanted to make up the deficiency by increasing the tax on corporate profits, which then stood at 38 percent. He said nothing in his speech about the further inflationary pressures that might be engendered by a $3.2 billion increase in consumer purchasing power; that point was to be made by his critics.

Viewed cynically, the speech was a generous shopping list which would benefit all groups in the community whose support the Democratic party already possessed or might conceivably win: wage earners, farmers, Negroes, conservationists, public power advocates, citizens of foreign birth who were regarded as especially concerned with the fate of displaced persons in Europe. Only business corporations, whose taxes would be increased, were excluded from Truman's proposed benefits—and they did not control many votes.

Viewed less cynically, Truman's message, despite its impoverished rhetoric, projected much the same expansive vision of American society that later animated the more felicitous utterances of John F. Kennedy and Lyndon B. Johnson. There was no talk of "New Frontiers" or of a "Great Society" (Truman's "Fair Deal" did not make its first appearance until 1949), but the President envisaged going far toward "stamping out poverty in our generation" and nearly doubling the prewar standard of living during the next decade. His proposals in the areas of expanded social security and aid to education were to recur in Democratic manifestos for a dozen years thereafter; indeed, not until the Johnson administration was a thoroughgoing program of federal aid to education enacted. Truman's medical program was also far in advance of his time; his plan, which was not fully spelled out in his speech, involved compulsory medical insurance for everyone, similar to social security coverage. It reappeared in truncated form in the Kennedy and Johnson plan for "medicare" for the aged, which was not finally enacted until 1965. Similarly with civil rights; the measures which Truman alluded to in his State of the Union address, and which he spelled out in a special message on February 2, foreshadowed the substance of much of the Civil Rights Acts of 1964 and 1965.

At the time, the speech hardly seemed of historic significance. Audience response was tepid, with no applause until Truman was halfway through; as usual, his flat, understated delivery did not inspire enthusiasm even from strong partisans. The Republicans began to applaud when Truman pledged emphatically that he would enforce the Taft-Hartley Act, though he still disagreed with it; they also joined in applause when he urged military strength upon the country. Otherwise, the handclapping was limited to brief outbursts by the Democrats when Truman outlined his domestic proposals.

On one occasion, laughter arose from the Republican side when three youngsters, children of members, unwittingly joined in Democratic applause for Truman's tax program.[3]

After the speech, Republicans spoke derisively of it. "A labored effort to promise all things to all people," said Senator H. Alexander Smith. "My God, I didn't know that inflation had gone that far!" exclaimed Representative Harold Knutson, chairman of the House Ways and Means Committee. "Tom Pendergast paid two dollars a vote and now Truman proposes to pay forty dollars." In the view of Representative Carroll Reece, Republican national chairman, "President Truman could have saved a great many words by simply writing a note to Henry A. Wallace stating 'Dear Henry: Come home, all is forgiven. . . .'" The day after Truman's speech, Senator Robert A. Taft delivered a half-hour reply over the ABC radio network. "The Federal Government comes forward again as Santa Claus himself," Taft charged. He estimated that Truman's new proposals would cost $5 billion a year. "Where is this money coming from?" Taft predictably inquired.[4]

Democratic politicians by no means unanimously favored the speech. In a compilation of the first twenty-three Democratic comments, the *New York Herald-Tribune*[5] reported that seventeen Democrats "generally" favored it while six ranged from "against" to "halfway for." Senator Claude D. Pepper of Florida thought the message was "magnificent," while Senator Alben W. Barkley of Kentucky, the minority leader, expressed more moderate enthusiasm by calling the speech "comprehensive." Truman had obviously evoked no crusading zeal in the troops; 1948 was going to be a long, hard campaign.

Press comment was less than ecstatic, even from journals favorably disposed toward Truman. Both the *Washington Post* and the *New York Times* liked much of the speech, but criticized the $40 tax credit as demagogic gimmickry which would compound the country's inflationary problems if it were ever enacted. *PM,* the liberal New York tabloid, gave the speech one of its few rave notices in a page-long editorial by Max Lerner.[6] Calling it "a whacking good document," Lerner wrote: "Not only does it have a large measure of Roosevelt's fighting liberalism; it even has some of his cockiness of tone." Like many commentators, Lerner suggested that Henry Wallace's third-party candidacy had given Truman "a leftward nudge," but he thought the nudge had not been overly important, given the fact that Truman had been moving in that direction anyway.

The State of the Union speech was followed by a succession of messages to Congress designed to keep the President's program in the headlines. Truman was thereby exploiting one of the major prerogatives of Presidential office which no congressional rebuff could deny him: the power to generate publicity, for any utterance of a President is news. Few Presidents have bombarded Congress with more unsolicited counsel than Truman did in the first months of 1948; around the White House, the staff slogan for the technique was "hit 'em every Monday." [7] Charles S. Murphy, an administrative assistant who handled congressional liaison, was in charge of the message-writing operation. On January 12, the day the budget message was issued, he wrote a memorandum to the President outlining eighteen more subjects for congressional messages—everything from civil rights to the St. Lawrence seaway. [8]

Thereafter the messages came in a relentless barrage, not all of them on Monday. On January 14, Truman issued his Economic Report to the Congress; on January 19, the governmental Reorganization Plan 1 of 1948; on January 26, a plan for a waterway that would link the St. Lawrence River to the sea; on January 29, a proposal for curbs on grain used in making ethyl alcohol. Nine more messages descended on Capitol Hill between February 2 and March 1: civil rights, extension of certain wartime controls, highway construction, assistance to Greece and Turkey, the International Telecommunication Convention, assistance to China, U.S. participation in the United Nations, housing, extension of the Reciprocal Trade Act. Some of these messages concerned relatively minor matters, but most of them sought to dramatize the gulf between the President's aggressive leadership and Congress' mean-minded obstructionism. For there was never any doubt that Congress would give the President little that he asked, except in the area of military preparedness and foreign aid. Congress performed as predicted.

By far the most important message was the February 2 one on civil rights, which ultimately led to the Dixiecrat breakaway and to a solidification of Negro support for Truman which had been one of the primary goals set forth in the Clifford memorandum. The message, however, was more than a campaign improvisation. Its origins went back to December 1946, when Truman created by executive order a prestigious Committee on Civil Rights, headed by Charles E. Wilson, then president of General Electric. Ten months later, the committee issued an exhaustive report calling for a variety of federal initiatives seeking to end discrimination in employment, protect the right to vote, suppress lynching, and effect more equitable naturalization procedures, among other things. The committee's report, "To Secure These Rights," was widely publicized and created a mood of aggressive expectancy among civil rights activists.

Truman's message incorporated ten of the recommendations of the Wilson committee. Asking the Congress to enact "modern, comprehensive civil rights laws, adequate to the needs of the day," he proposed a massive legal attack against most forms of discrimination which had afflicted Negroes in the eight decades since emancipation. He called for anti-lynching legislation, an end to segregation in interstate transportation, the establishment of a Fair Employment Practices Commission to secure equality in job opportunities, stronger statutory protection for the right to vote and "the right to safety and security of person and property," self-government for the District of Columbia, the establishment of a permanent Commission on Civil Rights. For his own part, Truman promised an executive order restating government policy against discrimination in federal employment as well as further steps to eliminate "the remaining instances" of segregation in the armed forces.

To the present-day reader, there are some evident gaps in the document, for it contains no proposals to insure equality in education, housing, and public facilities, such as hotels and restaurants. In 1948, however, these omissions were no cause for complaint, if indeed they were noticed by anyone but the civil rights professionals, for Truman's message contained far more than it omitted. As a Presidential paper it was remarkable for its scope and audacity; F.D.R. had never enlisted his immense prestige in any comparable crusade to aid Negroes, although he did create a wartime FEPC. It was hardly relevant that the Eightieth Congress was unlikely to heed Truman's exhortations; the message was nonetheless an historic one—and was so regarded at the time.

Southern congressmen bitterly denounced it. The outcry was magnified a few days later at a long-planned Conference of Southern Governors in Wakulla Springs, Florida. Though civil rights had not been on the agenda, the President's message inevitably became the center of attention. One of the more impetuous governors, Fielding L. Wright of Mississippi, urged the convening of an all-southern political conference to consider a bolt from the national Democratic party. His resolution was rejected; instead, a committee was set up to study the impact of the President's proposals. Another meeting would be held forty days later to see if progress had been made in restoring sanity to Washington.[9]

Meantime, on February 19, the annual Jefferson-Jackson Day Dinner was scheduled to be held in Washington. This is a ritualistic assemblage of party leaders convened partly for the purpose of raising morale and largely for raising money; $100 per plate is the traditional admission charge. In Washington, the ticket sale had gone so well that the 2,900 guests had to be divided between the Statler and the Mayflower hotels. The President addressed both throngs. At the Mayflower, the most dramatic event was a silent rebuke to Truman administered by Senator and Mrs. Olin D. Johnston of South Carolina—a large empty table strategically placed near the dais. Mrs. Johnston had secured the location because she had been a vice-chairman of the dinner committee; she and her guests then decided not to attend "because I might be seated next to a Negro," as she told the press. Senator Johnston, however, prudently sent a friend to make sure that no one else sat at the table, which had cost him $1,100.[10]

The dinner in Little Rock, Arkansas, that same evening also made the headlines. Some 850 party leaders, led by Governor Ben Laney, dutifully listened to Attorney General Tom Clark eulogize both the President ("the world's best hope") and the Democratic party ("the party of hope"), then on a motion of the Governor took a standing vote as to whether the proceeds of the dinner should be sent to the Democratic National Committee, as originally planned, or retained in Arkansas as a protest against the President's civil rights program. The chairman called the vote a tie and referred the matter to the party's state committee. Soon afterward, the voice of Harry Truman came over the loudspeaker, relayed by radio from Washington. About 400 diners got to their feet and quietly filed from the room.[11] Ironically, Truman did not say a word in his Jefferson-Jackson Day address about civil rights.

Four days later, on February 23, a committee of the Conference of Southern Governors called on Senator McGrath, in his capacity as chairman of the Democratic National Committee.[12] The group was led by Governor J. Strom Thurmond of South Carolina, who before his involvement in the Dixiecrat cause had been considered something of a liberal; the other governors on the committee were R. Gregg Cherry of North Carolina, Beauford H. Jester of Texas, and Ben Laney of Arkansas. Also present, as an observer, was Governor William Preston Lane, Jr., of Maryland, the chairman of the Conference of Southern Governors. Before the meeting, Lane privately told McGrath that he did not think the problem was as serious as the volume of southern protests might indicate; he would do what he could, as a kind of "friend of the court," to help patch things up.

With McGrath was Jack Redding, publicity director of the Democratic National Committee, who thoughtfully suggested that a stenographic record be kept, from which he was later to derive an amusing account of the confrontation. According to Redding, Governors Cherry and Laney were thoroughly relaxed about the affair, engaging in pleasantries with McGrath and acting as if they were involved in a friendly disagreement. Thurmond's attitude was entirely different. He was tight-lipped and unsmiling, permitted himself only a formal greeting, and refused even to sit down, despite frequent entreaties.

When McGrath opened the meeting, Thurmond began to read from a list of prepared questions in the aggressive tone of a district attorney. At first McGrath replied at length, quietly countering the southerners' contention that the President's proposals were an unconstitutional invasion of states' rights. It soon became apparent, however, that there could be no meeting of minds, for the southern demand came to little less than Presidential capitulation, and McGrath's responses became more and more abrupt. Thurmond, for example, asked, "Will you now, at a time when national unity is so vital to the solution of the problem of peace in the world, use your influence as chairman of the Democratic National Committee to have the highly controversial civil-rights legislation, which tends to divide our people, withdrawn from consideration by the Congress?"

"No," said McGrath.

The meeting broke up after an hour and three quarters, the southern demands having all been rejected. The governors then issued a statement declaring that "the Southern states are aroused and the present leadership of the Democratic party will soon realize that the South is no longer 'in the bag.' " [13]

In retrospect, it seems surprising that Truman and his advisers did not anticipate the vehemence of the South's response. Clifford's November memorandum flatly asserted that the South would remain loyal no matter what program the President enunciated. The White House was not alone in its miscalculation. On February 4, two days after the civil rights message, Charles Murphy called on the Senate minority leader, Alben Barkley, with a draft of an "omnibus" civil rights bill which the administration was eager to have introduced as soon as possible. Barkley told Murphy that he had an open mind toward the project, but he advised that the bill should not be introduced just yet, for the southerners were still "mad." He suggested that the administration hold off for a few days, at least until after the governors' conference in Florida. Barkley, however, was not apprehensive about the southerners' reaction, characterizing their anger as mere "froth." [14] His political antennae were as defective as those in the White House.

When the "froth" refused to settle, the administration quietly retreated. Truman never modified his civil rights proposals, but the omnibus bill which Murphy had been pressing was never introduced. Moreover, the administration was embarrassingly dilatory about initiating the action which Truman had promised to step up the campaign against discrimination in federal employment and against segregation in the military forces. In a memorandum written on March 29, nearly two months after the civil rights message, George Elsey[15] noted the sad fate of the proposed Presidential executive order on federal employment. Donald Dawson, a White House administrative assistant in charge of personnel, had been originally delegated by Clifford to draft the order. "The result was weasely and unsatisfactory," Elsey wrote, whereupon the assignment was given to Stephen J. Spingarn, an assistant general counsel in the Treasury. Spingarn's superior told him not to work on it and the chore was passed to Charles Murphy. Murphy then decided that the prudent course was to hold the matter in abeyance; his opinion had been reinforced, Elsey noted, by McGrath, Oscar Ewing and other "politicos."

In the end, both the executive order on federal employment and the one relating to the armed services were not released until July 26—nearly two weeks after the Democratic convention, which saw the passage of a militant civil rights resolution over the administration's opposition, and nine days after the designation of the States' Rights ticket in Birmingham, Alabama. Short of going back on his February 2 message, Truman had done all that he could to keep the Dixiecrats in the party. Truman's memoirs, written years later, are understandably silent about the lengthy period of gestation which his two executive orders underwent.

The southern rebellion which began in February was only one of Truman's problems. Since the first of the year, troubles had crowded in on him from all sides—some the consequence of his own actions, others the result of developments beyond his control. On the left, Henry Wallace's candidacy was causing increasing anxiety. True, in January Wallace had been scorned by the Congress of Industrial Organizations; anti-Communist liberals, led by Americans for Democratic Action, were opposing him; in New York State the Amalgamated Clothing Workers had broken with the pro-Wallace American Labor party, reducing its labor support to the left-wing unions. Nevertheless, predictions were widely made that Wallace would poll several million votes; even if he polled less, he could easily throw New York, Illinois, Michigan and California to the Republicans.

Democratic apprehensions became more acute after February 17, when a by-election was held in the Twenty-fourth Congressional District in New York City. The Twenty-fourth was a decaying, low income area bordering on the East River in the borough of the Bronx; ethically, it was 55 percent Jewish, 18 percent Negro; politically it had long been safely Democratic. Back in 1946, the Democratic nominee had won with a 15,000 plurality over the American Labor party candidate, who placed second. Confident about the by-election, Democratic boss Ed Flynn nominated a colorless lawyer named Karl J. Propper; the Liberal party, then the second of New York's "third" parties, put up Dean Alfange, who had a statewide reputation; the Republicans fielded a token candidate. By contrast, the ALP had an attractive and aggressive candidate in thirty-seven-year-old Leo Isacson, a labor lawyer who had served a term in the State Assembly.

Isacson embarked on an energetic campaign, stressing civil rights issues before Negro audiences, denouncing the administration for its inconsistent course on Palestine when he spoke before Jewish groups; everywhere he inveighed against inflation, demanded strong rent controls and, much as Wallace did, championed the cause of peace against the belligerency imputed to the White House. Waging a highly professional campaign, the ALP sent thousands of election workers from all over the city into the district, canvassing almost every tenement flat and working the sound trucks in Yiddish, English and Spanish. For the campaign windup, Henry Wallace, the famous Negro singer Paul Robeson, and Vito Marcantonio, the fiery left-wing congressman, all invaded the district. By contrast, the Democratic effort was routine. Late in the campaign, Flynn became alert to the danger and prevailed upon Mayor William O'Dwyer and Eleanor Roosevelt to speak in the Twenty-fourth. But candidate Propper was a lost cause; when the returns were in, the ALP's Isacson had taken almost 56 percent of the vote; the Democratic candidate had only 31 percent.[16] It was of little help to Democratic morale to argue that a by-election was a special case, enabling a minority party to concentrate all its forces in a single district. The majority party might have done the same thing. The plain fact was that Truman's support was being eroded from the left at the same time that it was being undermined in the South.

Disenchantment with the President was also spreading among voters who basically agreed with his policies. Early in January, Truman abruptly fired James M. Landis, a distinguished New Deal figure, as chairman of the Civil Aeronautics Board, by refusing to reappoint him when his term expired. Truman offered no explanation. The graceless way Truman handled the affair—he did not proffer a word of thanks for Landis' services—aroused widespread criticism.[17] Later in January, the President rejected Marinner S. Eccles for a new term as chairman of the Federal Reserve Board and replaced him with a Republican, Thomas B. McCabe of Pennsylvania. Eccles, however, agreed to remain on the board, for his term as a member had another ten years to run. His demotion was widely attributed to the hostility of John W. Snyder, the conservative Secretary of the Treasury and the President's devoted friend. Eccles had also offended the banking community by his proposal that banks be forced to build up secondary reserve funds as an anti-inflation measure and by his advocacy of a radical reorganization of the banking system that would centralize control in the Federal Reserve Board. Eccles' policies were hardly understood by the average newspaper reader; he was widely regarded, however, as opposed to "Wall Street" domination of the banking system[18] and, like Landis, he was a long-time New Dealer. To liberals, the firing of Landis and the demotion of Eccles were only the latest in a long series of inexplicable episodes by which Truman had eliminated most of the leading figures who had served Roosevelt. Nostalgic New Dealers once again felt betrayed.

Truman's public relations problems were further compounded by an investigation of commodity speculation by the Senate Appropriations Committee. The previous October, Truman had denounced commodity speculation as a prime cause of inflation. In January, Harold Stassen testified before the Senate committee that eleven government "insiders" had profited to the extent of $4,000,-000 by speculating in commodities since the war. He named only three of the eleven, and claimed that Edwin W. Pauley had run up $1,000,000 in profits; Stassen implied that Pauley had benefited from high-ranking government tipsters.[19] The charge was widely reported, for Pauley was a good friend of Truman, as well as a special assistant to the Secretary of the Army and a State Department adviser on reparations. Pauley freely conceded that he had made $932,703 in commodity deals over a three-year period, but denied that he had benefited from inside information; [20] no wrongdoing was ever proved against him, but, as always, the public airing of unsubstantiated charges was damaging.

Stassen's other major target was Brigadier General Wallace H. Graham, Truman's personal physician, who came off second best. Stassen charged that Graham had been less than candid in stating that he had gotten out of the commodity market after Truman had issued his blast. Now, called before the Senate committee, Graham conceded that he had been inaccurate; he had not ended his commodity trading until seven weeks after Truman's statement. Nor had he "lost his socks," as he had often said; he had actually made a profit of $6,165 in some five months of commodity trading, thereby doubling his investment. On the stand, Graham presented a picture of pained naïveté. Although he had traded on margin, he claimed not to know the meaning of the term. He said that he also had not realized that cottonseed oil and cotton were called commodities. Graham was only a puny operator, but his performance was a painful embarrassment for the administration. The day after his appearance, the White House announced that he would continue in his post.[21] Pauley decided to resign his army assignment.[22]

Any President, of course, is vulnerable to embarrassment by friends and retainers. Truman's difficulties tended to be intensified by a remarkable tolerance for human frailty, where his friends were concerned. Other embarrassments he brought upon himself. Early in the year, correspondents got word that Truman was planning to add a second-floor porch to the White House, located behind the pillars of the south portico. An uproar ensued. The Commission of Fine Arts denounced the plan. Congressman Frederick Muhlenberg of Pennsylvania, an architect by profession, declared that the White House "was a heritage of the American people, not lightly or casually to be altered at the whim of any tenant." The *New York Herald-Tribune* called the President "Back-porch Harry," suggesting that it was "scarcely an appellation that a man would like to carry into a Presidential campaign, even if he were impervious to the odium of violating good taste, propriety, and historical feeling." [23]

But Truman persisted with his plan. At a lively press conference on January 15, he pointed out that "There was the same opposition to putting bathtubs in the White House, and a cooking stove, and gaslight." Correspondent May Craig thereupon observed that these

innovations had not changed the structural appearance of the building. "Oh yes, but they did, in some instances," Truman replied.
"Entirely changed the interior of the White House when they put in
bathrooms . . . Mrs. Fillmore put the first bathtub in the White
House, but they almost lynched her for doing it." But Mrs. Craig
could not be put off. "Mr. President, the Republican comment is
that you are only a temporary tenant, therefore you are not—"

Truman was equal to that too: "No President has been anything
but a temporary tenant. That will continue, I hope, as long as our
Republic lasts."

The press derided Truman for his architectural folly for many
weeks. Even his friends took to calling the porch, "a monument to
a Missouri mule." [24]

Throughout January and February, while his trouble
increased, Truman genially fended off questions as to whether he
would run for reelection. At his January 22 press conference, a
correspondent alluded to the multiplicity of Republican contenders, but pointed out that so far there were no Democratic candidates. "Have you any idea when there will be any announcement?"
he asked.

"No, I haven't the slightest notion," said Truman.

The next question was "Will there be one?" to which Truman
replied airily, "Oh, eventually of course there will be one before the
Democratic convention meets in Philadelphia, but I don't see there
is any hurry about any announcement."

As late as March 1, at a press conference in Key West, Florida,
where he was taking a brief vacation, Truman responded to what
the correspondents called the jackpot question with the comment
that he was "so darned busy with foreign affairs and domestic
affairs and other situations that have developed that I haven't had
any time to think about any Presidential campaign . . ." Nobody
believed that he had not been able to spare a moment for his political plans, but it seemed likely that any announcement would be
many weeks off.

Thus it came as something of a surprise, a mere eight days later,
when Senator McGrath emerged from a White House meeting with

the President to announce that if nominated, Truman "will accept and run." McGrath, as he later recalled,[25] was equally surprised that he had been designated to make the announcement. For some time he had favored an early declaration by the President, for, with dissatisfaction about him growing more vocal, McGrath feared that other candidates might emerge who would receive delegate commitments which would later be embarrassingly difficult to pry loose. Soon after the President returned from Key West, McGrath called on him to press his appeal. "Well, Howard, if you think so, let's do it," Truman finally said. McGrath suggested that the President make his statement at his next press conference, but Truman preferred that McGrath inform the press as he left the White House. McGrath did so.

In March, the President further alienated support by two acts clearly animated by considerations of national interest. On March 17, he asked Congress to reimpose a peacetime draft as a prelude to Universal Military Training. Appearing before a joint session of the House and Senate, the President spoke of the critical situation in Europe resulting from the recent Communist coup in Czechoslovakia, renewed Soviet pressure on Finland, the civil war in Greece, and the "determined and aggressive effort" of a Communist minority to take control of Italy. Since the end of the war, said Truman, "the Soviet Union and its agents have destroyed the independence and democratic character of a whole series of nations in Eastern and Central Europe" and were planning to extend this "ruthless course of action" throughout the continent. To protect the freedom of Europe, Truman urged Congress to hasten action on the Marshall Plan, but argued that economic aid was not enough. The United States urgently had to increase its military strength in order to support European resistance to aggression. Hence the need for selective service legislation to keep the armed services up to their authorized strength; once that was accomplished, conscription could give way to a program of Universal Military Training which, according to prior proposals, would subject all eighteen-year-olds to a year's active duty followed by several years' enrollment in the reserves.

On several previous occasions, Truman had urged UMT on the

Congress; Congress had always rebuffed him. In 1947, the original wartime draft had finally been allowed to lapse. Despite the foreign situation, the reintroduction of peacetime conscription was inevitably one of the most unpopular proposals which any President could make. "There was scarcely anything Harry Truman could have recommended that could have aroused more controversy," *Time* reported.[26] "For the United States to accept conscription in time of peace is a momentous political act, a violation of very deep traditions and habits of mind," Freda Kirchwey warned in *The Nation*.[27] Politicians saw Truman not only losing the pacifist vote—which was of no great consequence—but the vote of half the mothers of America as well.

Two days later, the Jewish vote seemed in even greater jeopardy when the administration reversed its position on the partition of Palestine. The previous November, the United States as well as the Soviet Union had endorsed partition as the best solution when the British ended their mandate over Palestine. The country was to be divided between a Jewish state and an Arab state, linked in an economic union, with Jerusalem internationalized. The Zionists favored the plan, the Arabs opposed it and threatened a war over the issue when the British relinquished control on May 15, 1948; before long the Arab states began to mobilize troops on the borders of Palestine.

The Truman administration, however, refused to pledge itself to the use of military force to impose partition; one of its major anxieties, it was reported, was that a UN force would necessarily include Soviet as well as U.S. troops, thereby allowing the Russians to establish a military presence in the Middle East.[28] The Pentagon also argued, according to Truman's memoirs,[29] that the United States could not spare more than a token force to police the Middle East; there was also considerable anxiety that if the Arab states were alienated, they would deny the United States access to their oil supplies. From November through March, Truman was under enormous pressure from both his State and Defense Department advisers to change U.S. policy. The President finally gave way and on March 19, Warren Austin, the chief U.S. representative to the United Nations, made a speech in the Security Council in which he withdrew U.S. support for partition and instead proposed a temporary United Nations trusteeship over Palestine when British control ended.

Zionists felt betrayed; the Arabs were triumphant. Many non-Zionists shared a sense that the United States had chosen oil over lives, for Palestine had been the hoped-for refuge for hundreds of thousands of Nazi victims still scattered in the DP camps of Europe. Democratic politicians despaired of the electoral effect of Truman's action. *Collier's* Frank Gervasi quoted one unnamed Democratic senator as saying, "The antagonism of the Jews may produce a revolt, in those cities where their populations are largest, as damaging to Truman in November as was the anti-Catholic movement in 1928 to Al Smith." [30] (The prediction proved to be unfounded, for two months after his switch on partition Truman partly repaired the damage by extending diplomatic recognition to Israel within an hour after its provisional government was proclaimed on May 14.)

"How to lose friends and alienate people," the satirical reverse switch on the old Dale Carnegie slogan, increasingly came to exemplify Truman's impact on the electorate. By the beginning of March, there was a growing impression that Truman was doomed to defeat; by the end of the month, the impression had solidified into a conviction. Gallup polls taken in March indicated that Truman would lose to either Dewey, Stassen, Vandenberg, or MacArthur; Taft was the only man Truman could beat. [31] In April, a nationwide Gallup poll reported that only 36 percent of the American people approved Truman's performance as President—a sharp decline from the 55 percent who approved in October 1947. Fifty percent disapproved of him in April, as compared with only 29 percent in October. [32]

The certainty of Truman's doom inspired perhaps the most ludicrous development of the entire campaign—the effort to discard him in favor of General Dwight D. Eisenhower. Before the anti-Truman movement had run its course, it enlisted the most diverse elements in the party—southern segregationists, the liberal militants of Americans for Democratic Action, big city "bosses" such as Jacob M. Arvey of Chicago and Frank Hague of Jersey City, the three politically active sons of F.D.R. (James, Franklin, Jr., and Elliott), a variety of labor leaders, and the Liberal party of New York. All were united in the belief that not only was Truman a sure loser but that his position at the head of the ticket guaranteed the defeat of many local candidates who might otherwise win.

The effort to ditch Truman was being quietly discussed by early March. On March 10, James Loeb, the executive secretary of ADA, circulated a memorandum to his colleagues in which he reported that "one of the staff members of the CIO Political Action Committee approached me unofficially with the suggestion that the liberal and labor people start campaigning for someone else, because a Truman nomination would be disastrous to the whole liberal-labor coalition, to say nothing of success in the campaign." Loeb suggested that the "wave of seemingly justified defeatism should be given serious attention by the ADA Executive Committee and the National Board." [33]

The day after Loeb sent his memorandum, *Time*,[34] in a cover story about Clark Clifford, reported a Washington rumor that Philip Murray, president of the Congress of Industrial Organizations, and Jack Kroll, head of the CIO's Political Action Committee, were devising a strategy both to persuade Truman to withdraw as a candidate and to persuade Eisenhower to run in his stead—an "extraordinary idea," *Time* found it. *The Nation* simultaneously appeared on the newsstands with an article—"Must It Be Truman?" by Dale Kramer—which reported that "Those tremors recorded on the political seismograph are Democrats asking each other: Will President Truman step aside and let the nomination go to a man with brighter prospects of victory?" Kramer attributed the desire to be rid of Truman to three motives—"personal irritation with the President, political desperation, and the dispassionate conviction that Mr. Truman is simply not equipped to deal with the monumental problems of the times." [35]

By the end of the month, the rebellion began to erupt in all parts of the country. In Chicago, Jack Arvey announced that he would no longer support Truman; he had not picked a candidate, he said, but suggested that Eisenhower "comes closest to representing the ideals of the Democratic party." [36] In New York, Franklin D. Roosevelt, Jr., a vice-chairman of ADA, called upon the Democratic convention to draft Eisenhower. Declared Roosevelt: "Circumstances require a man who will convince the Russian leaders that the constant aim of our policy is to secure . . . lasting peace . . . and who, at the same time, will take all necessary steps to stop further aggression . . . by the USSR against the free peoples of the world. The American people have such a man in General Eisenhower." Roosevelt was not dismayed by the fact that in January Eisenhower had foresworn all political aspirations; Roosevelt argued that thereafter the Communist coup had occurred in Czechoslovakia and "we have entered a period as critical as that after Munich. The American people have a right to call the General back into active public service." [37]

Two days later, Elliott Roosevelt issued a similar statement. That same week, Alabama's two senators—John Sparkman and Lister Hill—publicly urged Truman to withdraw. Their defection was considered significant, for both were well known as liberals; Hill had nominated Roosevelt for a third term at the 1940 convention. Labor leaders began to make similar noises. Max Zaritsky, president of the AFL hatters' union, stated that Truman had "completely lost" the confidence of the workers.[38] Louis Hollander, head of the New York State CIO, commented that "I hope the President will not be a spite candidate"—like Henry Wallace.[39]

Meeting in Pittsburgh on April 12, the National Board of ADA repudiated Truman's candidacy and urged that the nomination go to either Eisenhower or Supreme Court Justice William O. Douglas. A few days later, at a Jackson Day dinner in Los Angeles, Senator McGrath was boisterously booed when he ended his speech with a peroration that compared Truman to F.D.R. "His heart is just as sincere, his purposes are fought for just as courageously, his stand is for the right. . . . Can we ask for more than this in leadership?" Amidst the boos and the clanking tableware, the crowd chanted "Yes! Yes!" Eisenhower was their man.[40]

Meantime, Eisenhower expressed a total lack of interest in a Democratic draft. "I wrote a letter and I meant every word of it," he told the press. But his Democratic admirers could not be persuaded to desist. "He may be pulling the door a little closer to him, but I didn't hear the lock click," said Senator Claude Pepper.[41]

The draft-Eisenhower movement was to continue to the eve of the Democratic convention. It was a ludicrous adventure, but hardly inexplicable. Eisenhower's Democratic admirers not only had no notion of his party preferences, but were equally in the dark about his views on domestic issues; the General, after all, never had any need to voice his opinions on the Taft-Hartley Act, agricultural price supports, tax policy or Truman's anti-inflation program. Indeed, there was no way of knowing from the record whether he was a liberal or a conservative. What was clear was that Eisenhower was a man of peace and bountiful goodwill. He was also immensely popular among voters of both parties. Even if he was not a liberal, he could win (as the 1952 election later was to prove). Victory is a prize that all politicians cherish, but what was so entertaining about the unrequited Democratic passion for Eisenhower in 1948 was that it was shared by so many liberals who normally claim to value principle above power.

In April, when Truman's prospects looked bleakest, an event occurred which would ultimately affect the entire style of his campaign. For months Truman's staff had been perplexed by the problem of improving his performance as a speaker. Although he had been in public life for over two decades, he had never mastered the art of reading a speech. He would bow his head over his manuscript and plow straight ahead in an uninspired drone of words; modulation, shifts of pace and emphasis were all beyond him. Someone, probably Clifford or Elsey or Murphy (no one can remember just who) got the idea that the President ought to try an extemporaneous speech before a large audience, for it was a common observation that he was often quite engaging when speaking off the cuff before small groups in the White House. The President was agreeable and the experiment was scheduled for his appearance before the convention of the American Society of Newspaper Editors in Washington on April 17.

Truman first delivered a prepared speech about his anti-inflation program, then went off the record for an extemporaneous talk.

He was lively, colloquial, relaxed, and remarkably effective; the editors applauded generously and in the weeks that followed there were occasional references in the press to how well he had done.

Truman recalls the incident in his memoirs: "After reading an address to the American Society of Newspaper Editors in April, I decided to talk 'off the cuff' on American relations with Russia. When I finished my remarks about thirty minutes later, I was surprised to get the most enthusiastic applause that I had ever received from a group made up mainly of Republicans." [42] Truman's account is basically accurate, except for an omission characteristic of his memoirs: he gives no indication of the careful staff work that made possible his seemingly sudden decision. When he launched into his extemporaneous talk, he had before him detailed notes on the topics to be covered, neatly arranged in outline form under main subject heads, subheads and sub-subheads. The outline was prepared by Charles Murphy, whose papers at the Truman Library in Independence, Missouri, contain two copies of the document, one typewritten, the other in Murphy's hand.[43]

Truman adhered to the suggested sequence of topics, from the immediate postwar relations with Russia to an exhortation to the editors: "Let us all work together." His improvisations were his own and had the characteristic flavor of the man. Speaking of the obstructionism of Soviet Foreign Secretary Molotov at the founding meeting of the UN in 1945, Truman recalled that "I had to send Harry Hopkins to Moscow to see Mr. Stalin to please call Mr. Molotov and tell him to behave and sign the Charter, which he did." About Stalin, he observed, "I like old Joe—not a bad guy when you get a chance to talk face to face" (a comment which he was to repeat publicly two months later in somewhat altered form). He was disarmingly modest about himself; referring to the problems of aircraft production, he remarked, "With all the information I got I would be rather dumb if I didn't know something about it. Some people may think that, anyway." [44]

Truman followed his ASNE success with three other off-the-cuff speeches in Washington. On May 1, he addressed the National Health Assembly dinner at the Statler Hotel, performing on this occasion without an outline. George Elsey noted in a memorandum that the speech was "satisfactory" and added, "We are all encour-

aged by this effort & hope Pres will keep it up." Truman was insist-
ing, however, that he would not speak over radio without a manuscript, as both Clark Clifford and Charles G. Ross, his press
secretary, were urging him to do when he addressed the National
Conference on Family Life on May 6.[45] In the end, Clifford persuaded Truman to risk the experiment and he carried it off well.
Though a large crowd was present in the Departmental Auditorium,
Truman appeared relaxed and displayed a happy sense of timing.

In a detailed analysis of the audience response, Elsey commented that the President was interrupted eight times for applause
or laughter in the course of a 13½-minute speech—a remarkable accomplishment for Truman. The crowd loved such a homey
Trumanism as "Children and dogs are as necessary to the welfare
of the country as Wall Street and the railroads" and also responded with laughter to the moderate self-derogation of "People
talk about the powers of a President, and what a powerful executive he is, and what he can do. Let me tell you something—from
experience!" A President's powers were not all that remarkable; his
principal power, said Truman, was "to bring people in and try to
persuade them to do what they ought to do without persuasion."
More laughter. Hardly any sparkling wit in these lines, but what
charmed the crowd was the homespun informality not normally
associated with the office of President.[46]

Gaining confidence by each effort, Truman next tried an impromptu political talk. Appearing before a dinner meeting of a
thousand young Democrats at the Mayflower Hotel, the President
delivered what the *New York Times* called a "fighting" speech "in
the new Truman manner." [47] He talked with pugnacious assurance
about his own reelection, he ridiculed and taunted the opposition
and altogether gave the illusion of a leader who never doubted that
he was in the ascendancy. "I want to say to you," he announced,
"that for the next four years there will be a Democrat in the White
House—and you are looking at him!" The crowd roared its approval, whereupon Truman quipped, "I was not mistaken when I
said what I did about those bright young faces here tonight!"

These oratorical exercises were part of Harry Truman's preparations for his remarkable "nonpolitical" tour in June. In his memoirs, Truman writes, "Early in May I had an idea—perhaps the

only one that the critics admitted was entirely my own. In order to circumvent the gloom and pessimism being spread by the polls and by false propaganda in the press, I decided that I would go directly to the people in all parts of the country with a personal message from the President." [48] A coast-to-coast train tour, lasting two weeks or more, was projected.

Truman's account is accurate as regards the purpose of the trip, but his recollection of its origins is faulty. As previously noted, Clifford's memorandum of November 1947 proposed such a trip. Throughout the winter and early spring, Truman's political advisers were quietly developing plans. In February, Oscar L. Chapman, the Under Secretary of the Interior, presented the President with a plausible excuse for a cross-country tour. The excuse itself was not contrived. Robert Gordon Sproul, president of the University of California, wanted the President to deliver a commencement address on the Berkeley campus on June 19. As is customary in these matters, Sproul tried to determine the likelihood of Truman's acceptance before sending a formal invitation. He spoke first to Paul S. Taylor, a Berkeley professor of economics who was also a consulting economist to the Interior Department. Through an intermediary, the matter soon reached Chapman, who liked the idea.

On February 17, Chapman placed a long distance call to Sproul to make certain that the university would also offer an honorary degree to Truman; Taylor had thought that was the plan, though he was not certain. Sproul assured Chapman that a degree would be forthcoming, although the university's board of regents first had to approve it. Some entertaining byplay then occurred, with Chapman suggesting that Sproul would have trouble with at least three of his regents. Sproul replied that there were enough regents who would favor giving the President a degree; he insisted he had no fears on that score. Chapman conveyed his intelligence to the White House and the President ultimately approved the project. [49]

Apart from the distinction of its degree, the University of California had the advantage of being some 2,500 miles from Washington, which would enable the President to stop at dozens of places en route to greet the voters and proselytize for his program. The trip would be by rail, which in 1948 was still regarded as a normal mode of Presidential travel, although Truman usually flew. By calling it "nonpolitical," not only would the proprieties be observed but the cost of the trip would be borne by the government rather than by the impoverished Democratic National Committee. (The President had an annual travel allowance of $30,000.) Five major speeches were planned—in Chicago, Omaha, Seattle, Berkeley, and Los Angeles. Clifford was in charge of preparing texts, with Murphy's and Elsey's assistance (in the end the Los Angeles speech was delivered from an outline). The back-platform talks were to be off the cuff, using local color supplied by the newly created Research Division of the Democratic National Committee.

The Research Division had been set up at the behest of the White House speech writers, who during the winter realized the need for a group of experts to research the issues of the campaign, document the opposition's record, and provide the raw materials for the scores of speeches that the President would be called on to deliver.[50] The new group, which was to play an important part in the campaign, was headed by William L. Batt, Jr., a young Harvard graduate, army veteran, and liberal activist who in 1946 had made a quixotic effort to become elected as a Democratic congressman from a Republican "main line" suburb outside Philadelphia. He had been in the army with David Morse, the Under Secretary of Labor, who recommended him to Clark Clifford. Clifford had persuaded Howard McGrath to allow the Research Division to function under the National Committee's auspices, but it was clear from the outset that Batt's group would really be an adjunct to the White House staff—a fact which provoked some resentment on the part of Jack Redding, the committee's publicity director.[51] The Research Division's independence was symbolized by the fact that it was not located in the committee's offices in the Ring Building (there was actually no room for it there) but in a Connecticut Avenue bank building near Du Pont Circle. Batt drew up a budget of around $50,000 and hired a staff of five or six professionals, plus secretaries.[52] One of his best recruits was David D. Lloyd, then research director of Americans for Democratic Action, who so impressed Truman's brain trusters that he was added to the White House staff after the campaign.[53]

The June trip was a strange affair. Covering eighteen states, it was as ambitious as a major campaign tour, yet it often seemed improvised and amateurish. It had only one advance man, Oscar Chapman, who hopped around the country a mere three to five days ahead of the traveling party.[54] In the first few days, the trip blundered from one small disaster to another, all of them amply chronicled in the press. The crowds were initially only mildly curious. Then in the Far West, the President suddenly caught on; the crowds increased; and the trip ended as a small triumph.

Perhaps the most professional aspect of the operation was the elaborate physical setup provided on the sixteen-car train. The President traveled in the rear in a luxurious special car, with armor-plated walls, called the Ferdinand Magellan; it had been built by the Association of American Railroads for President Roosevelt and contained sleeping quarters, bath, galley, a dining room and a walnut-paneled sitting room. A new public address system had been installed on the back platform. For working quarters for the President's staff, a conventional dining car had been converted into a suite of offices, complete to reception room. Another dining car was transformed into a newsroom. The Signal Corps had a car of its own in which it installed radio and cryptographic equipment. Wherever the train went, it was in continuous radio contact with Washington; when it stopped, land telephone lines were immediately hooked up.

The train carried 125 people: the President's immediate staff, Secret Service men, Signal Corps technicians, Western Union representatives, railroad personnel, and 59 reporters and photographers—a record press party for a Presidential tour.[55] The President's personal entourage was limited to official White House aides, among them Clifford, Murphy, Ross, and appointments secretary Matthew J. Connelly. In keeping with the ostensibly nonpolitical nature of the trip, no representative of the Democratic National Committee accompanied the President; even McGrath was left at home. The opposition was hardly impressed. Carroll Reece, chairman of the Republican National Committee, remarked that the trip was as "nonpolitical as the Pendergast machine." [56]

The train left Washington's Union Station at 11:05 P.M. on June 3. On hand to bid farewell were Secretary of State George C. Marshall, Secretary of Defense James Forrestal, Secretary of Agriculture Charles F. Brannan, Attorney General Tom Clark, and Senator McGrath. The President was jaunty and cheerful. "If I felt any better, I couldn't stand it," he told reporters.

The first day, June 4, passed without any untoward incident. On his way to Chicago, the President made back-platform speeches and greeted local political leaders at Crestline, Ohio, and Fort Wayne and Gary, Indiana. At noon in Crestline, he displayed the bantering, folksy tone which was to enliven many of his utterances. He confided "how intriguing it is . . . for the President to get away from the White House and get to see the people as they are. The President, you know, is virtually in jail. He goes from his study to his office and from his office to his study, and he has to have guards there all the time."

He also joked slyly about the nature of his trip: "On this nonpartisan, bipartisan trip that we are taking here, I understand there are a whole lot of Democrats present, too." He then went on to endorse Frank Lausche for election as governor of Ohio. Ex-Governor Lausche stood nearby, beaming.

At Fort Wayne at 2:20 P.M., Truman proceeded quickly from some local pleasantries to a short lecture on how to keep the peace of the world, in the course of which he berated the Congress for not providing the Universal Military Training program which he had been continually urging since 1945. Ten minutes later, at Gary, he set the political tone of the tour with a bitter attack on Congress for not controlling inflation. "This Eightieth Congress has not seen fit to take any action," he declared. A new Congress was the only solution and he expressed the hope that "maybe we'll get one that will work in the interests of the common people and not the interests of the men who have all the money."

In Chicago, two leading Democrats—Mayor Martin H. Kennelly and Senator Scott Lucas—met Truman at the railroad station and drove with him in an open car, through a fluttering downpour of paper, to the Palmer House. The estimated 100,000 persons on the street were friendly but hardly enthusiastic. The President was in a jovial mood, even when the motorcade turned the corner of Jackson Boulevard and State Street and Truman confronted banners urging "Democrats Dump Truman—America Needs William Douglas or Eisenhower." Truman waved at the demonstrators, who seemed both surprised and embarrassed.[57]

He had a crowded evening, first attending a private banquet given by the Mayor. Truman reminisced a bit about Chicago. "In earlier years," he said, "I came to Chicago on shopping trips with Mrs. Truman. I enjoyed looking in the windows. No one paid any attention to me then. I suppose a lot of people wish I was looking in windows again. But they won't get their way because a year from now I'm going to be right back in the same trouble I'm in now." [58]

After dinner, he drove to the Chicago Stadium for the major event of the day, an address before twenty thousand persons celebrating the centenary of the first Swedish settlement in the Midwest. The speech, carried over a nationwide radio hookup, began with a tribute to the Swedish pioneers, then discussed the plight of the 800,000 displaced persons in European refugee camps for whose benefit Truman urged more generous immigration legislation than Congress seemed in the mood to pass. He next addressed himself to the problem of how best to combat communism. Outlawing the Communist party, he argued, was no solution. "As far as the United States is concerned, the menace of communism is not the activities of a few foreign agents or the political activities of a few isolated individuals. The menace of communism lies primarily in those areas of American life where the promise of democracy remains unfulfilled." All of which led him to a plea for his full domestic program: "Let us adopt legislation that will provide our citizens with the homes they need, the opportunity for universal good health and universal free schooling, the extension of social security, the full rights of citizenship, an equal chance for good jobs at fair wages and a brake on inflation that will hold the purchasing power of these wages at a high level." It was a typical Truman speech, full of the predictable liberal clichés, and read with his usual lack of distinction. It aroused no cheers.

The next day the train moved west to Omaha, Nebraska, where

the President's World War I outfit, the Thirty-fifth Division, was holding its annual reunion. The morning was devoted to fun and games. The President was riding in an open car as the reunion parade began. He had traveled about a block when his old buddies of Battery D took up the cry, "Come on, Harry, we're walking!" Truman jumped out of the car without opening the door, and fell into step at the head of the column, next to his old barber, Frank Spina, who carried the guidon. Dressed in a double-breasted tan gabardine suit and brown-and-white shoes, the President marched briskly for half a mile, grinning and waving his hat at the crowds lining the sidewalks. He then took up a position on the reviewing stand, where he was entertained by such hijinks as an old soldier turning somersaults and marching past on his hands and another carrying a pitchfork at present arms. One enthusiastic cowboy rode by on a horse and rather inexpertly tried to lasso the President. The rope fell over his shoulder; Truman quickly disentangled himself and shook hands with the prankster.[59]

That evening the first of a long series of mishaps occurred. Although the police estimated at least 150,000 people had been out on the streets to greet Truman, fewer than 2,000 appeared to hear him speak at the Ak-Sar-Ben Coliseum (Nebraska spelled backward), which seated 10,000. Photographs were published throughout the country showing the small crowd up front and the endless rows of empty seats stretching behind. The President's embarrassment made far more of an impression than did his stern speech assailing the Republicans for betraying the interests of the farmers. (Later, it was explained that the meager turnout had occurred because Edward McKim, an old Omaha buddy of the President who was handling the arrangements, had failed to publicize the fact that the meeting was open to the public; most people assumed that it was only for the reunioneers of the Thirty-fifth Division, under whose auspices the President spoke.)[60]

Meantime, Truman was unexpectedly creating ill will among local politicians, largely because of slipshod liaison. Nebraska's state chairman, William Ritchie, complained that he had no chance to talk with Truman and had been given "the bum's rush." Ritchie was caustic about the President: "I'm convinced that he cannot be elected. He has muffed the ball badly. He seems to prefer his so-called buddies to the persons who have done the work and put up the money for the party." [61] The Montana state chairman was soon to be equally unhappy, because Truman had refused to allow local party leaders to travel through the state on his train—an immemorial custom on Presidential campaigns. The prohibition was designed to lend plausibility to the nonpolitical character of the trip.[62]

Perhaps the most disconcerting blunder of the trip occurred in the small town of Carey, Idaho, where Truman arrived to discover that the local citizens were expecting him to dedicate the new Wilma Coates Airport. Someone thrust a wreath in his hands; though he was unprepared for the ceremony, Truman was game. He saw an honor guard of uniformed men standing at attention, and apparently got the impression that the airport was named after a local war hero. "I'm honored," he began, "to dedicate this airport and present this wreath to the parents of the brave boy who died fighting for his country . . ." A tearful woman, standing nearby, interrupted to say that Wilma was a girl. Startled and embarrassed, the President began again: "Well, I'm even more honored to dedicate this airport to a young woman who bravely gave her life for our country." Mrs. Coates again had to correct the President: "No, no, our Wilma was killed right here." The sixteen-year-old girl, it developed, had been killed in a civilian plane crash. The shaken Truman apologized to the bereaved parents.[63]

As the train rolled on, Truman's verbal slips mounted; speaking off the cuff, without even an outline to guide him, he often seemed incapable of censoring himself. In Pocatello, Idaho,[64] he unexpectedly confided, "I have been in politics a long time, and it makes no difference what they say about you, if it isn't so. If they can prove it on you, you are in a bad fix indeed. They have never been able to prove it on me." All of which seemed to be a totally gratuitous reference to his past association with the Pendergast machine.

His exuberance often led him to shed all the dignity of Presidential office. Presented with a pair of spurs in Grand Island, Nebraska, he exclaimed, "These spurs are wonderful. When I get them on, I can take the Congress to town!" Given some cowboy boots in Kearney, Nebraska, he remarked, "I really can take Congress for a ride now." [65] His humor was rarely subtle. In North Platte, Nebraska,[66] he commented that there were nine hundred members of the Lions Club in town for a convention. "You ought to have some cages," he advised. "I hope nobody gets clawed."

His most celebrated verbal indiscretion occurred during a back-platform appearance in Eugene, Oregon, on June 11. He gave a rambling little talk, in the course of which he spoke a few words about his pursuit of peace and about the Potsdam conference in 1945 at which he met Joseph Stalin. Then came the memorable lines which sent the reporters scurrying to their typewriters: "I like Old Joe! He is a decent fellow. But Joe is a prisoner of the Politburo. He can't do what he wants to. He makes agreements, and if he could he would keep them; but the people who run the government are very specific in saying that he can't keep them."

Truman's utterance created a sensation, as much for its jovial friendliness as for its contradiction of a view our Soviet experts had long held: that Old Joe ran the Politburo and was the undisputed dictator of Russia. In Washington, Charles E. Bohlen, counselor of the State Department and later ambassador to the USSR, relayed a message to Clark Clifford, through George Elsey, in which he said he was mystified by the President's remark. Robert A. Lovett, Under Secretary of State, also telephoned Clifford about the matter. Clifford undertook to attempt to persuade the President not to repeat his statement.[67] He never said it again in public.

Truman, however, seemed unperturbed by his bobbles, for there was little doubt that his back-platform appearances were pleasing the crowds. He always included some local reference—the Idaho potato, Montana mining, the Grand Coulee Dam—often exclaimed that "half the state" seemed to be out to see him that morning, spoke a few sober words about the need to secure peace or to spend money on reclamation projects, and would end by introducing Mrs. Truman—"my boss"—and his daughter Margaret. ("I am henpecked by another member of my family whom I would like to introduce to you.") Neither of them would say a word, but they always got a big hand; the women in the crowd were especially pleased to see the Truman ladies.

A typical Truman performance, midway in the trip, occurred in Sacramento on June 12. "My grandfather, you know, owned the site of Sacramento," Truman informed the crowd. "He was a freighter from Westport, which is now part of Kansas City, Missouri, to Salt Lake City and San Francisco. They made a deal one time and obtained twenty-seven Spanish leagues of land in the Sacramento Valley on a part of that site that Sacramento City is upon." Then his grandfather's partner had decamped with the assets of the freighting company and the Sacramento ranch had to be sold in order to pay grandfather's debts. "Now think of that! I probably would not have been President of the United States if the old man had kept that valley. . . .

"I was invited to come to California by the President of the University of California to make the graduation address . . . and at the same time to receive a degree from that university. I am most happy that the President of the university invited me. That gave me an excellent excuse to make a nonpolitical trip across the country and tell the people what I think. . . . And I am extremely happy that I have had the opportunity to see as many people as I have on this trip, and to explain to them the policies of the President of the United States, so that when these issues are drawn and when these conventions meet, and when they make their platforms, the record of the President of the United States will be one platform, and the record of the policy committee of the United States Congress will be the other. And then you will have a chance to take your choice and see which one you want. . . .

"When I ride up and down the streets in these great cities, people stand on the sidewalk and say, 'Hi, Harry.' Now there isn't another head of a state in the world to whom that can be done. That means that the people are the government of the United States. They elect the President, they elect the Vice-President, they elect the Congress, and when they don't like what the Congress does or the President does, when the time comes they can turn him out and try another one, who may not be quite so good, but at least it's a change. In this instance, I don't think you will want to make a change when the time comes, but we will discuss that when I go on my political tour." Laughter and applause.

Truman's informality continually amazed the press. Twice he appeared late at night in pajamas and bathrobe. In Missoula, Montana, he told a crowd, "I understand it was announced I would speak here. I am sorry that I had gone to bed. But I thought I would let you see what I look like, even if I didn't have on any clothes." [68]

The following week, Truman's train nosed into Barstow, California, sometime past midnight. The crowd at the railway station was dismayed to see the Presidential car shuttered against the night. But suddenly Truman appeared on the rear platform, attired in a blue dressing gown and blue pajamas. He was met with a roar of surprise and pleasure.

A female admirer, out in the throng, asked whether he had a cold. The President denied it. "But you sound like it," she insisted.

Truman grinned. "That's because I ride around in the wind with my mouth open." [69]

Mixed with the jocularity came increasingly vituperative attacks on the Republicans. In a speech in Butte, Montana, on June 8, in which he criticized the Congress for failing to enact an anti-inflation program, Truman referred to a statement once made by Senator Taft that the way to reduce food prices was for people to eat less. "I guess he'd let you starve," said Truman. "I'm not that kind."

In Spokane on June 9, a reporter for the *Spokesman-Review* asked him how he liked being in a Republican stronghold. Truman responded by denouncing the reporter's paper as being, together with the Chicago *Tribune*, "the worst in the United States." Both papers, he added, had gotten just what they wanted in the Eightieth Congress—"the worst we've ever had since the first one met." The epithet of the "worst Congress," headlined across the country, prompted Republicans to retort in kind. The House Majority Leader, Charles A. Halleck, called Truman "the poorest President" since George Washington.[70] Representative Cliff Clevenger of Ohio called him a "nasty little gamin" and a "Missouri jackass." [71]

The following day, in Bremerton, Washington, Truman charged that "this Congress is interested in the welfare of the better classes. They are not interested in the welfare of the common, everyday man. . . . The poor man is having to pay out all his money for rent and for clothing and for food at prices that are certainly outrageous." At that point, a loud voice rang out in the audience: "Pour it on, Harry!"

"I'm going to—I'm going to!" replied Truman. In a few days, he said, Republican congressmen would gather in Philadelphia "to tell you what a great Congress they have been! Well, if you believe that, you are bigger suckers than I think you are."

The asperity showed even in some of Truman's back-platform repartee. In San Bernardino, he was given a gift basket of eggs. "At least they didn't throw them at me," he joked. Someone called out: "What about throwing them at Taft?" To which Truman shot back: "I wouldn't throw *fresh* eggs at Taft." [72]

The joviality and the bombast made effective political vaudeville. "His reception has been uniformly cordial," Richard L. Strout reported in the *Christian Science Monitor*. "Most reporters on board feel that this warmth has increased as the journey progressed. Just why is a matter of speculation, but it may be that word has gone round that a scrappy fighter is making an uphill fight." [73] From Montana westward the crowds grew in size and enthusiasm. In Butte, 40,000 people crowded the downtown section to give Truman a boisterous welcome; 10,000 filled an outdoor stadium for his speech.[74] In Seattle, the police estimated the street crowds at 100,000—the largest outpouring in thirty years, more than Roosevelt had drawn.[75] At Berkeley[76] some 55,000 were on hand in an outdoor arena for his commencement speech—a sober, well-reasoned discussion of foreign affairs and of the impasse in our relations with the Soviet Union. (*Time,* no idolator of Truman, called the address "one of the best speeches of his career, delivered with dignity, poise and eloquence.")[77]

Two days later, in Los Angeles, the President received the most enthusiastic welcome of the trip. Between 750,000 and 1,000,000 people lined the flag-draped route, some five miles in length, between the railroad station and the Ambassador Hotel. A mounted sheriff's posse, in black and yellow uniforms, led the parade; airplanes roared overhead; a sky-writing plane wrote a welcome in smoke; confetti and torn telephone books rained down on the motorcade. Truman rode through the streets like a homecoming hero.[78]

Opening his speech before the Los Angeles Press Club, he exclaimed that the city's reception had "topped them all." He then had a little sport with Senator Taft's comment, in a recent speech, that "The President is blackguarding the Congress at every whistle-stop in the country. . . ." Said Truman, with a delighted grin: "Los Angeles is the biggest whistle-stop!" He then went on to up-braid Congress for its delinquencies, and to urge that it act on no less than eight major issues—from housing to health insurance—before adjourning five days later. "If they haven't time, they ought to take it," said the President.

After Los Angeles, Truman headed back to Washington, with four more days of back-platform talks in Arizona, New Mexico, Kansas, Missouri, Illinois, Indiana, Ohio, Pennsylvania, Maryland. When he reached Washington at 12:55 P.M. on June 18, he had been away for 15½ days, had covered 9,504 miles and delivered 73 speeches.[79] "I have seen, I imagine, about two and a half millions of the people," he told an audience in Dodge City, Kansas, two days before the end of the trip. "I have talked to a great many people, and a great many people have talked to me, and I think I have found out what the country is thinking about. I think I have definitely fixed the issues which are before the country now. It is merely the fact: are the special privilege boys going to run the country or are the people going to run it?"

Whatever he had discovered about the country's mood, Truman had clearly found an effective political style. So ended the first phase of his reelection campaign, which had begun six months before with the State of the Union address.

# CHAPTER 5
# The Republicans Nominate a President

The Republican convention began on Monday, June 21. "We are here to nominate the Thirty-fourth President of the United States," declared the keynote speaker, Governor Dwight H. Green of Illinois, on the first evening of the convention. Such a confident assertion is part of the ritual of every Democratic and Republican Presidential convention; the proprieties demand it; the delegates expect it—no matter how bleak the party's electoral prospects. In Philadelphia in 1948, however, there was no hint of bravado in the keynoter's boast, no synthetic boisterousness about the crowd reaction; to most people in the vast, steamy hall, the cliché for once expressed the truth. The Republicans were not merely nominating a candidate; for the first time in sixteen years they were handing him the keys to the White House.

On the eve of the convention, Dewey was clearly in the lead, a position which he had secured after his victory over Stassen in the Oregon primary. Taft was regarded as Dewey's principal opponent, for Stassen was now a long shot, a status which he was naturally reluctant to acknowledge. But Dewey was not so far ahead as to be unbeatable; the delegates had no reason to think of themselves as supernumeraries in a scenario which had already been written. Dewey was generally credited with no more than 300 to 350 votes on the first ballot, whereas 548 votes were needed to win.[1] The authoritative James A. Hagerty of the *New York Times* calculated that the three leading candidates controlled two-thirds of the convention's votes. The remaining third was largely pledged to nine "favorite sons"—all but two (Governor Earl Warren of California and Senator Arthur Vandenberg of Michigan) token candidates

91

with not the remotest chance of victory.[2] As a gesture of esteem, they would get the votes of their states at least on the first ballot. Meantime, their delegations' leaders would have time to deliberate, to be wooed and to bargain before deciding which of the leading candidates to favor on the second or third ballots.

Success for Dewey, Taft, or conceivably even Stassen was thus likely to hinge on how the favorite-son states decided to switch. Substantial blocs of votes were involved: 73 in Pennsylvania, 56 in Illinois, 53 in California, 41 in Michigan, 35 in Massachusetts, 35 in New Jersey, 29 in Indiana, 22 in Tennessee, 19 in Connecticut. Two days before the convention, Dewey's managers predicted that he would attract enough additional support to win on the fourth or fifth ballot.[3] Stassen had already announced that he would win on the ninth ballot.[4] Supporters of Vandenberg and Warren made no predictions. Their only hope was that a prolonged convention dead-lock would lead to the emergence of their man as a compromise choice.

Warren had long been an avowed candidate for the Presidential nomination. When he arrived in Philadelphia, he announced that he was not at all interested in the Vice-Presidency.[5] Vandenberg played a more enigmatic role. For months he had resisted the en-treaties of friends to declare his candidacy. He was sixty-four, in less than robust health, and apparently content with his post as chair-man of the Senate Foreign Relations Committee.[6] But while he did not want the nomination, he was equally unwilling to exclude him-self definitively. Two days before the convention opened, Governor Kim Sigler of Michigan announced that Vandenberg was "available as a candidate for the Presidency, should that be the demand of the people." Sigler made it clear, however, that Vandenberg would not seek to persuade the people.[7] To the dismay of his friends, Van-denberg held to that resolve after he arrived in Philadelphia. Apart from one visit to the convention hall, he remained in seclusion, received only a few friends and did no politicking. It was a self-defeating way of rendering oneself "available."[8]

So unclear was the situation on the eve of the convention that there was even speculation about a third dark horse—Joseph W. Martin, Jr., of Massachusetts, a conservative of no discernible en-lightenment, intellectual distinction or popular appeal (outside his own constituency), whose principal claim to consideration was the high regard in which he was held by House Republicans who shared his distaste for welfare measures and foreign spending. Recently Martin had been one of the leaders in the House move, which had been partially successful, to reduce appropriations for the Marshall Plan.

To the internationalist wing of the party, Martin symbolized a frightening isolationist ground swell among Republicans. This phenomenon led many internationalists to see the convention in apocalyptic terms, a view reflected (not to say furthered) in the syndicated column of Joseph and Stewart Alsop. On June 21, for example, they wrote: "The stage is set at Philadelphia for the final struggle between . . . the backward-looking and modern-minded Republicans. The issues have been made brutally plain by the recent behavior of the leaders of the House of Representatives. The situation is too uncertain, moreover, to rule out altogether an isolationist victory, in the form of the nomination of Senator Robert A. Taft, or Speaker Joseph W. Martin, or even Senator John Bricker." [9]

The high stakes and the unpredictable outcome created a sense of suspense, but hardly of solemnity. The American political convention may be one of the crucial mechanisms of the democratic process, but it is equally a carnival, designed to amuse the participants and enrich the merchants of the host city. Before the convention began, Philadelphia's hoteliers, restaurateurs, nightclub owners and shopkeepers looked forward to $35,000,000 in additional revenue. Some 200,000 visitors were expected, creating a seller's market that allowed the hotels to increase their rates by 50 percent; with appropriate horror, newspapers reported that double rooms were now costing $12 a night. To attract the convention, the city of Philadelphia had given the Republicans a $250,000 gift. (The Democrats, who were to convene in mid-July, received a similar amount, but Henry Wallace's third party, due the last week of July, got nothing.) The city also appropriated $650,000 to spruce up its convention hall—new roof, freshly painted interior of blue and gold, better lighting and acoustics. The ventilating system was also improved, but a modern air-conditioning plant was too expensive. Provision was also made for extensive television coverage. This was to be the first Presidential convention in which television was to play a major role, for there were now an estimated 400,000 TV sets along the eastern seaboard, the furthest reach of the coaxial cable which brought live transmission. In an auditorium adjacent to the convention hall, several television lounges were set up to accommodate an overflow crowd of six thousand.[10]

Several days before the convention opened, the leading candidates established their convention headquarters—Dewey's at the Bellevue-Stratford, Taft's at the Benjamin Franklin, Stassen's at the Warwick. The Dewey forces took over the hotel ballroom, mounting three huge photographs on the stage—a color picture of the Governor, flanked on one side by the state capitol in Albany and on the other by the national capitol. Every visitor to Dewey headquarters was deluged with gift samples of candy, cosmetics, cigarette holders, matches donated by friendly manufacturers, together with a shopping bag with Dewey's name imprinted on all sides. Every two hundredth visitor received a door prize.

At Stassen headquarters the loot was cheese, parceled out from four 300-pound Swiss cheeses sent by admirers in Wisconsin, a strong Stassen state. Stassen's cause was also boosted by a dazzling blonde in nautical costume, rowing a boat on the lobby floor of the Bellevue-Stratford; when not rowing, she distributed Stassen buttons. Tacked to the bow was a sign reading, "Man the Oars and Ride the Crest / Harold Stassen—He's the Best." The Taft forces also had a mascot who never failed to stir interest—Little Eva, a baby elephant a mere four feet tall, who was paraded in and out of hotel lobbies with the Taft band and glee club. Everywhere it went, the glee club sang a song which likened Taft to a four-leaf clover.[11]

Stassen was the first candidate to arrive in Philadelphia, on the Thursday before the convention opened. On Sunday, Dewey, Taft and Warren all arrived. That afternoon Taft held a remarkable press conference in the Crystal Room of the Benjamin Franklin. The Senator and his campaign manager, Representative Clarence J. Brown of Ohio, settled down on a pink sofa against the wall, under two huge photographs of Taft. Just as the press conference began, the photographs fell from the wall, landing atop Taft's and Brown's heads.

The Senator had no sooner regained his composure when an Indian mahout walked up with the baby elephant, who for the occasion was wearing a blanket imprinted with the legend, "Win With Taft." Delighted with the confrontation, the cameramen urged

Taft to shake Eva's trunk. Taft did so, grinning gamely. "Shake it again," a cameraman urged. "It's your baby." And the Senator complied.

Turning finally to the business at hand, Taft estimated that he would have 300 votes on the first ballot. "The race is largely between myself and Mr. Dewey," he remarked, "and I think I have the better chance." But he refused to predict on what ballot he would win. He also emphatically denied rumors of a deal between himself and Stassen. They had not conferred, "and there is no bargain in prospect," he said.[12]

There was a greater crush at the Dewey press conference, with some five hundred reporters and photographers in attendance, but no falling pictures or intruding elephants. Dewey, dapper in a tan lightweight summer suit, sat behind a battery of microphones on the ballroom stage, responding to questions with crisp good humor. "Are you available for the Presidency?" a Cleveland reporter asked him. "For the benefit of the gentleman from Ohio, the answer is yes," said Dewey. Did he expect to be nominated? He did indeed. On what ballot? "I don't know," said Dewey, then added, "An early one, I should think." Asked about the record of the Eightieth Congress, with which a liberal Republican could hardly have been happy, he commended it generously, particularly on foreign affairs. It was a diplomatic response, designed to appeal to conservatives. He did not believe, however, that Congress had completed its work on civil rights. Whatever the state of its unfinished tasks, he was emphatically opposed to summoning Congress back into session after the party conventions. A special session would be "cruel and inhuman punishment," he said. On whom? "Both the candidate and Congress," he retorted, flashing a smile.[13]

The following morning the convention formally opened at 11:07 A.M. The first session was mercifully over before 1:00 P.M., for even in the forenoon the enormous hall, with its fourteen thousand seats under the huge batteries of klieg lights, began to resemble a vast communal sweat box. The major speech at the morning session was by B. Carroll Reece, the national chairman; it had a timeless quality, best typified by a long quotation about the principles of the Republican party which had first been uttered by Elihu Root at the Republican convention of 1904. In heralding the Republicans' return to power, Chairman Reece spent so much time retrospectively denouncing the New Deal (for "unbelievable waste, curtailment of freedom, debasement of the currency, chronic unemployment") that the inattentive listener could easily have gotten the impression that the party was still running against F.D.R. The crowd applauded politely.

That evening the hall was packed for the keynote address. Despite the heat, an air of gaiety and triumphant expectation was stimulated by the rousing tunes of the organ and of the sixty-two-piece brass band. "This was the richest, the noisiest, the most exuberant quadrennial Republican meeting since Franklin D. Roosevelt won the White House," Meyer Berger wrote in the *New York Times* the next day.[14] After the stirring musical buildup, Governor Green's keynote address was something of an anticlimax. It had all the familiar pieties ("Here in Philadelphia wise men shaped the Constitution. . . . We in this convention hail once more that immortal charter . . ."), the familiar denunciations of the New Deal ("the sorriest series of broken promises in the history of our nation"), the familiar panegyrics to the record of the Eightieth Congress. The one new theme for a Republican keynote was a call to cleanse the government of subversives ("We shall ferret out and drive out every Red and pink on Federal payrolls"). It was a shapeless, wide-ranging speech, compensating in bulk for what it lacked in inspiration. It was cheered at the end, but the effort seemed to have exhausted both Governor Green and the crowd.

Then came ex-Congresswoman Clare Boothe Luce, petite, blond, immaculate-looking under the harsh lights, with an endless fund of blunt wit and sarcasm that left the crowd alternating between laughter and applause. She scorned Truman—"a gone goose . . . a man of phlegm, not of fire. He just can't read those old Bob Sherwood lines with the oomph they need for the curtain calls in November." The Democratic party was "less a party than a podge. It is a mishmash of diehard, warring factions" made up of a Jim Crow wing, a Moscow wing "masterminded by Stalin's Mortimer Snerd, Henry Wallace" and a center "or a Pendergast wing . . . run by the wampum and boodle boys, the same big city bosses who gave us Harry Truman in one of their more pixilated moments."

She tore into the Democrats on foreign policy. "On the great issue of war or peace the Democrats are divided . . . Wallace says that Truman wants war at any cost. Truman says that Wallace wants peace at any price. Both may be right. . . . 'I like Old Joe,' says Mr. Truman . . . Good old Joe! Of course they liked him. Didn't they give him all Eastern Europe, Manchuria, the Kuriles, North China, coalitions in Poland, Yugoslavia and Czechoslovakia?"

It was a rousing bit of vaudeville, of a sort which few politicians could perform, and it was to remain the rhetorical high point of the convention.

On Tuesday, the delegates elected Representative Joseph W. Martin, Jr., as permanent convention chairman, approved the report of the credentials committee which had voted to seat the sixteen-man Dewey delegation from Georgia rather than the rival Taft delegation—it was Dewey's first victory of the convention—and in the evening indulged in a remarkable display of nostalgia and affection when ex-President Hoover came forward to address the throng. Hoover's appearance at the podium touched off a sixteen-minute demonstration, with the delegates parading through the aisles, waving their state standards and singing "The Battle Hymn of the Republic." [15] Mr. Hoover then delivered a quiet lecture in which he assured his admirers that "You are here to feed the reviving fire of spiritual fervor which once made the word *American* a stirring description . . ."

While the fires of spiritual fervor were being tended on the hot convention floor, the real business of the gathering—the selection of a Presidential candidate—was being pursued in air-conditioned bars and quiet hotel rooms. The Dewey command post was on the eighth floor of the Bellevue-Stratford Hotel, in Suite 816, where the triumvirate of Herbert Brownell, J. Russel Sprague, and Edwin F. Jaeckle directed the operation.

In appearance and personal style, Dewey's three top men seemed to span the political generations. Brownell, forty-four, was the youngest of the group. He was a slender, balding man with the dry and understated manner of a college professor; though quietly affable, he was no glad-hander and sometimes gave the impression of being a dedicated calculating machine, the technocrat in politics. By contrast, Ed Jaeckle, fifty-one, the Republican leader of

Buffalo, looked every inch the big city political boss, for he was a hulking, paunchy man with a beak nose, a thatch of white hair, and an outsized joviality that matched his frame. Russ Sprague, sixty-one, was the oldest, a suave, well-tailored gentleman who seemed to be a throwback to a more genteel era of Republican ascendancy, which still prevailed in his native Nassau County, New York, where he had long been party leader.

For Brownell, Jaeckle, and Sprague, the convention was the culmination of four years' work. They were beautifully organized, with liaison men assigned to every state delegation and with a file card on almost every delegate to the convention. Dewey's Albany aides, members of the New York delegation, and other reliable supporters were all given missionary assignments among the unconverted. The pursuit of delegate Chester Gillespie of Cleveland was typical. Gillespie was pledged to Stassen on the first ballot. A Negro, he was a friend of Judge Francis E. Rivers, a leading Negro Republican from New York City. Judge Rivers was thus logically assigned to Gillespie. Meeting him on the first day of the convention, Rivers stressed Dewey's contribution to the civil rights cause, for New York had been the first state to pass a law against discrimination in employment. Gillespie was even more impressed when he was invited to meet Dewey, who received him for a midnight chat that lasted half an hour. By the time he left, Gillespie had pledged himself to switch to Dewey on the second ballot. Thereafter, Judge Rivers met Gillespie at breakfast each day and rarely let him out of his sight.[16]

While these quiet incursions were going on in the enemy camp, the Dewey strategists were preparing their major offensive. Their first breakthrough occurred on Tuesday. At his morning news conference, Brownell told reporters to expect a big story later in the day when the announcement would be made of who would nominate Dewey. Soon afterward, it became known that Senator Edward Martin of Pennsylvania was in conference with Dewey, Brownell and Sprague in Room 807 of the Bellevue-Stratford. The press realized that something important was in train, for Martin was the "favorite son" candidate of the seventy-three-man Pennsylvania delegation, which was openly split between a pro-Dewey faction led by Martin and ex-Senator Joseph A. Grundy, and another faction led by Governor James H. Duff, which favored Vandenberg. Martin's favorite-son candidacy was a compromise to keep the delegation's vote intact until the leaders could resolve their differences and come down decisively on one side or the other.

Martin conferred with Dewey for an hour. Then he returned to his headquarters in the Warwick Hotel, where he issued a statement that he was withdrawing as a candidate for President and would instead make the nominating speech for Dewey. This was a major coup, for Martin's move not only guaranteed Dewey an additional 35 to 50 votes on the first ballot but had the psychological advantage of indicating an irresistible trend toward his candidacy. The press promptly labeled the breakthrough a "blitz." Brownell, who was normally not given to hyperbole, claimed that Martin's announcement would have "the effect of a new, improved atomic bomb." [17]

The beneficiary of the bomb, Thomas E. Dewey, found his afternoon press conference jammed with eight hundred reporters, television and radio technicians. He strode in smartly, posed for photographs for a full five minutes with a jubilant smile on his face, responded with a resonant "I feel swell" when asked how he felt. With the manner of a man who has already won, he expressed gratitude to Senator Martin, whom he characterized as an old friend, but blandly denied that he had sought to launch a "blitz." On the other hand, he was happy to oblige the press with a list of the many delegations which had been waiting upon him—Alabama, Indiana, Maine, Nebraska, North Dakota, South Dakota, Oklahoma, Oregon, Wyoming, Rhode Island. When asked about his views on a Vice-Presidential candidate, he vigorously denied that he had made any deals with anyone: "There has been no understanding, arrangement, bargains, or deals for anything of any kind or character—for Vice-President, for Cabinet offices, jobs or patronage." It was a statement which signified that Dewey had changed the character of the American political convention.[18]

The Martin coup shook the opposition and did as much as anything to create the legend of Dewey's "ruthlessness"—which basically meant superior tactics and greater efficiency, as well as shrewd trading of future jobs for present support, if one believed the rumors. Cynics took understandable delight in pointing to the incongruity of the alliance between Dewey, the enlightened, liberal Republican, and such an unreconstructed relic of the Old Guard as eighty-five-year-old Joe Grundy. But such bizarre alliances are the stuff of convention politics.

Harold Stassen, characteristically, put up a brave front after the Martin *démarche*. The Pennsylvania announcement, he told a news conference, was an indication of "desperation," a clear "mark of weakness"—presumably because Dewey had felt the need to display second-ballot strength on the first ballot. Said Stassen: "That sudden announcement of the Grundy-Dewey deal, without a caucus, coming from a smoke-filled room before the balloting began, is no sign of strength. It is the opening move at the start of one of the most exciting sessions in the history of the Republican Party." [19]

Before the excitement was to reach the convention floor, the delegates had one more chore—the adoption of the party platform, which was unanimously approved on Wednesday. In foreign affairs, the platform was determinedly internationalist and in domestic matters it was far more liberal than the Eightieth Congress (to which it nonetheless paid abundant tribute), favoring federal aid for housing, a long-range farm program, reclamation projects dearly prized in the West, and a variety of civil rights measures. In deference to southern sensibilities, however, the platform committee agreed to drop an earlier plank favoring a Fair Employment Practices Commission. Conservatives were appeased by the omission of any reference to federal aid to education and by a meaningless compromise that involved support for reciprocal tariff reduction while "at all times safeguarding our own industry and agriculture."

Nominating speeches for Presidential candidates were scheduled for Wednesday night; while the delegates were bracing themselves for the oratorical deluge, Dewey's strategists triggered four more announcements. The most important came from Representative Charles A. Halleck of Indiana, who stated that he was withdrawing as a favorite-son candidate, that he would second Dewey's nomination, and that all of Indiana's 29 votes would go to Dewey on the first ballot. (Previously, Taft and Stassen had been expecting some Indiana support after the first ballot.) Earlier in the day, Governor

Alfred E. Driscoll of New Jersey announced his support for Dewey, assuring him of 22 of New Jersey's 35 votes on the second ballot. Senator James P. Kem of Missouri also joined up, as did Governor Robert F. Bradford of Massachusetts, bringing Dewey the bulk of the votes in their delegations.[20] Dewey was now clearly going to get well over 400 votes on the first ballot, far more than his nearest rival.

The recruitment of Indiana was almost as surprising a development as the Martin announcement. Halleck, the House majority leader, was a prewar isolationist and a conservative in domestic affairs who might logically have been expected to support Taft. That Halleck endorsed Dewey was a tribute to the skill of Dewey's strategists; it was also a consequence of Halleck's ambition. Halleck, then forty-seven, wanted to be Vice-President. He thought Dewey was going to be President and, as he is quite candid in stating, he thought he had made a deal.[21] Dewey, on the other hand, consistently maintained that he had no commitments to anyone.[22]

One fact is not in dispute. It was important to capture Indiana if the Dewey "blitz" was to maintain its momentum. For some time, Dewey's managers had an even bigger prize in mind—Illinois, with 56 delegate votes—and considerable effort had been made to persuade Governor Green, another "favorite son," to swing his delegation to Dewey after the first ballot. But Colonel Robert R. McCormick, the eccentric and irascible publisher of the Chicago *Tribune,* to whom most Illinois Republicans were beholden, detested Dewey and insisted that the delegation remain solid for Taft. So it did, with Governor Green making the announcement on Wednesday that Illinois would support Taft after the first ballot. Once it was clear that Illinois was unattainable, Indiana became a crucial objective for Dewey.

What is in dispute is just what was said to Halleck. According to Halleck,[23] there was a meeting in one of the Dewey suites at which Brownell, Jaeckle, Sprague, Leonard Hall, Mason Owlett and one or two others were present. He was offered the Vice-Presidential nomination if he did two things: swing the entire Indiana delegation to Dewey and make a seconding speech in his behalf. "The offer was unequivocal," says Halleck.[24] Dewey was not present.

Dewey has repeatedly denied that he ever authorized anyone to make such an offer to Halleck.[25] Brownell maintains that he was not present at the meeting with Halleck and suggests that Halleck might have misunderstood an expression of esteem and possibility as a flat offer.[26] Jaeckle in effect confirms Halleck's story. He says[27] that the plan of Dewey's strategists was to allow Halleck to draw the "inference" that he was being offered the Vice-Presidency without actually making a commitment in unambiguous language. Jaeckle says that he was opposed to the scheme, for he always believed that Warren would be the choice.*

While the Dewey offensive was rolling forward, with strategically timed announcements and endless rumors about new support—"They have literally manufactured the whole conversation of this convention," [28] the Alsop brothers wrote—the opposition was frantically trying to put together a defensive alliance. On Tuesday night, Taft, Stassen, and Pennsylvania's Governor Duff met secretly at the apartment of John D. M. Hamilton, a Philadelphia lawyer who had been national chairman in the mid-thirties. In this crisis atmosphere the ideological gulf between Taft and Stassen was quickly bridged—though it was hardly irrelevant when it later came to devising strategy. They traded estimates of each other's delegate strength, found themselves in substantial agreement, and shared their alarm at the way Dewey was stampeding the convention in advance of the first ballot.[29]

They held another meeting the following morning at Hamilton's apartment, agreed on the urgency of a coalition to stop Dewey, and decided to convene a larger group that afternoon. The new recruits were Governor Kim Sigler of Michigan, spokesman for the Vandenberg group; Harold E. Mitchell, Connecticut national committeeman who had 19 votes pledged to Senator Raymond E. Baldwin; and Preston Hotchkiss, who represented Governor Earl Warren.

The newspapers had learned of the morning meeting and resolved that the afternoon session would not go unobserved. The problem was that the press did not know where the meeting was to be held. Reporters stood guard at every exit to Stassen headquarters and followed the candidate when he descended in an elevator.

---

* Another Dewey adherent present at the meeting, who after nearly two decades refused to be quoted on the matter, stated flatly to me that a commitment had been made to Halleck.

On the street, he disappeared into a limousine, whereupon a group of newsmen leaped into a jeep and gave chase; the jeep was followed by a line of cabs and motorcycles. Stassen's limousine had a good head start, but the pursuers finally caught up by swerving through a filling station and driving along a stretch of sidewalk. The convoy halted before 2031 Locust Street, an apartment house in which Hamilton lived on the eleventh floor. The press dashed into the elevator with Stassen, only to retreat when the candidate insisted on going upstairs alone.[30]

The flurry of activity resulted in no new strategy. The obvious way to try to stop Dewey would have been to combine behind one candidate. Personal ambition in large part made that solution impossible. Neither Taft, Stassen, nor Warren wanted to decline in favor of one of the others, nor were Vandenberg's supporters willing to relinquish his claim. Moreover, given the policy differences between Taft and his three rivals, it was not certain that their supporters would switch allegiance on command—for the sole purpose of denying the nomination to Dewey.[31] Dewey was hardly loved, but he was by no means universally detested by delegates whose first allegiance lay elsewhere. On the other hand, it was obvious that Dewey lacked the strength to win on the first ballot; if he could be kept from reaching a majority on the second or third, his support was likely to erode and thus one of the other four candidates might have a chance. Thus the only strategy that emerged was for each man to stand firm, holding his own delegates behind him.

Speaking to the press after the final conference, Senator Taft explained that "we decided it was not our job to agree on a candidate. The real purpose was to keep everything open so the nomination will develop in a free and uncontrolled way. The Dewey blitz is already stopped. I feel very encouraged. I feel that if the delegates have a perfectly free hand I will be nominated in due time." He insisted that Dewey would not get more than 400 votes on the second or third ballot.[32]

At 9:20 P.M. on Wednesday night, the formalities of nominating a Presidential candidate began. Under the best of circumstances, a nominating session is a test of an audience's endurance and masochism, even when only three or four candidates are to be presented. Tonight there were to be seven—each entitled to a fifteen-minute nominating speech, a floor demonstration, and several five-minute seconding speeches. When the roll call of the states began, Alabama, by prearrangement, yielded to Pennsylvania. Up to the podium strode Senator Edward Martin, freshly turned out in a white suit. Loud boos rolled down from the galleries. Three times Chairman Joe Martin rapped for order, shattering a water pitcher in the process. The galleries finally quieted down and the Senator was able to proclaim, "By every test there is one man who towers above all others. . . . He has the American people behind him. He has the fighting vision to wage a winning campaign. He can carry the crushing burden of the Presidency." Martin concluded by announcing that it was "the greatest honor of my life" to present to the convention "America's next President—Thomas E. Dewey." [33]

The utterance of the candidate's name, always at the end of the speech, is of course the traditional signal for his supporters to leap into the aisles to dramatize their enthusiasm. The candidate's home state always leads the way. Veteran convention observers thought that the New Yorkers were a little slow in unfurling their banners and adjusting their standards; despite the convention band and another on the floor, the Dewey demonstrators were notably incapable of working themselves up into any frenzy of enthusiasm and the galleries remained unresponsive. But the demonstrators managed to troop around the hall for thirty-two minutes, which made it a respectable show.

Senator John Bricker of Ohio came next, nominating his colleague Taft ("I give you a man of great faith. A faith in divine guidance, a faith in his government, a faith in himself"), after which Representative George Bender took over the podium, ringing his cowbell and shouting "We want Taft! We want Taft!" as platoons of teen-agers leaped out among the delegates on the floor with balloons, cowbells, rattles, and placards with such slogans as "To Steer Our Craft, Let's Have Taft" and "To Do The Job, Name Our Bob." They loosed scores of balloons, which floated to the ceiling trailing Taft banners; they screamed and cavorted and snake-danced through the aisles and kept going for five minutes longer than the Dewey demonstration. Again, the galleries were indifferent. The Warren demonstration also failed to evoke audience interest, despite the presence on the platform of movie stars George

Murphy and Irene Dunne, chanting, without benefit of cowbell, "We want Warren!"

Stassen, it turned out, had the galleries. He also mounted the liveliest demonstration, with the rowboat containing the blonde being carried aloft by a dozen marchers, with two bands on the floor, and with a drum majorette, a group of Scottish bagpipers and an Indian chief up on the platform. In her enthusiasm, the drum majorette lost control of her baton, which twirled out of her hands and hit a delegate in the eye. After twenty-two minutes, the Stassenites retired. Speeches and demonstrations for Baldwin, Vandenberg, and MacArthur were still to come. It was nearly 4 A.M. when the session ended, with some six thousand people still in the hall.

The delegates were allowed to sleep late on Thursday morning; the balloting finally began at 2:35 P.M. The first vote took a mere thirty-nine minutes, for only two states—Maine and Wisconsin—demanded that their delegations be polled individually. (There had been a bit of confusion in Maine, with the delegation originally only being able to account for 12 of its 13 votes.) When the roll call was over, Dewey had 434 votes, Taft 224, Stassen 157, Vandenberg 62, Warren 59, MacArthur 11, Speaker Martin 18, Green 56, Driscoll 35, and all others 35. (Representative Everett M. Dirksen of Illinois received one vote.) Dewey had done better than his opponents had expected, whereas their strength was almost exactly what Dewey's strategists had predicted before the convention opened.

An hour and two minutes was required for the second ballot, for five states now wanted to be polled individually. Taft added 50 of Illinois' 56 votes, which had previously been cast for Governor Green; Dewey picked up 24 of New Jersey's 35 votes; he also got 10 votes in Iowa and anywhere from 1 to 5 additional votes in 25 other states. The second ballot count showed Dewey 515, Taft 274, Stassen 149. Dewey was a mere 33 votes short of victory.

As is usually the case, the result was apparent to scorekeepers on the floor ten or fifteen minutes before it was announced from the platform, thereby providing an interval for one or more states to switch their votes and gain the honor of putting over the winning candidate. Senator Raymond E. Baldwin, chairman of the Connecticut delegation, was now eager to switch to Dewey the 19 votes he had received as a favorite son. But he had made a commitment to Michigan and California not to break away until after the second ballot. To get a release from his pledge, he rushed around the convention floor, managed to confer with the Michigan delegation, which also wanted to break, but was unable to find Governor Warren. Then the chairman announced the results of the vote, making further switches impossible until the next ballot.[34]

At that point, the coalition went ahead with its previously agreed strategy and asked for a recess in order to regroup their forces. Governor Duff, who put the motion, proposed reconvening at 7:30 P.M. Angry shouts of "no" came from the Dewey delegations. On the convention floor, the Dewey strategists held a hasty conference. They could force a roll call on the motion to adjourn, but some of their own supporters might vote for it out of sheer weariness. If the motion passed over the Dewey groups' opposition, it would look as if their candidate was losing support. Far better to adjourn, even at the risk of sacrificing some of the momentum so far achieved.[35] William F. Bleakley, chairman of the New York delegation, got recognition from the chair and announced that New York was agreeable to a recess. The motion was put to a voice vote and Joe Martin announced that it had passed.

Back at the Benjamin Franklin Hotel, where he had been following the convention on television all afternoon, Senator Taft stepped into the corridor and talked to the press just after New York had agreed to the recess. "That certainly doesn't show any particular confidence in their ability to control the convention," Taft remarked. He had obviously not given up hope, going so far as to say, "I think it is wide open." A few minutes later, his campaign manager, Clarence Brown, puffed into sight, perspiring heavily and looking exhausted. "I don't know how things are going," he told reporters. "I'm just so damn tired, I don't know." [36] Taft then went into conference with Brown, Senator Bricker and other aides. There was only one chance left—that Stassen would withdraw in favor of Taft. Taft telephoned Stassen,[37] who flatly refused until after the third ballot. Soon afterward, Taft set to work on his concession statement.

When the convention reconvened, Bricker was first at the microphone, reading Taft's message releasing his delegates to vote for

Dewey—"a great Republican and will be a great Republican President." Then came Senator William F. Knowland, with Warren's concession of defeat, followed by similar statements from Harold Stassen, Governor Sigler, Senator Baldwin and Harlan Kelley, who had nominated MacArthur. The convention rules required the formality of a third ballot, which was unanimous for Dewey.

Like Taft, Dewey had spent the afternoon in his hotel. He had settled down in his suite to hear the returns when both his television and radio sets stopped functioning. In his shirt sleeves he dashed down the hall to the room of Bradley Nash, one of his headquarters staff, who had both a radio and a direct line to the convention floor. There he listened to the first two ballots. He returned to his own suite during the recess, conferred with his managers, and soon afterward learned that Michigan and Connecticut were going to switch to him on the third ballot. At 7 P.M., Earl Warren telephoned to say that he was withdrawing.

Dewey showered and changed his suit and returned to Nash's room to listen to the evening session. While Senator Bricker was in the middle of his little speech, Dewey stepped out into the hallway to talk to the press. He was solemn and composed, but his voice quavered slightly as he said, "I am humbly grateful for the confidence of the elected representatives of the Republican party and I hope God gives me the strength to merit it." A few minutes later, he collected his wife and rode downstairs. On the street, his limousine and a police escort had been waiting since midafternoon, for Dewey's staff had expected victory on the second ballot.[38] It was cool now, after a sudden thunderstorm had inundated the city. A few minutes before, a rainbow had arched over the sky.

Shortly after 9 P.M. Dewey faced the massed delegates. "I come to you unfettered by a single obligation or promise to any living person," he announced, trying with one assertion to dissipate a week's rumors. He spoke generously of his rivals, told how moved he was by their gracious statements of concession. No words of partisan combativeness followed, no denunciation or even mention of the Democratic administration. Instead, Dewey spoke of unity —unity of party, of the country, and of the world. "The unity we seek is more than material," he said. "It is more than a matter of things and measures. It is most of all spiritual. Our problem is not outside ourselves. Our problem is within ourselves. We have found the means to blow our world, physically, apart. Spiritually, we have yet to find the means to put together the world's broken pieces, to bind up its wounds, to make a good society, a community of men of good will that fits our dreams."

It was a speech that a man might make who had already won the Presidency. The crowd applauded generously, but seemed unmoved.

Then Dewey returned to the Bellevue-Stratford, delivered a short speech to his workers in the ballroom, after which he appeared on a balcony over the hotel entrance to address five thousand supporters on the street below. These rituals over, he returned to his quarters. Ahead was a long night and a decision on who would be the Vice-President.

As is always the case, the decision was one for the Presidential candidate to make. Dewey was dismayed[39] to hear rumors that Stassen was planning to stampede the convention for the nomination; to head him off, and to obtain as wide a consensus as possible, Dewey convened a meeting in his suite around midnight to which he invited some twenty advisers and party leaders, including Sprague, Jaeckle, Brownell, John Foster Dulles, Roy Roberts, Governor Arthur Langlie of Washington, Governor Driscoll, Senator Vandenberg, Senator Martin, Governor Bradford and Senator Leverett Saltonstall of Massachusetts, Governor Thomas Herbert of Ohio.[40] The meeting broke up around 3 A.M. All the candidates were discussed. Halleck, whom the press had been touting as a leading candidate, had little support in the group.[41] A sharp editorial in the *New York Times* entitled "Surely Not Mr. Halleck!" had summarized the case against him. Not only did he have a consistent prewar isolationist record, but recently he had voted for crippling amendments to the Reciprocal Trade Act and helped lead the fight to cut appropriations for the European Recovery Program.

As the lengthy session came to an end, Earl Warren emerged as the leading contender, for he was not only an attractive figure with an excellent record as governor, but he was internationalist, liberal, and would give the ticket an appropriate geographical balance. Dewey telephoned Warren, who was asleep in his hotel, and suggested a meeting. Warren arrived at Dewey's suite around 4 A.M.

and remained for an hour and a quarter. Asked whether he would be available for the nomination, Warren indicated that he would be interested provided the Vice-Presidency would involve more than merely presiding over the Senate. Dewey sympathized with this condition and they agreed to talk again later in the morning.

Shortly before noon, Dewey again phoned Warren and told him he was the unanimous choice of all elements in the party. Warren then accepted. A large factor in his decision, he told a news conference that afternoon, was Dewey's agreement to make the Vice-President a kind of assistant President with administrative responsibilities and Cabinet status.[42]

The Warren nomination went through in thirty-two minutes. The Arizona delegation made some tentative moves to nominate Stassen, but was hastily dissuaded by party leaders. With Warren's name the only one before the convention, Joe Martin called for a voice vote, hastily banged down his gavel and announced that Warren had been nominated. Then he discovered that he had moved too quickly for the newsreel cameras and repeated the whole process.[43] A few minutes later, Warren appeared before the convention to declare, "For the first time in my life I know what it feels like to get hit by a streetcar. . . . Before you change your mind, I want to say that I accept the nomination."

For the Presidential nominee, there remained only the routine business of selecting a new chairman of the Republican National Committee. His choice was a surprise—Representative Hugh D. Scott, Jr., of Pennsylvania, a little-known member of the Grundy-Martin faction whose collective contribution to Dewey's cause was thus formally recognized. Scott was an affable politician with an impressive war record; he was an internationalist and a moderate who was not likely to compromise the Dewey image. Once the word came from Dewey, the National Committee formally elected Scott, who immediately announced that Herbert Brownell would be campaign manager. Dewey had made that decision as well.

"The face of the Republican Party, as shown by its candidates, had never appeared so photogenic, so confident, so politically winning," *Time* noted after the convention was over. "Barring a political miracle, it was the kind of ticket that could not fail to sweep the Republican Party back into power." [44]

## CHAPTER 6

# The Democrats Nominate a "Gone Goose"

The Democratic convention opened on Monday, July 12, in an atmosphere of sodden gloom; the Associated Press was not guilty of overstatement when it had reported a few days before that "The Democrats act as though they have accepted an invitation to a funeral." [1] All zest and suspense had been drained from the enterprise ever since it became apparent that the delegates had no alternative but to nominate Truman and, just as inevitably, see him go down to defeat. Under the circumstances, an observer might reasonably have concluded that only a sense of duty or a compulsive addiction to the rituals of American politics could have brought nearly sixteen hundred delegates to Philadelphia to suffer the heat of midsummer.

The contrast with the Republican convention, held three weeks before, was apparent on all sides. The Democrats had no bands in the hotel lobbies, no boisterous crowds clogging the entrances and fighting to get into the elevators at the Bellevue-Stratford. Bartenders and cabdrivers complained of a shortfall in trade. Hotel managers had the remarkable experience of receiving room cancellations during a convention week. The flags and bunting and the brightly lettered posters—ALL 48 in '48 and KEEP AMERICA HUMAN WITH TRUMAN—looked so incongruous that they only underscored the pathos of the occasion. So did the "Truman Victory Kits," which provided delegates with a notebook, mechanical pencil, lighter fluid and—whistle. ("For use in the Democratic graveyard," the irreverent quipped.) At the Democratic National Committee's posh dinner two nights before the convention opened, Senator Francis J. Myers of Pennsylvania made a brave effort to lift the gloom:

"Nobody is going to lie down and die just to confirm a report in the newspapers, and neither is the Democratic party. Who says we're dead?" The dispirited throng responded with a polite round of applause. Indeed, as the week wore on, the liveliest member of the Democratic party seemed to be the papier-mâché donkey, with its flashing electric eyes and wagging tail, which stood on the marquee of the Bellevue-Stratford.[2]

Until a few days before the convention opened, there had at least been the prospect of a rousing floor fight to deny Truman the nomination. The Eisenhower boom had gathered surprising strength since its beginning in March. The South, in rebellion against Truman's civil rights program, saw the General as its savior. So did the nostalgic New Dealers and youthful activists of Americans for Democratic Action who approved Truman's program but disdained his leadership and were certain of his defeat. Professional politicians in such Democratic strongholds as New York, Chicago, and Jersey City also favored Eisenhower, partly out of fear that Truman would carry their local tickets to defeat.

The diverse groups seeking to discard Truman made common cause over the July 4 weekend. Nineteen prominent party leaders, at the initiative of James Roosevelt, the California state chairman, sent a telegram to each of the 1,592 convention delegates inviting them to a caucus in Philadelphia on July 10, two days before the convention opened, to select "the ablest and strongest man available" as Presidential candidate. Though not mentioned by name, Eisenhower was clearly alluded to in a passage which stated that "It is our belief that no man in these critical days can refuse the call to duty and leadership implicit in the nomination and virtual election to the Presidency of the United States." The sponsors of the caucus constituted a bizarre coalition, among them being Jack Arvey of Chicago, Mayor William O'Dwyer of New York, Mayor Hubert H. Humphrey, Jr., of Minneapolis, Chester Bowles of Connecticut, Governor J. Strom Thurmond of South Carolina, Governor Ben Laney of Arkansas, Senator Lister Hill of Alabama and Governor William J. Tuck of Virginia.[3]

On July 5, a survey by the *New York Times* documented the extent of the anti-Truman revolt. In the South, the 168 convention votes of Arkansas, Georgia, Mississippi, South Carolina, Texas, and Virginia were all certain for Eisenhower; most of Florida's 20 votes and Oklahoma's 24 votes would probably also be cast for the General. Elsewhere in the country, the large delegations from California, Illinois, and New York were split between pro- and anti-Truman groups; New Jersey's 36 votes were all pledged to Eisenhower. Strong Eisenhower sentiment was also found in Indiana, Kansas, Pennsylvania, and Utah. All of which led the *Times*' James A. Hagerty to conclude that "President Truman is facing a hard and possibly losing fight for the nomination . . ."

It was not to be. The same day that the *Times* survey was published, Eisenhower issued a statement reiterating his January refusal to run: "I will not, at this time, identify myself with any political party, and could not accept nomination for any public office or participate in partisan political contest."

Eisenhower's words could hardly have been more forthright, yet for a few days his desperate admirers continued to agitate for his candidacy. James Roosevelt maintained that Eisenhower could not be counted out of the race "unless he refuses to accept after the convention nominates him." In New York City, ADA enthusiasts picketed Eisenhower's home with signs reading, "Ike, You Favor the Draft, We Favor it For You," and "Ike, You're A-1 With Us, Be 1-A in the Draft." James A. Roe, Democratic leader of New York's borough of Queens, announced that he would introduce a resolution at the opening session of the convention asking that Truman step down in favor of Eisenhower. "Despite Eisenhower's statement that he is not a candidate," said Roe, "no man can honestly turn down the nomination for President of the United States at a time of crisis." John M. Bailey, Democratic leader of Connecticut, pointed out that Eisenhower had never said that he would not serve if elected President. Bailey therefore proposed that the convention nominate the General without his consent and run a campaign without his participation.[4] Senator Claude Pepper, one of the most liberal southerners in the Congress, voiced the even more ingenious idea that the Democratic party be temporarily converted into a "national" movement that would draft Eisenhower as a "nonpartisan" candidate. "The Democrats must be prepared to let General Eisenhower be a purely national President," said Pepper. "He could not be expected to accept the nomination if it narrowed him to the limits of a party candidate. The Democratic party's rewards would lie in the tributes it would gain for its magnanimity in a time of crisis." Pepper also wanted the convention to invite Eisenhower to write his own platform and of course select his own running mate.[5]

Pepper's remarkable initiative resulted only in a long and emphatic telegram from Eisenhower, released on July 9, which stated that "No matter under what terms, conditions or premises a proposal might be couched, I would refuse to accept the nomination." He pleaded that Pepper not place his name before the convention[6] and Pepper reluctantly agreed. So did his other principal supporters. Jack Arvey and William O'Dwyer now issued a joint statement endorsing Truman and arguing, rather unpersuasively, that "The Democratic party has been strengthened, rather than weakened, by the movement to draft General Eisenhower. A political party never errs when it earnestly strives to serve the majority's will." [7]

A few opponents of Truman still sought to deny him the nomination. Leon Henderson, the chairman of ADA, took the lead in trying to shift Eisenhower's support to Supreme Court Justice William O. Douglas. A quiet boom for Douglas had been going on during the months when Eisenhower was being importuned to run; indeed, the impression was sometimes created that Eisenhower was being used by certain of his supporters as a stalking-horse for the Douglas candidacy. Douglas had long been a favorite of the liberal militants, as well as of some professional politicians like Mayor O'Dwyer of New York. A former chairman of the Securities and Exchange Commission, he had been a vigorous reformer and an effective administrator in the era when the SEC was still taming Wall Street. Though he had served on the Supreme Court since 1939, he was still regarded as a vibrant New Deal figure whose reputation had not been clouded by compromise. He had been seriously considered for the Vice-Presidency in 1944. In the summer of 1948, he was not yet fifty years old and there had developed about him some of the mystique of the untested popular leader whose day of greatness would surely come.

After Eisenhower's final declination, Leon Henderson stated that "the Democratic party must choose Douglas or invite a disaster that will imperil the future of progressivism in America." [8] To prevent that disaster, Henderson was even willing to join in a bizarre proposal to reinstate the two-thirds rule in balloting for Presidential nominees—an archaic rule, discarded in 1936, which had traditionally endowed the South with a veto power. (Henderson, however, would only have applied the two-thirds rule to the first three ballots, after which a simple majority would have sufficed. By that time, Truman would hopefully have been stopped.)[9]

It was all fantasy. ADA itself claimed only 120 delegates and there were only a handful of other Douglas stalwarts at the convention. Douglas was known as a civil rights supporter, and was thus as unacceptable to the South as Truman. Moreover, the Justice held no great appeal for the party pros in the North; unlike Eisenhower, he was by no means a sure winner. Douglas' own attitude was also discouraging. "I am not a candidate, have never been a candidate, and don't plan to be a candidate," he told a Philadelphia reporter who reached him by telephone in Wallowa, Oregon, where he was vacationing.[10] On Sunday, the day before the convention was to open, Henderson twice spoke with Douglas, who finally prevailed upon him to call off his draft movement.[11] (Truman, as we shall see, was simultaneously trying to prevail upon Douglas to be his Vice-Presidential candidate.)

At that point, Senator Pepper reappeared before the cameras for a brief comic turn. At a press conference in the abandoned Eisenhower headquarters opposite the Bellevue-Stratford, Pepper announced his own candidacy for President. He was now the only man available, he declared, who would carry on in the tradition of Franklin D. Roosevelt. "This is no time for politics as usual," Pepper warned, "for this nation is trembling on the brink of war and our national economy is threatened by an economic depression." It was his view that "Only a liberal candidate has the opportunity to win." He was a "practical" southern liberal, however, and he took the occasion to denounce Truman's civil rights program as "a snare and a delusion," inasmuch as it had no chance of accomplishing anything concrete in the South.

Pepper said he was encouraged by indications of support from twenty-two states, but he admitted that his only definite pledges involved 6½ votes from Florida, his home state. William Ritchie, the Nebraska state chairman, spoke volubly in Pepper's behalf, but both the ADA and the CIO withheld support.[12] As far as the press could discover, so did virtually everybody else, and by Tuesday

Pepper had taken himself out of the race. His candidacy, however, caused one brief flurry at the convention hall when a twenty-two-year-old girl on Tuesday tried to ride a horse onto the floor. Stopped at the door, she said that she was promoting the cause of Pepper for President. "Everybody likes horses, everybody likes Pepper" was her disarming explanation. A policeman told her that she should have tried a donkey.[13]

The anti-Truman revolt may have been doomed from the start, for even if Eisenhower wanted the nomination, the fragile coalition of northern liberals and southern segregationists backing him would probably have broken up, long before the first ballot, over the issue of civil rights—which in any event provided the only dramatic conflict at the convention. It is difficult to see how Eisenhower could have avoided declaring himself on civil rights and thereby sacrificing support either in the North or the South; with Truman determined to win renomination, and with his people in control of the convention machinery, the President would probably have bested the popular General. But the contest would certainly have made for a lively convention.

Instead, the convention opened on a subdued note. The delegates nearly filled the floor, but the galleries were sparsely populated when the first sessions began at 12:14 P.M., a mere fourteen minutes late. The delegates shifted restlessly in their seats, fanning themselves, gossiping with friends and commiserating over the party's prospects while the loudspeaker transmitted a metallic drone of words bearing the greetings of the city fathers, invocations of divine guidance, and intermittent denunciations of the Republican Eightieth Congress. Only the heat made it impossible to doze peaceably beneath the torpid flow of oratory.

That night, however, the convention suddenly came alive when Senator Alben Barkley of Kentucky arose to deliver the keynote address. Barkley, long the Democratic leader in the Senate, had been keynote speaker at both the 1932 and 1936 conventions in that dim and golden era when the party was unbeatable; he was seventy now, a powerfully built, round-faced man, usually jovial in manner, and still endowed with a vigor of voice and a gift for rhetorical flourish that could move the most apathetic audience.

Barkley spoke for sixty-eight minutes, praising the achievements of the New Deal, denouncing the derelictions of the Eightieth Congress, exhorting the delegates to renew the humanitarian crusade which America led in the world. It was an old-fashioned speech, delivered with revivalist fervor, full of rococo prose, hackneyed biblical references, and imaginative invective; at times it was also very funny. Deriding the ambivalent Republican attitude toward the New Deal, Barkley thundered, "What is this cankering, corroding, fungous growth which every Republican orator, save one, denounced with unaccustomed rancor, then in their adopted platform hugged to their political bosom as if it were the child of their own loins?" A dramatic pause, then: "It was recovery. The new Roosevelt administration breathed in the nostrils of every worthy American enterprise a breath of new life, new hope, and new determination."

Later he devoted himself to Dewey's promise to eliminate the cobwebs from the federal government. "I am not an expert on cobwebs," said Barkley, "but, if my memory does not betray me, when the Democratic party took over the government of the United States sixteen years ago, even the spiders were so weak from starvation they could not weave a cobweb in any department of the government."

In one particular, Barkley deviated from the custom of keynote speakers: he did not predict victory. Making a virtue of caution, he declared: "We shall not follow the example so egotistically set by our opponents from this rostrum, three short weeks ago, by announcing the result of the contest four months in advance."

When Barkley finished, a twenty-eight-minute demonstration broke out on the floor. Led by Kentucky, delegates from a dozen states bearing their state standards crowded to the front of the hall; the band swung into "My Old Kentucky Home" and the audience took up the tune. Meantime, a long line of dignitaries paraded across the platform to shake Barkley's hand and pose for photographs with him. The *New York Times* characterized the demonstration as "spontaneous." Few demonstrations of that duration are without advance preparation, but there was nothing synthetic about the affection displayed for Barkley. For one long moment he had blotted out the rancor and frustrations of 1948 and recreated the emotional vigor of the Roosevelt era. The mood he evoked was

perhaps more nostalgic than combative, but at least he roused the
convention from its apathy. For the first time, it actually sounded
like a convention.[14]

Barkley's reward was the Vice-Presidential nomination. He had
a number of rivals until Monday night, among them Senator Joseph
C. O'Mahoney of Wyoming, Representative John W. McCormack
of Massachusetts, Senator Brien McMahon of Connecticut, Governor Mon C. Wallgren of Washington. And Barkley was not without
disabilities. He was not only old, but he represented the "old look"
of the Roosevelt era; he also came from a state close enough to
Missouri to deprive the ticket of geographical balance. Barkley's
advantage, however, was that Truman had failed to get his first
choice—Supreme Court Justice Douglas.

Truman wanted Douglas precisely because of his popularity with
the liberal and labor elements in the party who distrusted the President; with Douglas, the ticket could appease and possibly even inspire the disaffected left. Truman extended himself to persuade
Douglas to run. In retrospect, the episode was ironical but at the
time it was merely pathetic; of what value, after all, was the Democratic Vice-Presidential nomination in 1948?

Truman first asked Clark Clifford to sound out the Justice, a
friend of his. After a telephone conversation, Clifford reported
back that Douglas wanted to think the matter over but was hardly
"enthusiastic." [15] On the Friday before the convention, as Truman
relates in his memoirs, he telephoned Douglas in his isolated vacation retreat in Oregon. Conversation was difficult because of a poor
telephone connection, but Truman gathered that Douglas wanted
to discuss the matter with his family and friends and telephone him
the following day. Douglas did so, this time asking whether the
President could not wait for his final decision until Monday, the day
the convention opened. The President said he would wait.[16] Meantime, with Truman's approval, Clifford called Mrs. Eleanor Roosevelt to ask her to intercede with Douglas. Mrs. Roosevelt agreed
that Douglas would strengthen the ticket and said she would try to
help.[17]

On Monday, Douglas finally rejected the offer, telling Truman,
"I am very sorry, but I have decided not to go into politics. I do not

think I should use the court as a stepping-stone." Truman replied: "I am disappointed. That's too bad." [18]

The way was now open for Barkley. Leslie Biffle, the Secretary of the Senate and an old crony of Barkley's, had been vigorously promoting his candidacy over the preceding weekend. It would have been a fruitless effort had Douglas accepted Truman's offer. After Douglas' rejection and the convention demonstration for Barkley, he became the natural choice. Truman's and Barkley's versions differ, however, as to how the selection finally came about.

According to Truman, "at about the time" he heard from Douglas on Monday, Barkley telephoned him from Philadelphia, with Biffle on an extension phone. Barkley asked whether Truman would have any objection if he attempted to get the Vice-Presidential nomination. "Why didn't you tell me you wanted to be Vice-President?" Truman replied. "It's all right with me." Thereafter, Truman adds, "the two of them went to work, and when the time came, the convention nominated Barkley." [19]

Barkley, in his memoirs, writes that the conversation occurred on Tuesday[20] (although he originally told reporters that it took place Monday night after the keynote address[21]). According to Barkley, the President called to offer his congratulations on the speech. "Why didn't you tell me you wanted to be Vice-President?" Truman said. "I didn't know you wanted the nomination." Barkley replied, "Mr. President, you do not know it yet." Barkley was apparently distressed at Truman's failure to make a direct offer. At that point, the President said, "Well, if I had known you wanted it, I certainly would have been agreeable." Barkley then conceded that the convention did seem eager to nominate him for the Vice-Presidency; he thought that he ought to accept. Truman thought so too.

At any event, on Tuesday morning Senator J. Howard McGrath told a press conference that he had talked with the President earlier that day and that "if the Democratic convention sees fit to nominate Senator Barkley, President Truman will be most happy to welcome him as his running mate." [22] That ended any doubts as to Truman's attitude. In the afternoon, Senator O'Mahoney, Barkley's chief rival, withdrew from the race and endorsed Barkley.

Speculation over the Vice-Presidential candidate was only a mild diversion for the delegates. By Tuesday evening, interest was beginning to shift to the bitter conflict impending over the civil rights plank in the party platform. At the time, only a minority of delegates were exercised over the issue. Before the fight was over, the convention was in an uproar, the party leadership suffered one of its rare defeats on a convention floor, and Truman—quite unwillingly—found himself with an issue which was to become one of the crucial elements in his victory.

The civil rights fight resulted from an ADA initiative begun months before. In March, James Roosevelt and Hubert Humphrey sent out an ADA letter to party leaders around the country urging that a strong civil rights plank be adopted at the July convention.[2⁸] Prior to the convention, four ADA members were named to the 108-man platform committee—Humphrey, ex-Congressman Andrew J. Biemiller of Wisconsin, former Senator Hugh B. Mitchell of Washington and Esther Murray of California.[24] Humphrey in addition became a member of the smaller drafting committee; he and Biemiller were to play the leading roles.

A strong civil rights plank was precisely what the administration wanted to avoid. For months, Truman had resisted pressure to backtrack on civil rights, but he had no desire further to inflame southern hostility. The chairman of the platform committee, Senator Francis J. Myers of Pennsylvania, and other administration spokesmen tried to placate both the North and the South by pushing substantially the same civil rights plank which had proved acceptable in 1944. This strategy had been worked out with the White House, but Truman's staff went to considerable pains to preserve the fiction that the platform committee was operating independently. Thus, before the committee began its deliberations, a draft of the entire platform was prepared by a task force in Washington under Clark Clifford's direction. It was not, however, sent directly to Myers, lest it affront his dignity; instead, the document was carried to Philadelphia on July 8 by George Elsey, whose orders were to deliver it secretly to Leslie Biffle.[25] Biffle, who was both a crony of the President and one of the Senate's inner circle, was presumably in a position to handle the transfer to Myers more diplomatically. On the Saturday prior to the convention, Clifford also conferred with Myers at the Drake Hotel in Philadelphia.[26]

Humphrey failed to get a strong civil rights plank out of the drafting committee, which presented a moderate plank to the full platform committee. It stated: "The Democratic party commits itself to continuing its efforts to eradicate all racial, religious and economic discrimination. We again state our belief that racial and religious minorities must have the right to live, the right to work, the right to vote, the full and equal protection of the law, on a basis of equality with all citizens as guaranteed by the Constitution. We again call upon the Congress to exert its full authority to the limit of its constitutional powers to assure and protect these rights."

It was a bland and unexceptional statement, which dismayed the militants because it was not specific about congressional action and because it was intentionally ambiguous in its last sentence. The assertion that Congress should "exert its full authority to the limit of its constitutional powers" could be taken as a truism by civil rights advocates, but southern segregationists could just as readily interpret it as meaning that little federal action was possible, for in their view Congress' constitutional powers were severely limited by the doctrine of states' rights.

Humphrey and Biemiller fought vigorously for a more emphatic endorsement of Truman's specific civil rights proposals. The debate was harsh and acrimonious, with the ADAers charging that the administration's plank was a "sellout to states' rights over human rights." Senator Scott Lucas, one of the chief administration spokesmen, was furious at the obstreperous minority and kept referring to Humphrey as a "pip-squeak."[27] Later, when Lucas ran into ADA leader Joseph L. Rauh, Jr., outside the committee room, he railed against ADA's meddling.[28] On Tuesday night, July 13, the platform committee approved the moderate plank by a large majority. Biemiller announced that the fight would be continued on the convention floor with the submission of a minority report.

The platform was not due to go before the convention until Wednesday afternoon, but on Tuesday night a preliminary skirmish occurred on the floor which indicated that ADA's support was far broader than its 120 delegates. On Tuesday, the credentials committee recommended that the Mississippi delegation be seated; its right to participate in the convention had been challenged because the delegation was committed not to support the party's Presidential candidate if the convention endorsed Truman's civil rights program and nominated Truman. George L. Vaughn, a Negro member of the credentials committee, took over the podium to present a minority report urging the exclusion of Mississippi. He outlined the case against the rebel delegation, then raised a clenched fist and shouted, "Three million Negroes have left the South since the outbreak of World War II to escape this thing. I ask the convention to give consideration—" An outburst of boos and catcalls from southern delegations drowned him out.

Senator Barkley, who was serving as temporary chairman, had difficulty restoring order. He called for a voice vote on the minority report. Now the North was aroused, with a number of delegates jumping to their feet to demand a roll call. But the floor microphones had been cut off and the chair could ignore the demand. Barkley proceeded with the voice vote and declared that the minority report had been defeated. The commotion continued on the floor. Near the platform, where the Illinois delegation was seated, Jack Arvey and Adlai Stevenson, the party's candidate for governor, were on their feet, shouting for recognition. Burly Jack Shelley, the California delegation chairman and a former football lineman, rushed up to the platform, scattering two policemen who were guarding the entrance. Like Illinois, California wanted to be recorded as voting for the minority report.[29, 30]

After the convention adjourned for the night, a tense and excited crowd of delegates met for a caucus at a clubhouse the ADA had taken over on the University of Pennsylvania campus, within walking distance of the convention hall. Biemiller and Rauh had already prepared an amendment to the majority civil rights plank that read: "We call upon Congress to support our President in guaranteeing these basic and fundamental rights: (1) the right of full and equal political participation, (2) the right to equal opportunity of employment, (3) the right of security of person, and (4) the right of equal treatment in the service and defense of our nation." This paragraph was to be substituted for the scorned final sentence in the majority plank requesting Congress to exert itself "to the limit of its constitutional powers" to protect civil rights.[31] In the light of the civil rights legislation which Congress was later to pass in the

1960's, the language of the minority plank of 1948 hardly seems either incendiary or overly ambitious. It did, however, call upon Congress for action in four clearly defined areas and it also, of course, eliminated the escape clause designed to placate the South. It was stronger language than the majority plank, but verbal nuances were less important than the political impulse which they symbolized: to press vigorously for a full civil rights program, even at the risk of sending the South into full revolt.

Rauh, Biemiller, and others believed that the minority plank would win if a roll call was taken. The great fear was that Representative Sam Rayburn, who had been elected permanent chairman, would repeat Barkley's performance and refuse to heed the demand for a roll call. Jack Shelley declared that he had already taken some action: he had warned Rayburn that the California delegation, seated right under the rostrum, would rush the platform *en masse* if a roll call was denied.[32]

Throughout most of the nightlong caucus, Hubert Humphrey remained indecisive about whether to address the convention in behalf of the minority plank. Personally he had much at stake: he was running for the Senate for the first time, with a good chance of victory; only thirty-seven, he had come up very fast, having been mayor of Minneapolis for over three years, and was now the dominant figure in his state party. If he won in November, he was likely to be one of the national leaders of the party in the post-Truman era. Since the civil rights fight had started, he had often been warned by administration spokesmen that he was sacrificing a brilliant future in a crackpot crusade. "You'll split the party wide open if you do this. You'll kill any chances we have of winning the election in November," Humphrey had been told. At the same time, he was under considerable pressure from his ADA colleagues to lead the floor fight, for he was a rousing speaker who was likely to dominate the debate. Humphrey's personal sympathies were firmly engaged in the cause, of that his colleagues never had any doubt; on the other hand, he was a professional politician who was being asked to challenge the entire national leadership of the party.[33]

Shortly before 5 A.M., according to Winthrop Griffith's biography of Humphrey, "Minnesota's Eugenie Anderson proposed that one short line be added to the paragraph suggested in the minority report: 'We highly commend President Harry Truman for his courageous stand on the issue of civil rights.' Humphrey said, 'That's it. I'll do it.' The others suspected that the insertion satisfied his desire to retain at least some link with the establishment of the formal party leaders and the Truman Administration." [34]

Dawn had broken by the time the ADA caucus disbanded. A few hours later, Biemiller, who was to introduce the minority report, telephoned Sam Rayburn and made an appointment to see him shortly before noon. Rayburn was hardly surprised to be told that there would be a minority report; before Biemiller could ask for assurances that a roll call would be allowed, Dan Moody, a former governor of Texas, joined them. He also had a minority report, in behalf of a states' rights amendment to the minority plank. Ironically, the South was as dissatisfied with the "moderate" plank as were the northern militants. "Do you want a roll call?" Rayburn demanded. "Of course," said Moody. Both sides were assured that their rights would be protected.[35]

All morning and into the afternoon the ADA crowd lobbied zealously for their amendment. Apart from appeals to principle, always of limited utility in a political convention, they had one powerful weapon—the Wallace threat.[36] For months, Henry Wallace and his third party supporters had been making a major issue of civil rights. If the Democratic convention rejected a strong civil rights plank, Negro defections to Wallace in the North might well result in the defeat of scores of state and local candidates. Such a danger to their local tickets was something the professionals understood very clearly. Truman was in any case a lost cause.

Administration spokesmen refused to see it that way. They alternately warned that the ADA rebels would split the party or be humiliatingly defeated. One of the most diligent lobbyists against the Biemiller amendment was David K. Niles, a Presidential assistant who specialized in the problems of minority groups. Running into Joe Rauh, Niles predicted ADA's defeat and deplored the effect on Humphrey's future. "You'll ruin the chances of the best political talent to come along in years," said Niles.[37]

The civil rights debate was preceded Wednesday afternoon by a series of routine political orations to which the delegates paid little heed. During these preliminaries, Humphrey and Biemiller seated themselves on the platform. At one point, the Bronx's Ed Flynn joined them. He was exceedingly cordial. "I hear you kids have a minority plank on civil rights," he said. "That's what we need to stir up this convention and win the election." Flynn then sent runers down to the floor to fetch Jack Arvey, Frank Hague, and David Lawrence, the leader of Pennsylvania's Democrats. After conferring with Flynn, they agreed to support the minority plank. They had all been buttonholed previously by the ADA "kids," but Flynn's advice carried great weight.[38]

Four minority amendments went before the convention—Biemiller's, Moody's, and two other states' rights amendments submitted by Tennessee and Mississippi. The southern amendments were presented first. Debate was limited to an hour. Moody, who made the major southern speech, was conciliatory in tone. "I have never bolted a convention and never intend to," he said. "My purpose here is an effort to appeal for the restoration of harmony in the Democratic party." Cecil Sims of Tennessee was equally placatory: "I agree with everything in the platform. I am asking only for a simple statement of reserved rights of states. . . . If we are defeated here today you are witnessing the dissolution of the Democratic party in the South."

Hubert Humphrey spoke last, delivering a crisp, fervent plea that stirred the convention and brought him his first national acclaim. "There are those who say to you—we are rushing this issue of civil rights. I say we are a hundred and seventy-two years late," he proclaimed. "There are those who say—this issue of civil rights is an infringement on states' rights. The time has arrived for the Democratic party to get out of the shadow of states' rights and walk forthrightly into the bright sunshine of human rights."

When Humphrey finished, the Illinois delegation, led by the towering, white-thatched Paul Douglas, scrambled into the aisles, followed by the California delegation and a dozen others.[39] The delegates cheered and paraded for ten minutes, although there was no music to spur them on and the floor microphones had again been turned off, to keep down the din. When the demonstration was over the Texas amendment was first put to a vote. It lost by 925 to 309. Then the two other southern proposals were rejected by voice votes. After the alphabetical roll of the states began on the Biemiller amendment, the outcome was first heralded when Illinois' 60 votes were cast for it. Indiana, Iowa, Kansas, Massachusetts, Michigan and, of course, Minnesota all supported the minority plank; later came all of New Jersey's 36 votes, all of New York's 98 votes, and all of Pennsylvania's 74 votes (the latter an implied repudiation of the chairman of the platform committee, Pennsylvania's own Frank Myers). The final tally showed 651½ votes for the minority plank to 582½ votes against it.

Cheers and boos rolled through the vast hall. During the uproar, the chairman of the Alabama delegation, Handy Ellis, stood waving his state standard in a wide arc and shouting for recognition. He wanted to announce Alabama's withdrawal from the convention, but Chairman Rayburn refused to recognize him. Instead, he called for the adoption of the full platform by a voice vote and then recessed the convention until the evening. So ended the great civil rights debate of 1948.

"The South had been kicked in the pants, turned around and kicked in the stomach" was *Time*'s summary of the two roll-call votes.[40] In administering that punishment and forcing a southern bolt, the convention also enabled Truman to hold the allegiance of the Negro ghetto—an asset whose significance was not to be fully appreciated until the November returns were analyzed. Truman was given a winning issue despite himself, for all his representatives at the convention opposed the minority plank—McGrath, Myers, Rayburn, Barkley. Truman's own state of Missouri voted solidly against the Biemiller amendment, as did McGrath's Rhode Island, Barkley's Kentucky, and of course Rayburn's Texas. Truman's memoirs, however, make no mention of the civil rights fight at the convention. Instead—incredibly—he takes credit for the plank that was passed. Referring to the proposals in his civil rights message of February 2, he writes, "I incorporated these recommendations into the 1948 platform of the Democratic party. . . . I was perfectly willing to risk defeat in 1948 by sticking to the civil rights plank in my platform." [41]

Apart from civil rights, the Democratic platform contained few surprises. In foreign policy, it supported the various initiatives of the Truman administration, spoke approvingly of the United Nations, and pledged a "sound, humanitarian" management of the Marshall Plan. In domestic affairs the platform proposed to repeal the Taft-Hartley Act, advocated a rise in the statutory minimum wage from 40 to 75 cents an hour, favored an increase of at least 50 percent in old age and survivors' insurance benefits. Federal aid to education was endorsed, with an initial appropriation of $300 million. Farmers were promised improvements in the traditional Democratic agricultural programs, including price supports, soil conservation, rural electrification. A multifaceted program for the development of natural resources, reclamation, and flood control, with regional development plans, was also advocated.

On Wednesday evening, the delegates assembled to nominate a Presidential and a Vice-Presidential candidate. The chore was regarded as so routine that the convention managers decided to wind up the proceedings on Wednesday night rather than continue into Thursday, as originally planned. At 7 P.M., Truman set off from Washington in his special train. Sitting with Clark Clifford and Judge Samuel I. Rosenman, one of Roosevelt's old speech writers, the President made final changes in his speech outline as the train clattered over the rough roadbed to Philadelphia.[42] Truman arrived at the convention hall at 9:41 and had to wait behind the scenes for four hours until the convention finished its business.[43] The 1948 convention, everyone was to agree, was the worst managed in years.

The evening session began about 7 P.M. Alabama's Handy Ellis was finally recognized on a plea of "personal privilege." Alabama's Presidential electors, he announced, had been instructed "never to cast their vote for a Republican, never to cast their vote for Harry Truman, and never to cast their vote for any candidate with a civil rights program such as adopted by the convention." Half of the delegation was also pledged to walk out if the convention affronted the South by its civil rights plank. "We bid you goodbye!" cried Ellis. Whereupon thirteen members of the Alabama delegation got to their feet and marched up the center aisle to the door, as did the entire twenty-three-man Mississippi delegation. There were a few cheers from the South, but most of the southern delegations sat glumly in their seats while the galleries booed. Outside the convention hall, there was a rainstorm, but the group posed dutifully for pictures. "Show a little life!" the cameraman yelled, and the rebels shouted slogans and waved their arms.[44]

Though they had lost the main fight, the remaining southern delegates were in no mood to accede graciously to the nomination of Truman. Georgia nominated Senator Richard Russell for the Presidency. Truman was nominated by Missouri. The floor demonstration for Truman lasted thirty-nine minutes, seven minutes more than the longest demonstration at the Republican convention.[45] It was well organized—apparently the only aspect of the convention that was—and possessed a fervor which could be interpreted more as a rebuke to the South than as an expression of affection for the President.

To no one's surprise, Truman won on the first ballot by 947½ votes to 263 for Russell (Paul McNutt, former governor of Indiana, received half a vote). What was unusual, however, was that no one moved to make Truman's nomination unanimous, which is the normal protocol. Any such proposal would have been shouted down by the South.

It was 12:42 A.M. on Thursday when Truman was finally nominated. Another hour was then devoted to nominating Alben Barkley for Vice-President; in his case, the convention bestowed the honor by acclamation. While the convention was thus occupied, Truman was patiently waiting offstage. He remained for a time in Howard McGrath's office in the convention hall, but the room became uncomfortably hot and the President moved outdoors to a ramp near the stage entrance. There he sat with Alben Barkley and Homer Cummings, once Attorney General under Roosevelt, chatting animatedly and watching the railroad trains go by.[46]

At 1:45 A.M., Truman and Barkley finally strode out onto the platform, while the band played "Hail to the Chief." Barkley was to speak first. While Rayburn was making his introductory remarks a matronly committeewoman hastened over to the microphone, interrupting Rayburn and announcing that she was happy to present the President with a floral Liberty Bell. It had been on the platform ever since the demonstration for Truman, awaiting this moment. As she spoke, there was a rustle under the bell and a flock of white pigeons—"doves of peace"—was suddenly loosed over the platform. The guests ducked but some suffered inadvertent damage to their clothes. One pigeon landed on the rostrum; Rayburn captured it and flung it over the crowd. It was the climactic bit of convention nonsense and the audience loved it.[47]

Barkley spoke first, with admirable brevity. Then the weary crowd steeled itself for a dose of Presidential oratory. But this was the "new" Truman. Instead of reading a set speech, the President spoke from an outline written in short, punchy sentences.[48] He expressed his appreciation for the nomination, then his strident, high-pitched tones electrified the audience. "Senator Barkley and I will win this election and make the Republicans like it—don't you forget it!" he declared. "We will do that because they are wrong and we are right."

He spoke of the achievements of sixteen years of Democratic rule—higher wages, higher farm income, bountiful benefits for all the people. If the farmers and labor "don't do their duty by the Democratic party, they are the most ungrateful people in the world!" For the Republican party he had only contempt: "Ever since its inception, that party has been under the control of special privilege; and they have completely proved it in the Eightieth Congress." After enumerating the Congress' failings, he spoke scornfully of the recent Republican platform, which espoused so many programs rejected by the Congress.

Then came the one surprise in Truman's speech: he would give the Republicans a chance to prove the sincerity of their platform promises. "My duty as President requires that I use every means within my power to get the laws the people need. . . . On the 26th day of July, which out in Missouri we call 'Turnip Day,' I am going to call Congress back and ask them to pass laws to halt rising prices, to meet the housing crisis—which they are saying they are for in their platform. At the same time I shall ask them to act upon other vitally needed measures such as aid to education, which they say they are for; a national health program . . . civil rights legislation . . . an increase in the minimum wage. . . . Now, my friends, if there is any reality behind that Republican platform, we ought to get some action from a short session of the Eightieth Congress. They can do this job in fifteen days, if they want to do it. They will still have time to go out and run for office."

When Truman finished, the delegates rose to their feet and cheered for two minutes. "There was no doubt that he had lifted the delegates out of their doldrums," *Time* reported. "He had roused admiration for his political courage." [49] And for a moment Truman had created the illusion—few people regarded it as more than an illusion—that the Democrats had a fighting chance in November.

Two days later, the long-feared southern revolt became official. On Saturday, July 17, disaffected Democrats from all parts of the South gathered in Birmingham, Alabama, for a rump convention. It was a continuation of a conference of States' Rights Democrats, as the rebels preferred to call themselves, which had first met in Jackson, Mississippi, on May 10. There it had been decided to convene again in Birmingham if the Democratic convention either nominated Truman or adopted a platform which was hostile to the South.

The rump convention had an atmosphere of amateur improvisation. Original plans called for a meeting in a hotel conference room, whose seating capacity was limited to three hundred. On Thursday afternoon, the site was switched to the municipal auditorium, which accommodated six thousand. Rules for delegate-selection were very relaxed; virtually anyone who presented himself as a supporter could get a delegate's badge.[50] The Alabamians and Mississippians who had walked out in Philadelphia clearly represented solid political support; large delegations attended from both states. The South Carolina contingent included three delegates to the Democratic convention, Governor J. Strom Thurmond among them. As for the rest of the States' Rights delegates, some of whom were college students or tourists passing through Birmingham, it was difficult to determine how much organizational strength they represented.[51] Most of the South's political leaders remained away; the absentees included "Boss" Ed Crump of Tennessee, Senator Harry Byrd of Virginia, and Herman Talmadge of Georgia. Governor Ben Laney of Arkansas came to Birmingham, but never went to the convention hall; in the end he issued a statement urging that the national ticket be supported.

The dubious authority of the gathering did not impair its enthusiasm. Delegates lustily cheered ex-Governor Frank M. Dixon of Alabama, the keynote speaker, who denounced Truman's civil rights program as an effort "to reduce us to the status of a mongrel, inferior race, mixed in blood, our Anglo-Saxon heritage a mockery." There were a number of boisterous parades, with much waving of Confederate flags, rebel yells, and a huge portrait of General Robert E. Lee bobbing above the throng.

The delegates unanimously selected Governor Thurmond for President and Governor Fielding L. Wright of Mississippi for Vice-President and adopted a brief "declaration of principles" which stated that the way to protect the American people "against the onward march of totalitarian government" was by guaranteeing the rights reserved to the states in the Constitution. The declaration deplored a "long train of abuses and usurpations of power by unfaithful leaders who are alien to the Democratic parties of the states here represented," denounced the civil rights plank of the Democratic platform, asserted that "We stand for the segregation of the races and the racial integrity of each race" and called for the defeat of Truman and Dewey "and every other candidate for public office who would establish a police state in the United States of America."

It was easy to deride the rhetoric of the Dixiecrats—the name preferred by headline-writers, who are always short of space—and to demonstrate that they represented only a minority movement among southern Democrats. But their breakaway had to be taken seriously by the national party. The Dixiecrat strategy was to try to persuade the various southern Democratic parties to accept their candidates as the official party nominees, in place of Truman and Barkley; where this was not possible, Thurmond and Wright would appear on the ballot under the States' Rights designation. The Dixiecrats' announced goal was a large enough electoral vote to deny either Dewey or Truman a majority, in which case the constitution provided for the House of Representatives to select the President, with each state having but one vote. They saw their candidate either emerging as President or at least getting more electoral votes than Truman, in which case they believed that the States' Rights faction would be regarded as the official opposition party in

Congress, with all the advantages in making committee assignments which that position affords.[52]

It was a heady strategy to inspire a minority movement. There was never any chance, of course, of Thurmond being elected President by the House of Representatives, for there was no reason to suppose that he would attract enough Republican votes. On the other hand, with Henry Wallace cutting into the normally Democratic bloc in the North, there was at least an outside chance that Thurmond might emerge with more electoral votes than Truman. Failing even that goal, it seemed likely that the South would at least have its revenge by ensuring Truman's defeat.

There was irony in Strom Thurmond's participation in the anti-Truman crusade. A forty-five-year-old ex-judge and World War II paratroop officer, Thurmond had a reputation as a liberal-minded governor. He had sought to abolish South Carolina's poll tax, institute the secret ballot in general elections and modernize the state constitution; he had received a good deal of favorable publicity, a few weeks after becoming governor in 1947, when he had moved swiftly to arrest a large group of suspects after a Negro was lynched. "We in South Carolina want the world to know we will tolerate no mob violence," he had proclaimed.[53] It was a favorite theme of his, but he always opposed a federal anti-lynching law as an unconstitutional invasion of states' rights.

When he appeared before the Birmingham convention, Thurmond declared that "if the South should vote for Truman this year, we might just as well petition the government to give us colonial status." Probably few delegates remembered another speech which he had delivered in Louisville, Kentucky, on October 2, 1947. At that time, he had urged the reelection of Harry Truman—who had won "the confidence of the American people throughout the nation" and who had "emerged as the hope of freedom-loving people everywhere." Said Thurmond: "As between President Truman, with his seasoned experience, demonstrated ability, and tact in international affairs, and any Republican who has the slightest chance of getting his party's nomination, the American people will have no difficulty in reaching the conclusion that they had better leave our future in the competent hands which have looked after it so well to this time." Thurmond sent Truman a copy of this speech and Truman thanked him for "the kind things you said." [54]

Truman's announcement that Congress would be called back into special session was a transparent political maneuver, as the President's own words indicated. It was nonetheless a brilliant maneuver, for it confronted the Republican party with an embarrassing challenge which could hardly be sidestepped. It skillfully exploited an initiative which every President possesses but which most would probably regard as inappropriate for so blatantly political a purpose. It was also unprecedented. Not since 1856, the press was quick to point out, had an emergency session of Congress been called during a Presidential election year. And never before, so far as anyone could remember, had a President announced a special session in a speech to a party convention. In his inimitable way, Truman had also added a homey touch to the proceedings by his puzzling reference to Missouri's Turnip Day. It developed that he had been alluding to an ancient Missouri saw, "On the 25th of July, sow your turnips wet or dry." [55] He had shifted the date by one day, for Congress could hardly be called back on a Sunday.

Truman's move evoked immediate expressions of outrage from Republican leaders. Representative Hugh D. Scott, Jr., the new Republican national chairman, charged that "It is the act of a desperate man who is willing to destroy the unity and dignity of his country and his government for partisan advantage after he himself has lost the confidence of the people." Senator Vandenberg, usually temperate in his speech, was no less scornful: "This sounds like a last hysterical gasp of an expiring administration." Senator C. Wayland Brooks of Illinois declared that "Never in the history of American politics has a Chief Executive stooped so low . . ." [56] Southern Democrats were equally indignant. In his distress, Senator Walter George of Georgia mixed a few tortured images: "The South is not only over a barrel. It is pilloried. We are in the stocks." [57]

The denunciations had been anticipated by the White House. So had the risks. The pros and cons of calling a special session had been debated since shortly after the Republican convention had ended. More than one person claims authorship of the project. In an interview with R. Alton Lee in 1961, Truman maintained that the idea was his,[58] though his memoirs are silent on the point. According to the Margaret Coit biography, Bernard Baruch suggested the plan to Truman, urging him to announce it in his acceptance speech before the convention.[59] Judge Samuel I. Rosenman, an old Roosevelt speech writer who occasionally aided Truman during the 1948 campaign, has recalled [60] a White House conversation with Truman, after the Republicans adopted their platform, in which he said to the President, "You ought to tell them that here is a fine platform you've adopted. I'm calling you into special session to pass it—and if you pass it, I'll sign it." Rosenman, however, does not claim to have been the first or the only person to have made the proposal to Truman.

The idea was clearly in the air. On June 28, for example, the *Washington Post* ran an editorial deploring the fact that a special session was unlikely, for Congress had left much unfinished business. The balance of evidence, however, suggests that the main credit for pushing the project should go to the bright young men of Bill Batt's Research Division, which, while nominally a part of the Democratic National Committee, enjoyed a freewheeling status of its own. According to Batt,[61] the tactic of recalling Congress to Washington emerged out of a discussion in his shop following the adoption of the Republican platform. At the next dinner meeting of the strategy group which met at Oscar Ewing's apartment (Batt was by then a member of the group), he enthusiastically advanced the proposal. The Ewing group had all sorts of objections to it. Batt reported the rejection to his colleagues at the Research Division, who urged him to make another effort to sell the idea. Batt then telephoned Clifford; Clifford suggested that he prepare a memorandum on the subject.

Clifford partly corroborates Batt's account. He recalls first hearing of the proposal at one of the Ewing dinners, but does not remember who brought up the matter.[62] George Elsey, however, has a distinct recollection that Batt originated the idea.[63] There also survives a copy of a two-page unsigned memorandum, dated June 29, 1948, entitled "Should the President call Congress back?", which is to be found in the Samuel I. Rosenman papers at the Truman Library.[64] Batt claims authorship for his group.[65] The memorandum's blunt, strident style, peppered with the stock liberal clichés of the time, is similar to the style of many Research Division memoranda which Batt signed; moreover Judge Rosenman, while expressing admiration for the analysis in the document, states that he is certain he did not write it.[66] There is no mystery as to how the memorandum found its way into the Rosenman papers, for it is in a folder having to do with Truman's acceptance speech, in the preparation of which Rosenman had a hand.

The document clearly sets forth the strategic considerations prompting the Turnip Day session. It begins: "This election can only be won by bold and daring steps, calculated to reverse the powerful trend now running against us. The boldest and most popular step the President could possibly take would be to call a special session of Congress early in August." The memorandum then analyzes the advantages of a special session and its dangers. The principal advantage would be to "focus attention on the rotten record of the 80th Congress, which Dewey, Warren and the press will try to make the country forget." The Republican candidates would be compelled to defend the record of Congress and would be embarrassed by the "steady glare of publicity on the Neanderthal men of the Republican party, the reactionary men such as Martin, Halleck, Wolcott, Allen . . ." The Republican party would be split on the major questions of the day and President Truman would have a chance to show himself, as on his western tour, as a zealous advocate of the people's interests.

The hazards were enumerated, only to be promptly discounted. If the Republicans "invite a Southern filibuster by introducing strong civil rights legislation," the President could call for a coalition of liberal Democrats and Republicans to break the filibuster and pass moderate legislation. If Congress did pass some decent legislation, "it will be up to the Democratic Publicity Department and campaign speakers to pound it home to the people that the President deserves credit." As for the danger that the people might be fooled by the passage of some "phony bills" in such fields as housing, price control, or aid to education, the memorandum saw little likelihood of such deception being effective.

Clifford was soon persuaded of the wisdom of calling a special session and talked more than once with Truman about it. In Clifford's view, the Democrats could not lose whatever the outcome. If the Republicans passed some constructive legislation, the President could claim responsibility for forcing their hand. If they resisted his demands, which was the likeliest course, they would only dramatize further the President's case against the Congress.[67]

Once Truman announced the special session, the Republicans understood that they were at a strategic disadvantage, but it hardly seemed to matter, given the general assumption of a Republican victory. Dewey adopted a characteristically cautious attitude, saying nothing. Not until five days after Truman's acceptance speech did a statement come from his campaign manager. At a press conference expressly called to hear this pronouncement, Herbert Brownell limited himself to two sentences: "The Republican platform calls for the enactment of a program by a Republican Congress under the leadership of a Republican President. Obviously this cannot be done at a rump session called at a political convention for political purposes in the heat of a political campaign." Brownell amiably refused any elaboration, though the reporters pressed him for thirty minutes. He denied that the statement could be construed as coming from Dewey, but admitted that he had consulted with the candidate; he spoke only for himself—a modest disavowal difficult to credit.[68]

Brownell plainly was trying to make the best of an embarrassing situation. He had no alternative but to echo the views of the Republican leaders of Congress, for he had already failed to persuade them to accept Truman's challenge and pass some useful legislation. He had conferred at length with Senators Taft and Vandenberg, Speaker Joe Martin, and other leaders, urging them to pass two or three measures which Truman wanted and which the Republican platform favored. He was particularly keen to liberalize the Displaced Persons Act, which discriminated against Jewish refugees and some Catholics as well, arguing that a failure to act would only hurt Dewey in the populous centers of the East. Taft, however, was adamant against acquiescing to Truman and none of the other leaders were willing to break with him on the issue. To Taft, a matter of principle was involved in Truman's political misuse of a Presidential prerogative; he refused to compromise. Brownell was appalled.[69]

Representative Hugh Scott attended a similar meeting in the Senate, at which Senators Taft, Vandenberg, Milliken and a few others were present. According to Scott,[70] Vandenberg said, "Bob, I think we ought to do something. We ought to do whatever we can to show that we are trying to use the two weeks as best we can. Then we have a better case to take before the public." He proposed a couple of pieces of legislation which he thought should be passed, but Taft would not agree. Scott also urged some affirmative action; Taft ignored him. Vandenberg then suggested that they at least approve the International Wheat Agreement, arguing that it was a good measure and would help with the farm vote. "Bob Taft would have none of it," Scott relates. " 'No,' he said, 'we're not going to give that fellow anything.' Anyone familiar with Bob Taft's method of ending a conversation will know that was the end of it."

Truman took advantage of the histrionic possibilities of the special session by appearing in person on July 27 to read his message to Congress. As he usually did with a major scripted speech, he had spent hours with his advisers editing the manuscript. At three points he changed "inflation" to "high prices." On the fifth draft, he added a little interpolation of his own, addressed to members of Congress, "Ask your wife how much more it costs to feed your family now than a year ago," [71] which he delivered in slightly altered form.

The bulk of the message was devoted to the need to check inflation and end the "acute" housing shortage. Truman repeatedly emphasized the urgency of the problem: "High prices are not taking 'time off' for the election. High prices are not waiting until the next session of Congress. High prices are getting worse. They are getting worse every day. We cannot afford to wait for the next Congress to act." To curb inflation, he urged the adoption of a variety of measures, among them an excess profits tax, powers to control consumer credit, greater authority to the Federal Reserve Board to regulate bank credit, the strengthening of rent controls, the authorization of price controls for scarce commodities, and provision for wage controls in situations where price controls would be imposed. To meet the housing crisis, he urged passage of the Taft-Ellender-

Wagner bill, previously approved by the Senate, which provided assistance to cities for slum clearance and low-rent housing projects, as well as aid for farm housing and the home-construction industry.

These measures constituted Truman's top priorities, but he also urged the passage of "other important legislative measures on which delay would injure us at home and impair our world relations." He wanted the minimum wage law raised to 75 cents an hour, a 50 percent rise in old-age retirement benefits, federal aid to education, the authorization of a loan for the construction of the United Nations headquarters building in New York City, Senate ratification of the International Wheat Agreement, amendment of the Displaced Persons Act, and the passage of various civil rights measures to carry out the recommendations of his February 2 message.

Before the day was out, the Republican leaders issued a detailed reply. After underscoring the transparent political purpose of the session, they argued that "The President's quarrel with the Eightieth Congress is not its failure to enact legislation, but a fundamental difference in government philosophy . . . The President would fix wages, fix prices, expand government spending, increase Federal taxes, socialize and nationalize medicine and generally regiment the life of every family, as well as agriculture, labor and industry." Nonetheless, the congressional leaders were not disposed to follow the reckless counsel of some of their followers and adjourn immediately. They would consider the President's anti-inflation program "to determine whether there are any additional powers which might be helpful in dealing with high prices . . ." The Senate would also consider the anti-poll-tax bill which had already been passed by the House. Clearly, inflation was so disturbing an issue that it was thought unwise to pay no heed to it. And the virtue of a Senate debate on a poll-tax bill, from the Republican point of view, would be that it would provoke a southern filibuster.

The two-week session took its predictable course. A filibuster did occur in the Senate. Routine committee hearings were held on some of the administration's measures. The only major piece of legislation to pass the Congress was a $65 million loan for the construction of the UN building. The Federal Reserve Board was granted two of the measures Truman had sought—power to control consumer credit and to increase bank reserves. A truncated housing bill was passed, which largely liberalized credit terms, guaranteed by the government, for private construction. The rest of Truman's program was scorned.

A few days after the special session adjourned, the White House issued a statement listing in great detail how Congress had failed to act on the President's program. On the same day, August 12, Truman denounced Congress' performance at his press conference. Prompted by a reporter, he agreed that it had been a "do-nothing" session and a "do-nothing" Congress. He now had another useful epithet with which to belabor the "worst" Congress. The special session had been a great success.

# CHAPTER 7
# The Wallace Crusade

Philadelphia was host to a third political convention in 1948—that of Henry Wallace's party, which assembled on Friday evening, July 23, and finished its deliberations on Sunday. The gathering bore certain physical resemblances to the Republican and Democratic conventions. It met in the same cavernous auditorium, under the same wilting floodlights, and with the flags and multicolored banners and cardboard state standards without which a convention would seem naked. The rituals of an old-party convention were followed—the keynote address, the roll call of the states for Presidential nominations, the floor demonstrations for the nominees. But while the forms were the same, the spirit was totally different, for there was never any uncertainty as to who the candidates would be or what the platform would assert; the only element of doubt concerned the name which would be given to the "new party," as it had been called until then. In the guise of a nominating convention, the Wallaceites were holding a three-day rally.

There were other differences as well. The delegates were younger and thinner than those attending the Republican or Democratic conventions; the average age was thirty and numerous teen-agers were present. Dress was informal, with many males attired in slacks and open-necked sports shirts. There was a notable lack of alcoholic consumption. One reporter wrote that the convention had the atmosphere of a soda fountain rather than that of a smoke-filled room.[1] A surprising number of guitars were spotted around the convention floor; each session opened with a community sing. Then the delegates would settle back and listen attentively to the speakers; there was less milling around and restless chatter than at the old-party conventions. Demonstrations seemed genuinely spontaneous.

141

The absence of smoke-filled rooms was no doubt due to the shortage of politicians to fill them. In attendance were only two congressmen, Vito Marcantonio and Leo Isacson of New York; and one senator, Glen H. Taylor of Idaho, who back in February had been designated as Wallace's running mate. A convention questionnaire showed that for 25 percent of the delegates, this was their first campaign, though there was a scattering of old-timers who had been active as far back as 1912.[2] One question was not asked of the delegates: how many were members of the Communist party? Such a question would have been regarded as the most egregious kind of "red-baiting." Yet it would have been highly relevant, for the Progressive party convention was dominated by the Communist party, as would be clearly evident before the weekend was over.

It was a situation without parallel in modern American political history. Once every generation, dating back to the 1890's, a major third-party effort has been launched to break through the rigidities of the two-party system: there were the Populists in 1892, the Bull Moose Progressives of 1912, the La Follette Progressives of 1924. All these ventures were born of widespread dissatisfaction, unrealistic hopes of victory, and more rhetorical zeal than practical political calculation; they all advocated reforms that were in advance of their times and they all failed as parties though not as instruments of popular agitation, for in the end many of their causes were adopted by the old parties. Each of these third-party efforts differed from the others, but they were all what they purported to be; none of them was controlled or manipulated by a clandestine political group which could never hope to win more than a handful of votes on its own.

The Progressive party of 1948 was thus unique among major third-party efforts, for it was from the outset a creature of the Communist party. Though its vote fell far short of expectations, it was the largest and most successful electoral effort ever launched by the Communists. This is not to say that most Progressive party members or voters were Communists. It is to say quite the contrary, for the degree of deception was the measure of the Communists' success. The great majority of Progressives were non-Communist. Many willingly collaborated with Communists but most of them were probably too unsophisticated politically to recognize a Communist.

This vast enterprise of deception would not have been possible without Henry Wallace, a man who had never been a Communist but who was quite willing to lend himself to their purposes in pursuit of his own. "Mr. Wallace himself is not Communist-controlled in a certain sense," Rebecca West wrote during the Progressive party convention. "I do not think he obeys specific instructions as to what to say and do. But obviously the Communists control him as one controls a mass of gaseous vapor when one enfolds it in a skin and allows it to be itself within those limits when one wants a balloon to go up." [3]

Wallace was an enormous prize for the Communists because he was a figure of international stature, a former Vice-President of the United States, and a man for whom the mantle of F.D.R. could be insistently claimed, however much his detractors disputed the honor. Iowa-born and bred, Wallace had been a renowned plant geneticist, farm editor and businessman before becoming Roosevelt's first and best-known Secretary of Agriculture. As wartime Vice-President, he handled some important administrative jobs but achieved greater renown for his rhetorical flights about our postwar future, proclaiming "the century of the common man." After the war, many liberals who despaired of Truman's inadequacies regarded Wallace as the great lost leader who should properly have inherited the Presidency after Roosevelt's death, a destiny he had been denied by a group of mean-minded politicians at the 1944 convention.

In many ways, Wallace was miscast as a popular leader. He was curiously aloof and distant, but without the air of mystery which a De Gaulle carries. In a crowd scene, he was distinctly inept at the small glad-handing gestures demanded of politicians. He read a speech poorly. His great strength, apart from his name and his honorable past associations, was the quality of sincerity and dedication which he conveyed in his better moments. A lean-faced, rumpled man with a self-conscious grin, he so clearly looked like a homespun midwestern product that it was easier to think of him as naïve than as devious.

To people who saw him close up, he was often enigmatic. He

could be painfully shy. Although he was a hardheaded scientist, he had an unworldly streak which found expression in a great interest in numerology and Eastern mysticism. Communication was not always easy with him, for he had a distracting habit of seeming to absent himself from a conversation while still being physically present. In a memoir about Wallace written after his death, Michael Straight discussed his "working relationship" with him on the *New Republic,* of which Wallace was for a time editor and Straight publisher:

"We would talk over the subject matter of an editorial; Jim Newman would write out a first draft. Jim and I would then sit on the sofa, Wallace between us, jingling a bunch of keys in his pocket. Jim would read a paragraph or two; gradually, Henry's eyelids would close, and his head would sink, inch by inch to his chest. The jingling would stop. Jim would read on to the end; we would wait. After a moment of silence, the jingling would start up again. Henry's head would jerk back; his eyelids would flutter. 'Fine,' he would murmur, 'that's fine.' " [4]

Glen Taylor, Wallace's running mate, was an even more improbable choice as a leader of American progressivism. A guitar-strumming singer who had never made the big time, he had been elevated to the Senate from Idaho in 1944 after a close election largely featured by his diligent handshaking and cowboy songs. He was an idolator of Roosevelt and broke with Truman over foreign policy. In the autumn of 1947, he decided to alert the American people to the danger of war by a Paul Revere horseback ride from the West to the East Coast. His trip was cut short by the special session of Congress in November, but he got himself photographed riding his horse up the steps of the Capitol. In Washington, he was regarded as one of those genial oddballs for whom the primary system could be held responsible, but he clearly possessed a large measure of political courage. He had anything but a safe Senate seat and, predictably, he lost it in the 1950 election in the backwash of the Progressive party's 1948 disaster.

The sequence of events which led to the Progressive party adventure began in 1946. Wallace's breaking point with the Truman administration came, of course, over foreign policy, though the record is clear that he had no plan to go into political exile when he made his Madison Square Garden speech on September 12. As indicated in Chapter 2, Wallace had Truman's approval before he delivered the speech; it may well have been his view that he could influence the Truman administration toward a more cooperative and understanding attitude vis-à-vis the Soviet Union. This was an era, it must be remembered, when many liberals had difficulty adjusting themselves to the harsh realization that Russia had broken the wartime compact and was engaged in an expansionist program in Eastern Europe contrary to all the undertakings she had given her allies. The United States government had come to this realization and was striving to counter the Soviet threat, but the curious thing was that many domestic critics were more dismayed by the American response than by the provocations which had prompted it. Wallace was one of those liberal critics who were more readily disposed to question the motives of their own government than to impugn the sincerity of a foreign government. It should be added that in 1946 he hardly spoke for the whole of the liberal community, but for a substantial portion thereof.

After Truman sacked him from the Cabinet, Wallace received a good deal of sympathy, even from people who despaired of his views. He was not at loose ends for long. Michael Straight offered him the post of editor of the *New Republic,* a liberal journal of some prestige but little circulation which immediately launched a successful promotion campaign. At this stage in his career, however, Wallace found weekly journalism too confining. "Before long it was clear that Wallace was not at heart committed to our enterprise," Straight has written. "He lived in his own world. He rarely read through the magazine, took little interest in the editors, frequently forgot their names." [5]

The political arena was more appealing and Wallace soon had an eager sponsor, an organization called the Progressive Citizens of America. With Wallace as the main convention speaker, the PCA had been founded in December 1946 principally as an amalgamation of two left-liberal organizations of "independents" whose origins went back to the 1944 election—a period when the wartime alliance with the Soviet Union had so muddled political distinctions that many liberals had no difficulty collaborating with Communists (most of whom, of course, disguised their anterior allegiance). By the time PCA was founded, the political atmosphere had significantly changed but there were still a good many non-Communists who were willing to share an organization with Communists and fellow travelers. The collaboration was rendered possible because the Communists in such a group never pressed for their ultimate program but championed the standard liberal causes; to a sophisticated observer, they could of course be identified by their unwillingness ever to criticize the Soviet Union, but many liberals regarded an effort to identify and exclude Communists as a heinous form of "red-baiting." Together with the party-liners, PCA included a considerable number of prominent non-Communists, such as columnist Frank Kingdon, radio commentator J. Raymond Walsh, editor Freda Kirchwey, CIO president Philip Murray (who soon withdrew), Jack Kroll, the head of the CIO's Political Action Committee and A. F. Whitney, president of the Brotherhood of Railroad Trainmen.[6]

C. B. Baldwin, an old colleague of Wallace from the Department of Agriculture, was executive vice-president of PCA, but Wallace's identification with the organization was not merely the consequence of friendship; the PCA ambiance, with its somber suspicions of what motivated American foreign policy and its disdain for Truman, was completely in accord with Wallace's political mood. Nor was his close association with PCA for want of any other political forum. In January 1947, soon after PCA was founded, another liberal group was established called Americans for Democratic Action. Its supporters included such distinguished figures as Mrs. Eleanor Roosevelt, Walter Reuther, David Dubinsky, Chester Bowles, Reinhold Niebuhr, Leon Henderson, Wilson Wyatt.[7] ADA was critical of the domestic failings of the Truman administration and it by no means offered blanket endorsement of every aspect of American foreign policy, but it had a realistic sense of alarm about the Soviet threat and it excluded Communists from membership. Indeed, it was in large part set up as a counterpoise to PCA—to provide a rallying ground for anti-Communist liberals who rejected all association with Communists.

Wallace did not join the Progressive Citizens of America, but he was its star performer throughout 1947. On March 13, the day after Truman asked Congress for economic and military aid for

Greece and Turkey to enable both countries to resist communism, Wallace broadcast a radio address under PCA's auspices denouncing the President's program, which subsequently, of course, became known as the Truman Doctrine. "March 12, 1947, marked a turning point in American history," Wallace declared. "It is not a Greek crisis that we face, it is an American crisis. It is a crisis in the American spirit. . . . When Truman offers unconditional aid to King George of Greece he is acting as the best salesman communism ever had. . . . The world is hungry and insecure, and the people of all lands demand change. American loans for military purposes won't stop them. . . . America will become the most hated nation in the world." At the end of the month, Wallace spoke again at a PCA protest meeting which filled New York's Madison Square Garden.

In April he traveled to Europe for a series of speeches in which he continued his criticism of the Greek-Turkish aid program. He received generous press coverage and was denounced in the U.S. Congress for ventilating a domestic quarrel while abroad. In May, after Wallace returned home, he went on a nationwide tour jointly sponsored by PCA and the *New Republic*. Immense crowds came out to hear him speak in Chicago, Detroit, Los Angeles and other cities, paying admission as for a theatrical event—a development that astounded political reporters. During May, an estimated 100,-000 persons paid more than $1.50 each, on the average, for admission to his rallies. The main thrust of his speeches continued to be directed against the Truman Doctrine—"A curious mixture of power politics and international carpetbagging." He warned that "Any attempt to force Europe to join an American armed camp—and that is the logical next step of the Truman Doctrine—will result in catastrophe, violence and bloodshed in Europe." In Los Angeles he asserted, "I am not afraid of communism. If I fail to cry out that I am anti-Communist, it is not because I am friendly to communism but because at this time of growing intolerance I refuse to join even the outer circle of that band of men who stir the stormy cauldron of hatred and fear." [8] Communists could applaud that remark.

Without committing himself, Wallace frequently dropped hints that a third party might be on the way. In Chicago, he declared "that if the Democratic party betrays its responsibilities to the people, the people will have to find other means of political expression." [9] In Los Angeles he told a gathering of the county Democratic Central Committee that "If the Democratic Party departs from the ideals of Franklin D. Roosevelt I shall desert altogether from that party." [10] In Denver, he amplified the statement to say that "If the Democratic party becomes the war party and the party of reaction by 1948, I shall take a Democratic vacation. If the cause of peace can be helped, I shall do more than take a vacation. The day is coming when labor will agree on a real labor party in cooperation with forward-looking farmers, businessmen, professional men and scientists." [11]

Nonetheless, there was some uncertainty that Wallace would finally break away from the Democratic party. Despite his hints, he stopped short of a firm commitment; it was possible to interpret his threats as an effort to exert pressure on the Truman administration as well as to see how much popular support he could amass before he took the final leap. In September, he disheartened third-party enthusiasts by stating that it was his intention to work within the Democratic party[12] and, indeed, any realistic assessment of the political atmosphere would have indicated that the outlook for a third party was becoming very bleak.

In 1946 and the early part of 1947, when Truman had so dismayed liberals and trade unionists, there had been considerable sentiment for a third party, though it had always been a minority sentiment. After Truman sought to break the railroad strike by an emergency draft bill, A. F. Whitney vowed that he would spend his entire union treasury (some $47 million), if necessary, to defeat Truman at the polls.[13] A National Educational Committee for a New Party was also formed in 1946, largely at the inspiration of former socialists; the members included a number of prominent trade unionists who held posts in such unions as the International Ladies' Garment Workers, the United Automobile Workers, the Amalgamated Meat Cutters and Butcher Workmen. Harry Truman ended these stirrings of rebellion by his shift to the left, signaled by his veto of the Taft-Hartley bill in June 1947. In the months that followed, he pressed domestic programs virtually indistinguishable from those advocated by his liberal critics. The bulk of the labor

ABOVE: The three Trumans a few weeks before the start of the 1948 campaign. (Pictorial Parade)  BELOW: Governor Dewey is escorted by the "cavemen" at Grant's Pass, Oregon, during the hard-fought primary campaign in May. (Wide World)

As in most of their pictures, Harold Stassen towers above Dewey (a sore point with Dewey's advisers) as they meet before their famous radio debate in Portland, Oregon, on May 17. (Wide World)

Dewey at the microphone during the debate, while Stassen awaits his turn. (Wide World)

ABOVE: President Truman marches with his World War I buddies through the streets of Omaha, Nebraska, on the second day of his "nonpolitical" tour in June. (Wide World) BELOW: Earl Warren, Thomas E. Dewey, and Robert A. Taft in friendly colloquy at the Philadelphia convention after Dewey won the Presidential nomination. (Wide World)

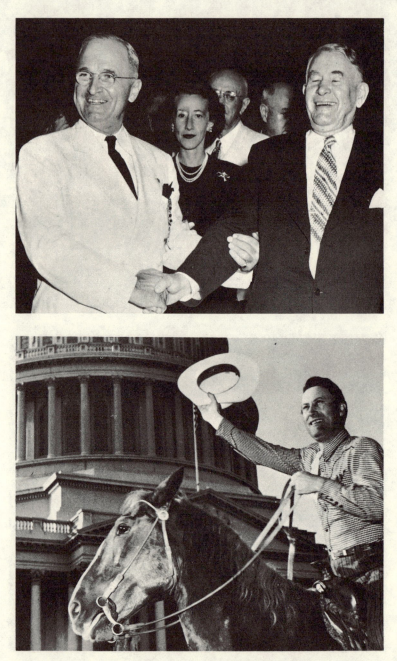

ABOVE: President Truman and Vice-Presidential nominee Alben W. Barkley after Truman's acceptance speech at the Democratic convention. (Pictorial Parade)   BELOW: Senator Glen H. Taylor and horse "Nugget" on the Capitol steps after his cross-country trip in November 1947 to alert the American people to the danger of war — and to get Senator Taylor on the front pages. (Wide World)

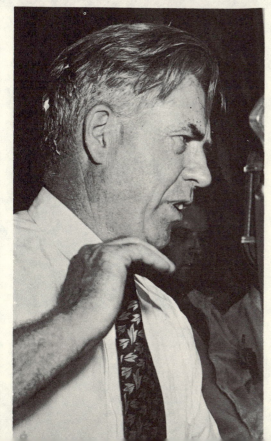

ABOVE: Henry A. Wallace, with Senator Taylor at his side, gives the crowd the big hello as he arrives for the opening of the Progressive party convention. (Wide World)   BELOW: An egg has just hit Henry Wallace behind the ear as he addresses a crowd in Greensboro, North Carolina, on August 30, 1948. (Wide World)

The Dixiecrat candidate, J. Strom Thurmond, in characteristic oratorical form. (Wide World)

The Socialist party candidates — Norman Thomas for President and Tucker P. Smith for Vice-President. (Wide World)

OPPOSITE PAGE, ABOVE: A typical Truman whistle-stop appearance in Richmond, Indiana, on October 12. (Wide World)
BELOW: Jubilation at Democratic headquarters in New York after Dewey's concession is announced. (Wide World)

ABOVE: The bitter-enders at Republican headquarters in New York in the early morning hours of November 3. (Wide World) BELOW: Dignified and self-possessed to the end, Dewey faces the press after congratulating Truman. It was perhaps Dewey's finest hour. (Wide World)

movement—with the notable exception of those CIO unions controlled by the Communists—lost all interest in a third party. And without labor support, it had always been assumed, a serious third-party effort could not be launched. In 1924, La Follette had the official endorsement of the AFL and the railway brotherhoods and yet only managed to poll 4,800,000 votes.

These considerations did not deter the Progressive Citizens of America, whose executive committee on December 15 proposed that Wallace run as a third-party candidate. He had already decided to do so early in December, according to Curtis D. MacDougall's exhaustive chronicle of the Wallace campaign, *Gideon's Army*.[14] On December 29, Wallace formally announced his candidacy in a radio address in which he said, "We have assembled a Gideon's Army, small in number, powerful in conviction, ready for action. We have said with Gideon, 'Let those who are fearful and trembling depart.' For every fearful one who leaves, there will be a thousand to take his place. A just cause is worth a hundred armies. . . ."

For all its pretentiousness, the speech had a ring of sincerity. There is no reason to doubt that Wallace believed that he was leading a crusade. In light of his dismal showing the following November, the question has often been asked why he became involved in so quixotic a venture. There is no certain way of knowing, but in December 1947 few people thought that he would receive only 1,150,000 votes. It rather seemed likely that he might equal or even surpass La Follette's showing. A Gallup poll published early in 1948 gave Wallace 7 percent of the vote,[15] which would have meant over 4.2 million votes if the total reached 58 million. On at least one occasion, Wallace himself spoke publicly of his expectation that the third party's chance would come in 1952, after the country went through another depression.[16] As for the impact of his candidacy on Democratic prospects in 1948, Wallace had no reason to be dismayed by the likely defeat of the man who had stolen the Presidency from him. As far back as December 1946, in his speech to the founding convention of PCA, Wallace had said, "We must make it continually clear to the administration that we, as progressives, would prefer the election of an out-and-out reactionary like Taft in 1948 to a lukewarm liberal." [17]

PCA's decision to run Wallace had been preceded by a similar decision by the Communist party. The Communists, understandably, made no public announcement, but their prompting was readily surmised by knowledgeable observers—if only because the Communist party, with over 60,000 members,[18] was the only substantial political force in the United States behind Wallace. Their spokesmen and newspapers enthusiastically supported him, and Wallace, in turn, deviated in no essential from the Communist party "line" on foreign policy, which at this point was principally directed against the Marshall Plan to provide economic aid to Europe. Moreover, without the disciplined corps of activists who constituted the Communist party apparatus in communities throughout the country, it would have been extremely difficult to collect the necessary signatures to get on the ballot in forty-five states (over 300,000 signatures were required in California, for example) and to undertake the multitude of other chores required to create a nationwide third party in a matter of months. Except in New York State, where the American Labor Party had been in existence for twelve years, the Communists provided the essential cadres around which local party organizations could be built.

The reasons the Communists wanted a third party are easy to understand. In the United States, they rarely had achieved any success unless they used another organization as a vehicle for their propaganda; the Communist brand name on their product simply put off the customers. Thus they had created a variety of "front" organizations in the previous dozen years to agitate for collective security, when Hitler was the menace, or for American nonintervention in World War II, when the Nazi-Soviet pact had been in force. Here and there, the Communists had also operated with some effectiveness within the Democratic party; they had supported Roosevelt in 1936, although they nominally had a candidate of their own, and again in 1944. The outbreak of the Cold War, however, had launched them on a policy of total opposition to every aspect of American foreign policy. A new organizational vehicle was thus necessary. A third party led by Henry Wallace seemed to offer limitless possibilities.

A behind-the-scenes view of the Communist instigation of the third party was not provided until three years later, when Michael

Quill, president of the Transport Workers Union, testified before a CIO committee investigating charges of Communist control filed against Harry Bridges' International Longshoremen's and Warehousemen's Union. (The Bridges union was ultimately expelled from the CIO, on grounds of Communist domination, as were several other left-wing unions.) Quill had been closely associated with the Communist party, although he apparently was not formally a member, for many years until he broke away in the early spring of 1948. He testified that on October 18, 1947, he had attended a meeting in New York City at which a number of leaders of left-wing CIO unions were present to confer with Eugene Dennis, general secretary of the Communist party, and two other leading party officials. According to Quill, Dennis told the group that the leaders of the Communist party "have decided to form a third party led by Henry Wallace and that Wallace would come out in the next few weeks and announce that he was a candidate . . ." The unionists were instructed "to start to petition and campaign now, to start the publicity, to line up endorsements for Wallace as soon as he announced himself on the radio."

Quill stated that he subsequently became very dubious about the wisdom of running Wallace—he feared that a split in the Democratic vote would lead to a Republican victory—but that his protestations to party officials got him nowhere. Gerhard Eisler, for example, explained to Quill that it was in the interests of the Soviet bloc that Wallace head up a third-party ticket.[19]

In January 1948, the night before a CIO executive board meeting in Washington, D.C., another caucus of left-wing union leaders was called by John Williamson, the Communist party's labor secretary. Williamson instructed the group to try to get the CIO board to pass a resolution endorsing Wallace; failing that, they were to attempt to block any anti-Wallace resolution.[20] The effort failed. By a three-to-one majority, the CIO on January 22 passed a resolution condemning the third party.[21]

PCA's announcement in mid-December that it had asked Wallace to run led to a series of resignations from the organization—the first being that of its co-chairman, Frank Kingdon. He had cast the only dissenting vote at the PCA board meeting on December 15 and soon afterward released a statement declaring that the lack of labor support for the new party was alone "enough to convince me that it would be folly to attempt an independent campaign." [22] In his column in the New York *Post* on December 31, he wrote, "Who asked Henry Wallace to run? . . . The call to Wallace came from the Communist party and the only progressive organization [meaning the PCA] admitting Communists to its membership." Kingdon's resignation was followed by that of Bartley Crum,[23] a prominent San Francisco lawyer who later became publisher of the New York *Star*, J. Raymond Walsh,[24] journalists Albert Deutsch [25] and A. J. Liebling,[26] the railroad trainmen's A. F. Whitney[27] and several others.

Immediately after the PCA announcement, Jacob S. Potofsky, president of the Amalgamated Clothing Workers, stated that the New York affiliates of his union would not go along with the Wallace candidacy.[28] The Amalgamated, a large and affluent union, was at the time the principal non-Communist element in the American Labor party, a New York State party which generally endorsed Democratic candidates. Potofsky's declaration, which hardly came as a surprise, meant that the ALP's labor support would be reduced to the hard core of Communist-led unions.

The liberal press—such as the newspaper *PM* in New York and the weekly journals of opinion, *The Nation* and the *New Republic* —all opposed Wallace's candidacy. *The Nation* pointed out that the great danger of such "quixotic politics" would be to split the Democratic vote to the advantage of the Republicans: "Perhaps we could afford to take a chance on electing Coolidge in 1924, but the world of 1948 presents a different picture. . . . By 1952, the fate of the American economy may well have been sealed and the question of war or peace decided. It is all very well for Communists to entertain the hope that after the deluge their turn will come, but why should Henry Wallace invite either consequence?" [29] The *New Republic* was equally dismayed and in January the announcement came of Wallace's resignation as editor, though he continued to write a weekly column until July.

The Communist origins of the Wallace movement received continuing attention from his critics. The International Ladies' Garment Workers' Union denounced Wallace's candidacy as "Communist-inspired" and charged that his opposition to the Marshall

Plan "resurrects the old course of appeasement" that led to World War II.[30] Walter Reuther, president of the United Automobile Workers, made caustic personal comments about Wallace. "I think Henry is a lost soul," he told a National Press Club luncheon in Washington. "People who are not sympathetic with democracy in America are influencing him. Communists perform the most complete valet service in the world. They write your speeches, they do your thinking for you, they provide you with applause and they inflate your ego as often as necessary. I'm afraid that's the trouble with Henry Wallace." [31]

Late in April 1948, in a speech in Atlantic City, CIO president Philip Murray stated that "the Communist party is directly responsible for the organization of a third party in the United States." He charged that the decision to found the party had been made at a Communist meeting in New York in October 1947.[32] Murray provided no further details, but within the week the *Washington Post* published a long article by Alfred Friendly which sought to document Murray's charges.[33] Friendly's article, which did not disclose its sources, was widely distributed by ADA and received much attention. In essence it told the same story which Mike Quill was later to elaborate before the CIO in 1950.

The denunciation of the Communist auspices of the third party, though damaging in the long run, initially did not seem to impair the enthusiasm which Wallace evoked as he toured the country in the winter and spring of 1948. There was still a magic to the Wallace name, still a cluster of nostalgic associations with the Roosevelt era, still a rousing appeal in the well-worn rhetoric about the century of the common man. Wallace began to campaign in February, with a midwestern tour, a trip to Florida, and several appearances in the Bronx to support ALP candidate Leo Isacson in his by-election campaign. He made a New England tour in March and April, then returned to the Midwest. Beginning in May, he campaigned on the West Coast, through the Rocky Mountain states and the Southwest, returning East in mid-June. In twenty-five days of his western tour, Wallace addressed 129,000 people in nine states and collected $269,593 in donations for his campaign fund.[34]

"His pilgrimage will probably be recorded in the history books as the strangest—and longest—campaign in U.S. annals," James

A. Wechsler wrote midway in Wallace's spring tour. "By the time the major parties . . . hold their conventions Wallace will have conducted the equivalent of nearly two full Presidential campaigns. . . . At virtually every stop the local left-wing stalwarts run the arrangements and control the scenery. They make little effort to keep their faces out of the pictures; it is the biggest show they have ever staged. But the political complexion of the audiences is definitely broader. It is a cross-section of American discontent and insecurity." [35]

Reporters were dazzled by the willingness of crowds not only to pay admission to hear Wallace but to empty their pockets for his cause once they were inside the hall. There was careful stage-managing for each of Wallace's one-night stands. First came the warm-up speeches by some junior member of the traveling troupe —such as the Negro actor Canada Lee—as well as one or two local dignitaries. There followed the "pitch" from William Gailmor, a suave, fast-talking New Yorker who had been an orthodox rabbi before becoming a radio commentator. Gailmor mingled jokes with political uplift, then appealed for funds. Luke P. Carroll appreciatively described his technique in an article in the *New York Herald-Tribune:* " 'The money you give is more than a mere political donation. It's a form of life insurance,' Mr. Gailmor told the audience. His next words depended on the town the show was playing. If it happened to be a large city where there was every expectation of a large 'take,' the radio commentator asked for individual $1,000 donations or pledges. This first request is scaled all the way down to $25 if the third party leaders feel that $25 is the most any one person will offer." Near the end of his routine Gailmor had an interesting gimmick. He would ask everyone to wave a dollar bill in the air, to impress the newspaper photographers. While the bills were held aloft, he would then make a huge joke of telling the ushers to collect them before they were pocketed.

With the fund-raising out of the way, Wallace would finally be brought on. "The hall is darkened," Carroll wrote. "A spotlight wanders over to the door and soon a man with an unruly forelock and a toothy grin strides onto the stage. He reads his prepared speech with little animation. And when he makes a parenthetical aside, the chuckle that follows seems to frighten him, for he immediately gets back to the business at hand. While the ovations are few and far between, he is always well received." [36]

While Wallace made a favorable impression on the audiences which paid to hear him, much of his press coverage was unflattering. For that he could in part blame his own gaffes. Testifying on February 24 before the House Committee on Foreign Affairs, he criticized the Marshall Plan on the grounds that it had become a big business operation that would be harmful to Europe. When Representative Sol Bloom, the ranking minority member, asked how his criticism could be distinguished from that of the Soviet Union, Wallace said, "I'm not familiar with the Communist approach and am unable to discuss it." He later added that he did not "follow the Communist literature." [37] Throughout the campaign, he was to make the same disclaimer of knowledge about Communist policy—which led to the frequent quip that Wallace was seeking the highest office in the land to deal with a worldwide problem about which he freely professed ignorance.

His comments about the Communist coup in Czechoslovakia were even more embarrassing. Initially, in a speech in Minneapolis on February 27, he argued that the Communist take-over was evidence that an American "get tough" policy "only provokes a 'get tougher' policy. . . . The men in Moscow, from their viewpoint, would be utter morons if they failed to respond with acts of pro-Russian consolidation." [38] On March 15, at a New York press conference, he went much further and attributed the Communist coup to a desire to forestall a right-wing revolution assisted by the American ambassador to Czechoslovakia, Lawrence S. Steinhardt.[39] This was an incredible charge, for which Wallace offered no evidence. (Steinhardt promptly pointed out that he had been away from Czechoslovakia for three months prior to the Communist coup.)[40] Wallace further startled his audience when a reporter asked him about the tragic, recent death of Jan Masaryk, the Czech foreign minister. Masaryk either had been murdered or had committed suicide—presumably because of his despair over the collapse of Czech democracy. Wallace's reply was remarkable. "I live in the house that John G. Winant lived in," he said, referring to the former U.S. ambassador to Great Britain, "and I've heard rumors why he committed suicide. One can never tell. Maybe

Winant had cancer. Maybe Masaryk had cancer. Maybe Winant was unhappy about the fate of the world. Who knows?" [41]

Perhaps Wallace's most memorable indiscretion involved no hostile needling from the press. In an extemporaneous speech to a small audience in Salem, Oregon, he spoke of the desirability of the government buying up submarginal agricultural land. "If the people insist on living on such land," he declared, "then the government should not let them have children. People who want to live on that kind of land have no right to have children." [42] Wallace's entourage was understandably horrified by the comment and at his next press conference he retracted it. [43]

By the end of his long preconvention tour, it was apparent that the Wallace campaign had made no progress. A variety of events, foreign and domestic, had conspired against him. The increasingly aggressive character of Soviet policy—first the Czech coup, then the Russian blockade of Allied access to Berlin which began late in June—undercut Wallace's argument that American "imperialism" was responsible for the Cold War. Truman's civil rights program and his baiting of the Republican Eightieth Congress effectively countered Wallace's thesis that there was no essential difference between the two major parties. The reiterated charges that his crusade was Communist-inspired unquestionably alienated many potential supporters. Through all these months, few prominent new recruits rallied to Wallace's side; the sole well-known New Dealer active in his behalf was Rexford Guy Tugwell, who had been one of F.D.R.'s original brain trusters. Wallace's organizational support was unimpressive. In the labor field, only those international unions later to be expelled from the CIO as Communist-dominated supported him. No AFL international union or major farm organization backed him. Among daily newspapers, his only support came from the two Communist papers—the *Daily Worker* in New York and the *People's World* in San Francisco—and the liberal *Gazette and Daily* in York, Pennsylvania.

In February, when Leo Isacson upset Tammany Hall to win the by-election in the Bronx, the euphoria among Wallace's supporters reached a peak it was never to attain again. But the Bronx election, as already indicated, was a special case—the ALP had concentrated its city-wide forces in one congressional district and the Democrats were temporarily vulnerable among Jewish voters because of the administration's uncertain course on the Palestine issue. By June, the Gallup poll gave Wallace a mere 6 percent of the popular vote, as compared with 7 percent in January.[44] By contrast, La Follette had received 17 percent in 1924. Wallace's managers, however, were comforted somewhat by the speculation that there was a substantial "silent vote" which did not show up in the polls—on the theory that many Wallace supporters were too timid or fearful to express their preferences to polltakers.

The party's convention in July failed to reverse the decline in Wallace's popularity, though the gathering was notable both for its size and enthusiasm. More than 3,200 delegates and alternates were in attendance, far more than the numbers at the Republican or Democratic conventions. The party's rules were of course designed to encourage maximum participation (a delegate could attend with as little as one-eighth of a vote) but there was no disputing the fact that many delegates were of modest means who had gone to considerable pains to attend. A great many had sat up on overnight buses or hitchhiked to Philadelphia; some pitched tents or slept in their cars to save on hotel rooms. Fatigue did not restrain their zeal or their massive participation in song whenever the signal was given by the platform. Equally impressive was the rally on the second night of the convention in Shibe Park, a baseball stadium, where 32,000 Wallace fans paid $.65 to $2.60 each to cheer his acceptance speech.

The convention was nevertheless a public relations disaster, for it bolstered the charge that the new party was Communist-controlled and that Henry Wallace was either unaware of the fact or indifferent to it. From the outset, most of the press was critical, not to say hostile, but no distortion of the facts was necessary to produce an unflattering portrait. At every turn, both Wallace and his party's managers played into the hands of their critics.

Wallace's press conference on July 23, the opening day of the convention, set the tone of bumbling ineptitude which was to characterize the entire three-day affair. Wallace began the proceedings by reading a letter written by George Polk, an American journalist recently murdered in Greece, and then lectured the puzzled journalists on the responsibilities of their calling. This irrelevance over, he next read a statement on his attitude toward Communist support— it was "a political liability" but "I will not repudiate any support which comes to me on the basis of interest in peace." He went on to say that "If you accept the idea that Communists have no right to express their opinions, then you don't believe in democracy," overlooking the fact that a repudiation of Communist electoral support hardly implied a denial of their right to free speech. Having stated his position on the Communist issue, he refused to entertain any questions on the subject.

Wallace may have thought that he had disposed of the most embarrassing preoccupation of the press, but he was immediately confronted by a question as to whether he had written the "Guru letters"—a series of mystical communications addressed to a cult leader named Nicholas Roerich, about which the right-wing columnist Westbrook Pegler had been belaboring Wallace for months.

Wallace refused to answer the question, saying, "I never comment on Westbrook Pegler."

Pegler then got to his feet, identified himself, and put the same question. "I never engage in any discussions with Westbrook Pegler," said Wallace. Undaunted, two other reporters asked the question, only to be slapped down with the comment, "I never engage in a discussion with a stooge of Westbrook Pegler." The redoubtable H. L. Mencken then arose to say, "Mr. Wallace, I can hardly be accused of being a stooge for Mr. Pegler. Why don't you answer the question?"

"I will handle that in my own way and in my own time," said Wallace, unyielding to the end.[45] It was a classic demonstration of how to ensure a bad press. The irony was that a simple admission of authorship of the disputed letters would hardly have involved a major public scandal.

The day before, Senator Glen Taylor, Wallace's running mate, had gotten through a press conference with greater aplomb but even less logic when the Communist issue came up. His contribution was a novel distinction between "pink" and "red" Communists. "I think the pink Communists, who believe in changes in our form of government by evolution rather than revolution, will support our party," said the Senator. "The red Communists will support Mr. Dewey because they hope that the best way to get a revolution is to have another Hoover administration." [46]

What was puzzling in all this was that Wallace and Taylor did not issue a brief, self-serving statement repudiating Communist support (without any expectation, of course, of alienating their unwanted admirers). The maneuver might have been too difficult to accomplish effectively, however, for a statement strong enough to impress their critics might well have brought outcries of dissent from the delegates if it had been uttered in their presence. Wallace had been booed when he had made some critical comments about the Soviet Union in his September 1946 speech.[47] He clearly did not enjoy audience hostility and there was no reason to believe that the Communists, who did not want to be repudiated, would cooperate in restraining their followers had he indulged in any comments which could be considered "red-baiting."

More astute management of the convention might have muted the Communist issue somewhat; instead it was inflamed. The matter caused no embarrassment at the opening session on Friday night, which was largely given over to a keynote address by a little-known Iowa lawyer named Charles P. Howard, whose principal distinction was that he was a Negro and, until recently, a Republican. On Friday night, the convention also unanimously decided to call itself the Progressive party.

On Saturday afternoon, with traditional convention hoopla, Wallace and Taylor were nominated by acclamation. At the Shibe Park rally that night, the party managers were not content with merely having Wallace and Taylor speak, as well as the accomplished pitchman, William Gailmor. They also gave prominent billing to Paul Robeson, the famous Negro singer, and Representative Vito Marcantonio. Both were models of fellow-traveling orthodoxy, who had faithfully complied with every shift of the Communist party line for more than a decade. Their presence on the platform inevitably plastered the red label on the biggest event of the convention.

The degree to which the convention was subject to Communist

control became fully apparent on Sunday, when the delegates spent nearly eight hours adopting the party platform. In almost every major particular, it paralleled the draft of the Communist party platform which had been published several weeks before—opposition to the Marshall Plan and the Truman Doctrine, demands for the ending of American "military and economic intervention" in Greece, Turkey, and China, the use of the United Nations as a mechanism for international aid instead of the Marshall Plan, repeal of the draft law and an end to the U.S. military buildup, destruction of the existing stockpiles of atomic bombs (which only the United States possessed at the time; the Soviet Union did not detonate a bomb until 1949).[48]

The platform committee was chaired by Rexford Tugwell, but he by no means was in control. Tugwell recalls that he was in frequent conflict with Lee Pressman, the secretary of the committee, over phraseology which Tugwell thought was too close to what the Communists favored.[49] Pressman, the former chief lawyer for the CIO and the steelworkers union, had for years been regarded as one of the most influential fellow travelers in the labor movement; not until 1950 did he publicly admit that he had been a Communist party member in the thirties for a period of a year.[50] (In 1950, he also resigned from the American Labor party, on the ground that it was Communist-dominated.)[51]

Tugwell also had a bitter dispute with Vito Marcantonio, who wanted a plank promising independence to Puerto Rico—a cause then being ardently championed by the Communists. Tugwell, a former governor of Puerto Rico, resisted the proposal and in the end a compromise was reached recognizing Puerto Rico's "right" to independence without promising it.[52]

Echoes of these disputes reached the press but the most damaging publicity was largely caused by two events on the convention floor. One was the exotic Macedonian issue. In the original draft of the platform, circulated the day before, the party was put on record as favoring for the Macedonians, as for the Armenians and Irish, a "unified homeland," in contrast to their present dispersion in Albania, Bulgaria, Greece, and Yugoslavia. After the draft platform was distributed, it was suddenly realized that the Macedonian Communists were supporting Marshal Tito in his conflict with the Soviet Union. The Progressive party was thus inadvertently saying a friendly word for the friends of heretic Tito. To avoid this embarrassment, the reference to Macedonia was deleted. Lee Pressman made the announcement to the delegates, without explanation. One curious delegate later insisted on an explanation. It was offered by author Louis Adamic, who delivered a wordy little speech in which he said that Macedonian-Americans had been split on the issue and hence the whole matter had been dropped. Over the opposition of several delegates, the convention then adopted a motion to drop the demand for a Macedonian homeland, thereby affording the *New York Times* an opportunity to comment, "So sensitive were the delegates to every change in the Communist line that it took one action today which seemed to put it on the side of the Communist Information Bureau in its conflict with Marshal Tito. . . ." [53]

The "Vermont amendment," which was to plague the party for the rest of the campaign, provoked extended debate. Three delegates from Vermont introduced an amendment which declared: "Although we are critical of the present foreign policy of the United States, it is not our intention to give blanket endorsement to the foreign policy of any nation." James Hayford, co-chairman of the Vermont delegation, declared that he had "no intention . . . to red-bait" but that "the great weak point of the platform as it now stands is that it lays us open to the charge of condemning the American foreign policy practically in toto, while saying nothing critical of the foreign policy of any other nation." Hayford thought his innocuous little amendment would set the record straight; he was supported by several other delegates, but lively opposition developed. The Vermont disclaimer was denounced as "the reflection of the pressure from outside," "a compromise with the smear campaign" and even, incredibly, "an insinuation against a wartime ally of the United States." When the matter was put to a voice vote, Vermont mustered a respectable volume of "ayes" but the "noes" clearly won. The enemies of the Progressive party could hardly have done it a greater disservice. [54]

And before the day was up, Henry Wallace had once again caught his foot in his mouth. A *Time* reporter asked how he ex-

## CHAPTER 8
# Strategies
# and Tactics

In every Presidential campaign year there is a deceptive lull after the conventions. Tradition, and the distractions of the vacation season, decree that the campaign proper not start until sometime in September. In the interim, the candidates relax, foregoing overt politicking but taking care to show themselves frequently in some informal pose for the benefit of newspaper photographers. The real story goes on behind the scenes, where strategy is pondered, campaign itineraries are drawn up, major speeches are planned; by mid-August the advance men generally start out on the road and the fund-raisers begin making their rounds.

The year 1948 deviated in no substantial degree from this pattern, except for the brief interlude of the special session of Congress. Truman derived the expected publicity advantages from this engagement, but Dewey was by no means neglected. A platoon of journalists trailed him as he moved between the state capitol in Albany and his farm in Pawling, with occasional side trips to New York City. There were only infrequent light moments, for Dewey was already exemplifying the dignity of his anticipated office before taking formal title to it.

He had many visitors. Soon after the Republican convention, Governor Warren and his family called on the Deweys in Pawling and spent two hours posing for photographs as they strolled over the grounds. John Foster Dulles, Dewey's foreign policy adviser, conferred with him in New York City, as did Senator Robert A. Taft. Late in July, Harold Stassen paid a visit to the farm and went swimming with the Governor in Quaker Lake. Dewey would not allow any photographs. "We're swimming for our benefit, not yours," he explained.[1] Two days later, General Dwight D. Eisenhower arrived for a "nonpolitical" conference. Dewey told the press that they had discussed European affairs and that both were in agreement about the necessity of a firm line against the Russian blockade of Berlin. Dewey also volunteered that the "General and I discussed a principal interest of both in farming and soil conservation. We talked about trench silos, pen stables and soil erosion." The General was asked by reporters whether his visit indicated that he would support Dewey's candidacy. "I have not identified myself with any particular party," he replied, adding a characteristic non-sequitur: "I think I reflect the Governor's views when I say we talked as two Americans." [2]

Preparations for the campaign went forward quietly; this was the second time around for the Dewey team, the 1944 campaign being the first, and the entire effort was characterized by the same remorseless efficiency which had secured Dewey the nomination. Campaign manager Herbert Brownell opened his headquarters in Washington; he was largely to be concerned with scheduling, radio arrangements, liaison with party organizations around the country.[3] Representative Hugh D. Scott, Jr., the new national chairman, set off on a nationwide speaking tour; it had been made clear to him from the outset that he was not to have any responsibility for running the campaign.[4] As in 1944, Elliott V. Bell, New York State's Superintendent of Banks, became head of Dewey's policy-making and speech-writing staff, which was installed on two floors of Albany's DeWitt Clinton Hotel. John Burton, the state budget director, was put in charge of research.

The staff setup represented a shift in the power configuration around Dewey. Until he won the nomination, his three most influential staff men were Brownell, Ed Jaeckle, and J. Russel Sprague. Then the job was supremely one of "practical" politics—winning primaries, cultivating delegates, outsmarting the opposition at the convention. Once the nomination was secured, the strategic decisions were of a different sort—the general tone and emphasis of Dewey's campaign, his positions on the great issues of public policy, the attitude he would take toward the Eightieth Congress, the way he would respond to Truman's attacks. In shaping the grand design of his strategy, Dewey heeded the counsel of Elliott Bell more than that of anyone else.

This is not to suggest that Bell was the "architect" of Dewey's "disaster," as Jules Abels put it in his book, *Out of the Jaws of Victory.*[5] If there was any architect, it was Dewey, for while he listened attentively to advice, in the end he made all the principal decisions. Nor was the basic strategy of the campaign something that only Dewey and Bell discussed. Various members of the Dewey brain trust contributed their views; Brownell came up from Washington several times during the summer to confer with the candidate. Later, when he was campaigning around the country, Dewey talked with Brownell every night by telephone.[6] Bell, however, was Dewey's chief speech writer and intellectual mentor, the latter a role which he had held for nearly a decade. He was also one of Dewey's oldest friends (as was Brownell).

Dewey and Bell had met at a lecture at the Columbia University Club in New York in 1929.[7] Dewey was then a young lawyer in a large New York firm, Bell a newspaperman who was later to become well known as a financial writer on the *New York Times.* The two men saw each other socially throughout Dewey's "racket-busting" years; Bell did not work for Dewey until 1939, when he headed up the research team to prepare Dewey for the 1940 campaign. When Dewey failed to get the nomination, Bell became Willkie's chief speech writer. After the election, Bell joined the editorial board of the *Times,* a position he held until Dewey, elected governor in 1942, appointed him Superintendent of Banks.

It was a rewarding relationship for both men. Through Dewey's patronage, Bell was able to display his talents in a wider arena than daily journalism afforded and Dewey had the benefit of one of the most brilliant minds in American public life. The two friends were dissimilar in many ways. Dewey had a great talent for absorbing facts and a restless curiosity about many things, but his book knowledge was limited and he found abstruse ideas uncongenial. He preferred to learn by listening rather than by reading. Bell, an eloquent conversationalist, had an intellectual turn of mind and was well versed in economic and political theory. He was politically an independent (he voted for Roosevelt in 1932) until Dewey's political fortunes made him into a Republican. A neo-Keynesian in his economic thinking, he would have made a far more liberal Secretary of the Treasury—the job for which many people thought he was destined—than Truman's appointee, John W. Snyder.

By the beginning of August, Dewey had determined the broad outlines of his campaign strategy. He would run a dignified campaign, emphasizing his own program, affirming the need for unity, and avoiding any slanging matches with Truman. He decided on this approach for several reasons, not the least of which was the nearly universal assumption that he was certain to win. The Gallup poll in early August gave Dewey 48 percent of the vote, Truman 37 percent, Wallace 5 percent, with 10 percent of the respondents undecided.[8] The Roper poll, published several days later, dropped Truman's percentage to 31.5, credited Dewey with 46.3 percent, Wallace with 3 percent; 19.2 percent appeared in the "no opinion" column.[9] The gap seemed much too great for Truman to bridge during the course of a campaign; moreover, the electoral vote was likely to be more lopsided, because of the Dixiecrat and Wallace defections from the Democrats.

Personal impressions confirmed the pollsters' findings. As Elliott Bell has recalled, "It was the prevailing view of all the experienced politicians, of all the newspapermen that I encountered, that Dewey couldn't win the campaign—he could only lose it." Bell remembers a constant stream of Republican politicians who would lunch with him and his group of speech writers at the DeWitt Clinton Hotel after calling on Dewey at the state capitol. "We always asked them what our strategy should be and they all said that as matters stood Dewey was in and the thing to do was not stir up too much controversy and run the risk of losing votes." [10]

It was clear that Truman was going to continue the uninhibited attacks which he had begun on his "nonpolitical" trip in June. For Dewey to respond in kind was considered both unnecessary and dangerous. The danger was to create sympathy for Truman, a superb performer in the role of underdog, and to alienate independent voters by awakening dormant fears that the Republicans were again planning to overturn the popular reforms of the New Deal.[11]

This assessment was reinforced by memories of what had happened in the 1944 campaign. Initially, Dewey and his advisers had decided to avoid any sharp attacks on Roosevelt and to run a "constructive" campaign; they calculated that to do otherwise would only encourage support for F.D.R., who had the advantage of not only being President but wartime Commander-in-chief. For the first two and a half weeks of the campaign, Dewey delivered a series of high-minded speeches in the Midwest and on the Pacific Coast. In Los Angeles, 90,000 enthusiastic partisans assembled in the Coliseum to hear him. "That crowd wanted Roosevelt fried in oil," Paul Lockwood has said. "Instead of that, Dewey got up and talked about social security. The speech fell like a wet rag on the deck." When Dewey's party returned to their hotel, Herbert Brownell telephoned from the East Coast to complain about the reaction of the "fat cats" to Dewey's temperate approach. They wanted a fighting campaign and were otherwise reluctant to finance it.[12]

The telephone pressure continued over the next day or two; it was reinforced by a scornful, denunciatory speech which Roosevelt delivered at a banquet of the teamsters' union in Washington. By the time he arrived in Oklahoma City for his next major speech, Dewey decided on a change in tactics. He would hit hard.[13] The Oklahoma City speech on September 25 was a model of aggressive political assault; Dewey, the erstwhile prosecutor, delivered it superbly. "Shall we . . . perpetuate one man in office for sixteen years?" he demanded. "Shall we expose our country to a return of the seven years of New Deal depression because my opponent is indispensable to the ill-assorted, power-hungry conglomeration of city bosses, Communists and career bureaucrats which now compose the New Deal?"

For the rest of the campaign, Dewey continued the attack. Committed Republicans relished his performance, but he was defeated on election day. In their postmortems, Dewey's advisers conceded that he would have lost in any event, but they were persuaded that he had been gaining at the outset of the campaign when he had followed the high road. In 1948, there was an understandable desire not to repeat the error.

There were other considerations as well which dictated a lofty course. Dewey faced a dilemma if he sought to debate Truman's charges about the Eightieth Congress. If he defended the Congress, he would delight conservative Republicans, but would dismay liberals and independents who saw merit in Truman's case. Moreover, he could hardly square his party's recently adopted platform with the congressional record in domestic affairs. It was equally unthinkable, of course, for Dewey to criticize a Congress controlled by his own party. The easiest solution was to avoid the issue, though from time to time he uttered some *pro forma* pleasantries about the Congress.

The moderation of Dewey's rhetoric was also motivated by more statesmanlike considerations. With the Berlin blockade in force since June, the campaign was played out against a backdrop of foreign crisis. Dewey's actions indicated that he had no desire to exacerbate a tense situation for partisan political advantage. He could easily have scored debating points with a detailed indictment of past errors and illusions in the conduct of American foreign policy, indulging in that measure of campaign exaggeration which is rarely regarded as inappropriate except in time of war; the blunders, real and imagined, of Teheran and Yalta and Potsdam could all have been exploited to embarrass the administration. Instead, throughout the campaign, Dewey expressed only restrained dismay about the past failings of the Democratic administration and stressed the unity of both parties behind the government's present policy. He frequently claimed credit for having instituted bipartisanship in foreign affairs during the 1944 campaign.

Of equal importance was Dewey's desire to avoid commitments, made in the heat of the campaign, which would plague him after he took office.[14] His speech writers labored under the slightly discomforting responsibility of knowing that they were setting words down on paper which would be uttered by the next President of the United States. The Alsop brothers wrote at the time of the Dewey strategists' "sober realization that the future is both unforeseeable and menacing. In these circumstances it is unwise to promise a world millennium the day after tomorrow. . . . And they do not wish to debar themselves in advance from using any expedients which events may later render desirable."[15]

It took a little time to cue in everybody to the restrained Dewey strategy. A few misleading newspaper stories appeared during the summer which predicted a hard-hitting, even a "rip-roaring" campaign.[16] On August 11, Hugh Scott returned from a cross-country tour to find that he had been innocently deluding party activists with promises of a "District Attorney" type of campaign. In Albany, Scott told the Governor that wherever he had gone he had been passing the word that Dewey and Warren "were both former prosecuting attorneys, they would read a bill of indictment against the administration a mile long and that they would have the administration on the ropes." [17]

The candidate quickly set the party chairman straight. "Dewey said the campaign wasn't going to be that way at all," Scott has recalled. "He said he wasn't going to get into the gutter with Truman and he might not even mention Truman's name." Scott and Dewey had an amusing exchange about the famous Oklahoma City speech, which Scott had been telling people would be the model for the 1948 campaign. Dewey called it the worst speech he had ever made; Scott demurred, calling it one of his best. But the party chairman, who was somewhat in awe of Dewey, made no strenuous effort to persuade him to conduct a "fighting campaign." In later years, Scott regarded his diffidence as "the biggest political mistake I ever made." [18]

Dewey and his advisers had one major anxiety about the campaign—that the Democrats would win control of the Senate. The Republicans had held a 51 to 45 majority since the 1946 election; if the Democrats won but four more seats, they would emerge with a 49 to 47 majority. During the summer, it was already apparent that the Republican candidates were in trouble in Iowa, West Virginia, Tennessee, New Mexico, Colorado, Montana, Wyoming, Minnesota. To lend a helping hand, Dewey's itinerary was arranged so that he could spend more time in many of these states than a Presidential campaign would normally have required. He would make both major speeches and numerous back-platform appearances. But as the front-runner, Dewey saw no need to tax himself excessively. He decided not to follow the example of Truman, who was going to open his campaign on Labor Day with several speeches in Michigan. Instead, he gave the Labor Day assignment to Harold Stassen. He also planned shorter and less intensive train tours than Truman's.

On the whole, it was a relaxed summer for Dewey and his entourage, with plenty of time for reflective speech-writing. Dewey took his speeches with the utmost seriousness and was never one to accept uncritically what his ghost-writers prepared for him; instead, he engaged in an active collaboration. Apart from Elliott Bell, who served as a kind of managing editor, Dewey had five principal speech writers during the campaign. Allen W. Dulles, then a prominent lawyer in private practice, dealt with foreign affairs and also handled liaison with his brother, John Foster Dulles, who was to be in Paris during most of the campaign as a delegate to the UN General Assembly. Merlyn S. Pitzele, the talented labor editor of *Business Week* and a former CIO organizer, was primarily concerned with labor, social security and civil rights issues. Stanley High, a *Reader's Digest* editor who had once been a Roosevelt speech writer, and Stewart Beach, an editor of *This Week* and an old friend of Dewey, were general assignment writers. Robert F. Ray, a young man who had written a dissertation on campaign speeches which had impressed Dewey, wrote an occasional speech and rehearsed the Governor before he faced his audiences.

The preparation of a Dewey speech went through several stages. Once the subject was set, research chief John Burton collected a fat dossier of material, including everything the candidate had previously said on the subject, so that inadvertent contradictions could be avoided. Then there would be a meeting with Dewey attended by two or three speech writers and perhaps an outside expert or two. A wide-ranging discussion would ensue, in which everybody's ideas were welcome, and at the end of the session a fairly clear idea would emerge of the policy line Dewey wanted to take. The ghost then retired to his typewriter and when he had a draft of the speech passed it on to Elliott Bell. Bell was an exacting editor who often required three or four drafts before he was satisfied. The manuscript then went to Dewey. If the Governor approved the contents, the speech was polished and cut to the required length.

After he got the manuscript back, Dewey usually called in his secretary, Lillian Rosse, as well as the speech writer and Bell. Dewey would go over the speech paragraph by paragraph, dictating word changes, revising sentences and whole paragraphs. Sometimes the changes were minor; on other occasions, a whole new speech emerged. At every point the speech writer could argue with the candidate. Dewey never lacked the power of making a decision but he encouraged debate. He rarely said "No" but rather, "I don't like that—why should I say it?" Frequently he could be persuaded. These sessions often lasted for several hours and gave the speech writer a heady sense of helping make the policy of the next U.S. government. After Dewey finished dictating, his secretary typed up a new version; the writer then went over it microscopically, making sure that the sentences were not too long and that there would be appropriate pauses for applause. If any substantive changes were made, Dewey would see the script again. A reading copy would then be prepared in jumbo type, after which Dewey would rehearse the speech with Robert Ray. All this effort resulted in a performance as polished as that of a professional elocutionist. Throughout the campaign nobody faulted Dewey on performance—only on substance.[19]

In preparing for the autumn campaign, the Democrats had no need, of course, to formulate a strategy. Since the first of the year, Truman had held with remarkable fidelity to the strategy suggested in Clark Clifford's memorandum of November 1947. The State of the Union address and the individual messages which followed had outlined the campaign issues; the President's June trip had pretested his campaign techniques; the special session of Congress had provided him with additional ammunition with which to belabor the opposition. For the remainder of the campaign, Truman would continue an unremitting attack on a Congress which had abdicated its responsibilities, plus an identification of Dewey with congressional delinquencies for which he was in no wise responsible. It was a strategy tailor-made for Truman, who had proven that in his folksy way he possessed demagogic gifts which a more accomplished performer might envy.

By the end of July, however, it was apparent that in one major particular Clifford's eight-month-old projection was wrong—the Solid South had split, threatening Truman with a loss of electoral votes which it was hard to see him making up elsewhere. Moreover, while the polls gave Wallace somewhat less strength in July than in January, it seemed likely that he would draw enough Democratic votes to make it impossible for Truman to carry New York, Pennsylvania, Michigan, Illinois, California and perhaps some other states  No new strategy could be devised to overcome these problems. Truman could only rely on the hope that his appeal to the country would prove so popular that he could somehow compensate for the losses caused by the Dixiecrats and the Wallaceites. No member of the Truman inner circle felt, during the summer, that the hope was anything more than a ritualistic piety. But Truman always expressed confidence in victory.[20]

As suggested in Chapter 2, the Truman campaign often created the illusion that it was an improvised show, with the President waging a one-man crusade against hopeless odds. Behind his artless platform performance, however, lay preparation as careful as anything on Dewey's side. Truman's success with extemporaneous speeches during his June trip led his advisers to recommend extensive use of this technique; Truman readily agreed. But little was to be left to chance. During the summer a procedure was worked out[21] whereby Bill Batt's Research Division compiled the necessary data for each back-platform appearance—appropriate local references, the issues of greatest local appeal—and prepared a speech outline to send to the train. On the train, George Elsey worked full time whipping the final outlines into shape; before the campaign was over, he prepared over three hundred of them. It was by far the largest literary contribution to the campaign.

Outline-writer Elsey had no prior experience in Presidential politics; he began the campaign as an amateur and emerged as something of a professional. As with his boss, Clark Clifford, his involvement owed much to accident. Elsey, a 1939 Princeton graduate, was a naval ensign back in 1942 when the fortunes of military assignment sent him to the White House map room. There he remained until the end of the war. In 1946, he began to work for Clifford, who was then naval aide, the association continuing after both men reverted to civilian status. As Clifford's assistant, Elsey functioned ably both as a speech writer and as a junior strategist, pursuits for which his professional training had not precisely prepared him; at Harvard, prior to his naval career, he had been doing graduate work in history. His brief period of scholarship, however, left him with an appreciation for the raw data of history and he frequently wrote memoranda to himself about the events in which he had a hand. At thirty, he was a shrewd, insightful observer, and much too young to be jaded.[22]

Throughout the campaign, Truman rarely spoke off the cuff

without an outline before him. Typically, it consisted of a series of topic sentences, each of which could launch him into an improvised passage; alternatively, he could read the sentences off consecutively if he was bereft of inspiration. Sometimes he did not follow the outline at all, but he always wanted one on the lectern. For the guidance of the outline-writers a staff memorandum was prepared entitled "Suggestions for Preparing Outlines for Brief Platform Speeches." The introduction to the speech was to contain some local reference, to establish a friendly rapport with the crowd, after which came the "Basic Proposition"; there were three such, at least one of which was to be stated in every talk: 1) "the only question in this campaign is a choice between the Democrats and the Republicans—a vote for Wallace or Thurmond is a vote for the Republicans"; 2) there was a decisive difference between what the Democrats and the Republicans stood for ("the Republicans serve the rich. . . . The Democrats serve all the people"); 3) the contrasts between the parties "make a direct and vital difference to the people. . . . It's a question of whether you'll have enough to eat and to wear. It vitally affects your chance for living in a world at peace." Following the presentation of the Basic Proposition came an issue to illustrate it—such as high prices, housing, reciprocal trade, with appropriate facts and figures to emphasize the contrast between the Democratic and Republican positions. Suggestions for the conclusion included a plea to register and vote in November and an expression of confidence in the future if the Democrats won.[23]

This simplistic approach represented no poverty of imagination on the part of Truman's advisers; it was all carefully calculated, both as to substance and style. Truman's entire campaign was designed to appeal to the material self-interest of his audiences. As Clifford has described it, there were four main targets: labor, the farmers, the Negroes and the consumer. Labor was to be promised liberation from the constraints imposed by the Eightieth Congress. The farmer was to be frightened with the loss of his prosperity if the Republicans won. The President's civil rights program was to be exploited to solidify the loyalty of Negro voters. High prices and the housing shortage were the issues designed to appeal to consumers.[24]

As for Truman's rhetoric, the pedestrian quality of his set speeches did not reflect the literary limitations of his ghost-writers so much as the limited range of the President's oratorical gifts. He was hardly the man for brilliant aphorisms, ironical understatement, elegantly serpentine sentences. "We tried to put it down on paper just as he would say it," recalls Charles Murphy.[25] "Truman couldn't possibly have delivered an Adlai Stevenson-type speech," Clifford points out. "It wouldn't have been in character. What we tried to get into his speeches was his courage, his convictions, his deep sincerity." [26]

Truman was not as painstaking as Dewey, but he devoted a good deal of time to the preparation of his major speeches. In Washington, he would usually have a conference with Clifford and perhaps some other advisers about the substance of the speech. When the draft was ready, Truman would go over it with several staff members in a session in the cabinet room that sometimes lasted for hours. Clifford, Murphy, appointments secretary Connelly, press secretary Charles Ross were the regulars at these sessions and other staff members attended on occasion.[27] The President was not a nit-picker, but he always strove for clarity and simplicity. He abhorred difficult or unusual words. "Can't we get something else for that two-dollar word?" he would frequently demand. After the speech was written, he often rehearsed it before two or three staff members.[28]

Through August and the first part of September, Clifford headed the speech-writing operation. When Truman went on the road, Clifford accompanied him and Charles Murphy took over the responsibility for the prepared speeches. Murphy, a relaxed, soft-spoken North Carolinian, had come to the White House in 1947 as an administrative assistant after a dozen years in the legislative counsel's office of the Senate. Prior to the campaign, his literary efforts on Truman's behalf had mostly involved the drafting of bills and legislative messages. He was one of the few people in the White House, apart from the President, who had been in Washington during the early New Deal and he never lost his youthful allegiance; he found Truman's populist simplicities eminently congenial. In 1950, when Clifford resigned as special counsel, Murphy succeeded him.

Murphy worked with a small staff of speech writers. Among them were David E. Bell, a young recruit from the Bureau of the Budget who in later years attained a prominent position in the Kennedy administration; David D. Lloyd, then a member of the Research Division; David M. Noyes, a former advertising man and top-level public relations strategist who had known Truman since his Senate days; Albert Z. Carr, a writer and former government official who had briefly served in the White House under Truman as a holdover from the Roosevelt administration; John Franklin Carter, a newspaperman better known by his pen name of Jay Franklin, who turned out prodigious amounts of copy in the later stages of the campaign.[29] Noyes and Carr, who were old friends, had been personally recruited by the President in midsummer and had a special relationship with him which on occasion allowed them to jump channels. They regarded themselves as being more militantly liberal than the regular White House staff and were responsible for some of the most vituperative language in Truman's speeches.[30]

In preparing for the campaign, finances were the most difficult problem for Truman's managers. Senator McGrath, the party chairman, received several rejections before he found someone who would accept the job as chairman of the finance committee. Not until September 14, three days before Truman's first major campaign tour, was McGrath able to announce that Colonel Louis A. Johnson, a former Assistant Secretary of War, would be finance chairman. Johnson had a good many business connections and was an energetic fund-raiser. He was rewarded for his efforts, some months after Truman's victory, by being named Secretary of Defense. It was one of the most undistinguished appointments which Truman ever made.

Throughout the campaign, the Democratic National Committee had to operate on a hand-to-mouth basis. On August 24, for example, publicity director Jack Redding sent an interoffice memorandum to McGrath listing $50,000 in "necessary monies needed immediately in addition to normal running expenses." Among the items were $10,000 for Truman's Labor Day broadcast on September 6, $10,000 for Truman-Barkley campaign posters, $17,000 for two Barkley broadcasts.[31] On September 30, Redding wrote a memorandum outlining "a plan for essential radio broadcasting" that allocated $360,000 for speeches made by Truman. To save money, it had been decided not to schedule any party broadcasts for the President between October 13 and 25, because Truman was due to speak during that period under the auspices of three outside groups—among them the American Legion—which would pick up the tab.[32]

Due to the straitened circumstances of the Democrats, the national networks often protected themselves by demanding advance payments for broadcasts. On a few occasions, the money was not available on time to pass through the committee's bank account and McGrath would carry $25,000 or $30,000 in cash to the broadcasting studios.[33] Truman sometimes ran over his allotted radio time and the National Committee lacked the money to keep him on the air. Thus, on October 7, Redding was compelled to telegraph Charles Ross on the President's campaign train: "FOR YOUR INFORMATION AND GUIDANCE THE PRESIDENT'S TALK LAST NIGHT RAN APPROXIMATELY TWENTY-SEVEN MINUTES AND THERE-FORE WE HAVE [*sic*] TO CUT HIM OFF THE AIR TO AVOID RUNNING OVER STOP CUT WAS MADE AT REASONABLY APPROPRIATE SPOT AND ON APPLAUSE STOP FINANCIAL PROBLEMS MAKE IT IMPERATIVE THAT PREARRANGED TIMING BE ADHERED TO CLOSELY FOR ALL NATIONAL BROADCASTS." [34]

Truman was not above taking a hand in fund-raising himself. At a White House gathering of affluent supporters in September, the President stood up on a chair to appeal for money to move his campaign train out of Washington's Union Station. Ten thousand dollars were needed immediately, and $15,000 soon afterward, to get the show on the road. The President's unexpected appeal stimu-lated two contributors to pledge $10,000 each immediately.[35]

Truman opened his campaign on Labor Day, with an energetic one-day tour of Michigan. His special train left Washing-ton on Sunday afternoon; the following morning he was in Grand Rapids, where he began the day's speechmaking at an 8:15 A.M. rally. There followed a back-platform appearance in Lansing at 11:05 A.M., the major speech of the day in Detroit's Cadillac

Square at 1:40 P.M., a brief stop in Hamtramck at 2:45 P.M., a speech in Pontiac at 4:00 P.M., another in Flint at 7:15 P.M. and a final rear-platform appearance in Toledo, Ohio, on his way back to Washington, at 11:55 P.M. "It is a great day for me. It is a great day for you. I am just starting on a campaign tour that is going to be a record for the President of the United States," Truman announced exuberantly at Grand Rapids. He had reason to be buoyed up at the size of the crowds. Some 125,000 persons heard him in Detroit. When he traveled by car from Detroit to Pontiac, the police estimated that 500,000 people greeted him along the thirty-five-mile route. There were 20,000 at the morning rally in Grand Rapids, 15,000 at Pontiac, 35,000 at Flint.[36]

The main rally in Detroit was a notable event, for it was jointly sponsored by the American Federation of Labor and the Congress of Industrial Organizations—a degree of unity between the rival federations which was more unusual in this era than in the 1950's. (The AFL and CIO did not merge until December 1955.) In his speech, Truman made an uninhibited appeal for labor support. "These are critical times for labor and for all who work," he declared. "There is great danger ahead." He reviewed the dismaying way labor had fared under Republican administrations prior to 1933 and the sizable gains brought by the New Deal. The Republican victory in 1946 began a period of retrogression, symbolized by the Taft-Hartley Act, which was "only a foretaste of what you will get if the Republican reaction is allowed to grow." He cautioned that the Republicans, if they won the election, would resume the old cycle of "boom and bust." Indeed, signs of it were already visible. "The 'boom' is on for them, and the 'bust' has begun for you." He went further. Not only were the workers' wages and living standards threatened, "but even our Democratic institutions of free labor and free enterprise" were imperiled.

He warned that "the reactionary of today is a shrewd man. He is in many ways much shrewder than the reactionaries of the twenties. He is a man with a calculating machine where his heart ought to be. He has learned a great deal about how to get his way by observing demagogues and reactionaries in other countries." Only a great outpouring of votes could forestall the calamities awaiting the country. "Labor has always had to fight for its gains. Now you are fighting for the whole future of the labor movement. . . . I know that we are going to win this crusade for the right!" At the end, the ex-haberdasher from Missouri sounded as if he were going to burst into "Solidarity Forever."

More than votes were involved in Truman's plea for labor support. The Democrats desperately needed the unions if they were to wage an effective campaign. In many parts of the country, the old-line Democratic organizations were in an enfeebled state. The big city machines of New York, Philadelphia, Jersey City, Chicago, Kansas City were no longer the efficient vote-gathering mechanisms that they had been in an earlier era. The unions had the resources to conduct voter-registration drives, set up precinct organizations, undertake door-to-door canvassing. In Michigan, the United Automobile Workers and the CIO all but took over the Democratic party organization. In New York, the Liberal party, largely financed by the International Ladies' Garment Workers' Union, was to be far more significant in Truman's campaign than the impoverished and dispirited Democratic party.

Before the Philadelphia convention, most of the leading trade unionists were eager to discard Truman. AFL president William Green, CIO president Philip Murray, even teamsters' union president Daniel Tobin, who used to head the AFL drive for Roosevelt, all stayed away from the Democratic convention. By early September, the bulk of the labor movement had pledged its support for Truman. On September 1, Philip Murray led a CIO delegation to the White House to notify the President formally of their endorsement. Truman was promised the backing of the four hundred state and local groups of the CIO's Political Action Committee, which had been of great help to F.D.R. in the 1944 campaign. Murray's visit was followed by that of George M. Harrison, president of the Brotherhood of Railway Clerks, who informed Truman that leaders of AFL unions representing 7,000,000 workers (the federation had 8,000,000 in all) would be active in his behalf.[37] The AFL itself, as was its custom (the 1924 election excepted) did not endorse any Presidential candidate. By contrast, the only national union to support Dewey was the 175,000-member AFL Building Service Employees.

As previously suggested, labor of course entertained no illusions about Truman's chances of victory. Nor did Truman personally arouse much more enthusiasm than he had before the Philadelphia convention. It was nonetheless unthinkable not to endorse the President, given his record during the past year and the character of the party platform. What was of great concern to the labor movement was increasing the liberal membership of the House and Senate and possibly winning Democratic control; in Michigan, Illinois, Connecticut, and elsewhere there also seemed to be a chance of gubernatorial victories. Inevitably, Truman would benefit from an all-out labor drive for the local ticket.

# CHAPTER 9
# The Long Campaign Trail

       Truman's first major tour of the campaign got under-
way on the morning of Friday, September 17. The President,
trimly turned out in his tan double-breasted suit, was animated and
self-confident as he said goodbye to Secretary of State George Marshall and Senator Alben Barkley. "Mow 'em down, Harry!" Barkley boomed. Truman grinned. "I'm going to fight hard," he vowed.
"I'm going to give 'em hell!" [1]

The exchange set the tone of the tour. In many ways, it was to be
a reprise of the June "nonpolitical" trip. The President was to
cover eighteen states, cutting through the heart of the Midwest,
crossing the mountain states to San Francisco, swinging south to
Los Angeles, then returning east via the southern route, through
Arizona, New Mexico, Texas, up to Oklahoma, and across Missouri, Indiana, Kentucky and West Virginia to Washington, D.C.
As in June, Truman would make a maximum number of back-
platform appearances, responding to what he assumed was an in-
satiable curiosity to see the President. Unlike the June trip, however, less was to be left to chance. Two advance men went on the
road—Oscar Chapman, the Under Secretary of the Interior, and
Donald Dawson, a Presidential administrative assistant who normally handled personnel matters. They traveled several days in advance of the train and took care to check out all details of local
arrangements—to avoid such disasters of the June trip as the partially empty hall in Omaha and the unexpected airport dedication
in Carey, Idaho. This time, as well, local politicians would be welcomed aboard the President's train. The political chores on the
train were generally handled by Matt Connelly and by William M.
Boyle, Jr., an old friend of Truman who was later to be chairman
of the Democratic National Committee.

181

Indeed, the politicians were so welcome that when Truman's train reached Chicago, at 2:15 A.M. on September 18, the President was awakened to greet Jack Arvey, the Cook County leader, who came aboard with a delegation of party officials. Truman received the group in pajamas and bathrobe, sitting on the edge of his bed. The visit symbolized reconciliation, inasmuch as Arvey had been one of the leaders of the preconvention dump-Truman movement. When he left the President, Arvey told reporters that they had just exchanged greetings and he had wished Truman well. "He looked sleepy and I felt like a heel getting him up," Arvey added.[2]

At midday on September 18, Truman arrived in Dexter, Iowa, for his first major speech of the tour at the National Plowing Contest. To an audience of over 80,000 gathered on Mrs. T. R. Agg's model farm, Truman delivered what was in effect his campaign manifesto to the farm country. Few observers realized it at the time, but the themes he underscored were to reverberate through the Midwest down to election day.

It was an aggressive, not to say strident speech, designed to evoke memory and fear. Truman reminded his audience of the economic horrors suffered under the Republicans: "You remember the big boom and the great crash of 1929. You remember that in 1932 the position of the farmer had become so desperate that there was actual violence in many farming communities. You remember that insurance companies and banks took over much of the land of small independent farmers—223,000 farmers lost their farms." Then came the New Deal, which lowered interest rates, reduced farm mortgage indebtedness by more than 50 percent, almost ended farm foreclosures. Today the American farmer was doing exceedingly well. He could continue to enjoy high prices and prosperity unless "the Wall Street reactionaries . . . these gluttons of privilege" won control of the government and proceeded to wreck the New Deal's entire agricultural policy.

"This Republican Congress," the President charged, "has already stuck a pitchfork in the farmer's back. They have already done their best to keep the price supports from working. Many growers have sold wheat this summer at less than the support prices because they could not find proper storage." He blamed the shortage

of storage bins on the actions of a Congress responsive to the interests of the grain speculators. This was only the first step, Truman
warned. "The Republican reactionaries . . . are attacking the
whole structure of price supports for farm products. . . . Republican spokesmen are now complaining that my administration is
trying to keep farm prices up. . . . They are obviously ready to let
the bottom drop out of farm prices." They had hurt the farmer in
other ways as well—by cutting funds for soil conservation, by kill-
ing the International Wheat Agreement (with its guaranteed export
market for five years), by trying to put a "death tax" on farm cooperatives.

In rhetorical violence, the speech surpassed any of Truman's utterances since his June trip. Some of the choicest invective was
contributed by David M. Noyes and Albert Z. Carr. Years later,
Clark Clifford said that he still cringed at the memory of that "pitchfork in the back," although he approved the phrase at the time.[3]
Repeatedly the President inveighed against Republican "gluttons of
privilege," a phrase that was less imaginative but served the
same purpose as the "economic royalists" whom Roosevelt
scorned throughout the 1936 campaign. There were other sledge-
hammer lines: "I wonder how many times you have to be hit on
the head before you find out who's hitting you? . . . These Republican gluttons of privilege are cold men. They are cunning men.
. . . What they have taken away from you thus far would be
only an appetizer for the economic tapeworm of big business."
This gruesome future could be readily avoided. "I'm not asking
you just to vote for me," said Truman. "Vote for yourselves! Vote
for your farms! Vote for the standard of living that you have won
under a Democratic administration!"

The vast crowd listened quietly and applauded politely at the
end. To many of the newspapermen present, there was a certain
incongruity between the impassioned language of the orator and
the jolly county fair atmosphere of the gathering. To Joseph Alsop,
"the obviously decent, moderate and flatly unemotional President
is almost comically miscast in the role of William Jennings Bryan."
His audience was "so prosperous, well-fed and optimistic that if he
dressed up as a blood-boltered [*sic*] ghost, and did the authentic

dance of death upon the platform, he would still fail to raise a single goose pimple." One mark of farm prosperity especially caught Alsop's eye: fifty private planes parked in a nearby field.[4]

Under the scorching sun of that September day it may well have been too hot for goose pimples to rise. But quite apart from his rhetoric, Truman's message was close enough to the truth to provoke anxiety. City folk might have difficulty following his speech, but farmers understood. The shortage of grain storage bins could cause painful losses. Under the price support system, the government guaranteed certain prices for various farm products. When the market price was above the support price, the farmer sold his crop through normal commercial channels. When the market price dropped below the support price, the farmer could get a crop loan from the government at the support-price level, pledging his grain as collateral. If the market price rose, he sold his crop and repaid his loan; otherwise, when the loan became due, he forfeited the collateral and kept the money. But to get a crop loan, the farmer had to store his grain in an approved facility. In a year of abundant crops, commercial storage facilities were soon filled, but in the past the Commodity Credit Corporation would have been in a position to provide additional storage bins.

In June of 1948, when the Commodity Credit Corporation's charter came up for renewal, Congress legislated a significant change which went almost unnoticed at the time: the CCC was prohibited from acquiring any new storage bins. If only a moderate harvest had occurred, the limitation would not have been significant. But 1948 was turning out to be a bumper year for wheat, oats, and corn, and farmers would clearly be hard hit if they had to sell at depressed prices. Few of them were expected to be in a position to provide their own storage facilities.

Truman was playing on another fear as well. On September 2, Harold Stassen, on a visit to Albany, had issued a statement blaming the Truman administration for trying to maintain high food prices despite bumper crops. Stassen's attack was directed at the timing of government food purchases for foreign-aid distribution and for the military forces; his point was that when prices were declining, the government tended to place huge bulk orders which drove prices back up. A more sensible policy, he suggested, would be to space out government purchases over a period of time.[5] Stassen said nothing about the price-support system, which had bipartisan backing, but both Truman and Secretary of Agriculture Charles Brannan responded with warnings that the Republicans were trying to undermine the farmers' price guarantees.

Brannan charged that "Mr. Dewey, through Harold Stassen . . . intends to destroy the farmers' price supports by falsely attributing to that legislation the exorbitantly high prices of certain foods. It is difficult to believe that they expect even the bulk of their Republican membership, particularly members in farm areas, to follow them down this dangerous road." Reporters reminded Brannan that Stassen had not mentioned price supports, but Brannan persisted in his attack.[6]  On September 17, Dewey issued a strong statement endorsing the price-support system "both for the present and the future." He insisted that the Democratic charge "was created out of thin air. It was an intentional fabrication designed to deceive the producers of America's food." Nonetheless, Truman repeated the charge in his Dexter speech. It was too useful a weapon to discard simply because it was untrue. Stassen's unfortunate statement was to plague the Republicans throughout the campaign.

The rest of Truman's case was far stronger, especially the grain storage bin issue. Its political significance, oddly enough, had only recently been noticed by Truman's strategists. The restrictions imposed on the Commodity Credit Corporation had passed the Congress in June with no Democratic outcry. Truman did not mention the matter on June 29 when he signed the act extending the CCC. On July 3, however, when he signed the Agricultural Act, he retrospectively criticized the storage features of the CCC bill but did not spell out its implications. In advance of the big harvests, Truman's agricultural experts were apparently unaware of the political time bomb that was quietly ticking away.

It was finally revealed late in August by W. McNeil Lowry, chief Washington correspondent of the Dayton *Daily News* and the other Cox papers, which were among the few newspapers supporting Truman. (Publisher James M. Cox, former governor of Ohio, had been Democratic candidate for President in 1920.) On August 6, Jesse Garrison, the farm editor of the Dayton paper, wrote Lowry about the new restrictions on storage bins in the CCC charter. Garrison had learned that Ohio farmers, who already had large wheat and oats crops, were worrying about where they were going to store their anticipated corn crop. The question for Lowry was how this had all come about.

In a little more than a week, Lowry pieced together an intricate story of how the grain lobby had managed to insert the storage-bin restriction into the CCC charter.[7] On Friday, August 27, the Dayton *Daily News* ran an eight-column banner across its front page: "Grain Dealers Act To Force Down Farmers' Price." Lowry wrote: "The whole course of the 1948 political campaign in the great corn and wheat states may ultimately be affected. From Ohio through South Dakota, farmers are asking where they are going to store the record 1948 grain crop and what price it is going to bring." Lowry sent clippings of his story to Brannan and Howard McGrath. He had a conference with Clark Clifford on the matter and gave him two copies.[8] A few days later, Brannan began to attack the Republicans on the issue. Truman's Dexter speech followed. Lowry's enterprise had uncovered one of the key issues of the campaign (although the Democrats would doubtless have ultimately awakened to it).[9] Lowry continued to write stories about grain storage bins throughout the campaign, but the rest of the daily press failed to grasp the importance of this arcane bit of farm economics. Immediately after the election, however, it received a good deal of attention in the journalistic postmortems.

After the Dexter speech, as Truman's train moved through the mountain states, he addressed himself to the issues of special concern to the West. Conservation of natural resources, reclamation projects, public power dominated his prepared speeches in Denver on September 20 and in Salt Lake City the following day. To an audience of 25,000 gathered before the state capitol in Denver, he attacked the Republicans for beginning "to tear down the whole western development program." They had slashed funds right and left, cutting back programs to bring water to the land and electric power to industry. As always, he had a horrible example to display before the crowd: "Right here in this state, the Colorado-

Big Thompson project is under way. It is an inspiring project, involving the transfer of water from one side of the Continental Divide to the other. The Republican Congress sharply reduced the funds for that project. When I pointed out the danger of that action and requested them to restore those funds, they refused to do it."

Similarly, in Salt Lake City he attacked the Eightieth Congress for protecting the interests of the private power companies by slowing down the construction of transmission lines from government hydroelectric projects. "Ask yourselves a question," Truman suggested. "Who benefits from the building of dams if the government does not also build transmission lines to carry the power from the dams to the people? Who benefits? The private power interests benefit, of course—at your expense!"

No major speech of Truman was limited to the main subject, but included a garniture of other issues, among them the high cost of living, the shortage of housing, the need for federal aid to education, for national health insurance, for expanded social security. Truman invariably lingered over three contrasting images—decay and distress under the Republicans prior to 1933; the high promise and fulfillment of the New Deal; the betrayal of the people's interests by the "do-nothing" Eightieth Congress. And he always provided an explanation for this dismaying state of affairs—the Republicans were the party of Wall Street, of reaction, of the "special interests." The repetitive quality of Truman's speeches made for dull reading in the press car, but the average voter had no need to ponder the texts.

Truman was at his best, everyone agreed, in his whistle-stop appearances. He subjected himself to an exhausting schedule, occasionally speaking a dozen times or more each day. On September 18, his first full day on the road, he began at 5:45 A.M. in Rock Island, Illinois ("I don't think I have ever seen so many farmers in town in all my life") and was not through until after an 8:10 P.M. appearance in Polo, Missouri. ("I didn't think I was going to be able to do it but the railroad finally consented to stop.")

Truman's impromptu talks held to no set sequence, but they usually contained the same ingredients: a plug for the Democratic candidate for Congress or the Senate, a passing reference to the local college or baseball team (sometimes only the local weather was worthy of note), a brief exposition of some problem of local or national concern (housing, farm price supports, public power) which the Republicans had managed to muck up, and a plea for his audience to register and vote. The final turn in his routine was to introduce his wife and daughter. "And now I would like you to meet Mrs. Truman," he would say, at which point the blue velvet curtain behind him would part and the First Lady would appear to smile at the crowd. "And now my daughter Margaret" or, in southern states, "Miss Margaret." Margaret was an object of great curiosity because of her well-publicized singing career.

As on his June trip, Truman combined invective with folksy informality. No language was too extravagant to characterize the misdeeds of the Republicans. He informed the throng in Roseville, California,[10] that the Republican Congress "tried to choke you to death in this valley" by cutting off appropriations for publicly owned electric power lines. In Fresno,[11] he announced that "You have got a terrible Congressman here in this district. . . . He is one of the worst obstructionists in the Congress. He has done everything he possibly could to cut the throats of the farmer and the laboring man. If you send him back, that will be your fault if you get your throats cut."

Truman always voiced an uncomplicated view of the economic philosophy of the opposition. In Merced, California,[12] he remarked that the "Republican policy is to let the big fellows get the big incomes, and let a little of it trickle down off the table like the crumbs fell to Lazarus." In Colton, California,[13] he put the matter more pungently: "Republicans are just simply tools of big business. They believe that there is a top strata [sic] in the country that ought to run the government and that ought to profit from the government. . . . They'll tear you apart."

He could be equally blunt when it came to lecturing the voters on their responsibilities. In Colorado Springs, on September 20, he reminded his audience that "In 1946, you know, two thirds of you stayed at home and didn't vote. You wanted a change. Well, you got it. You got the change. You got just exactly what you deserved. If you stay at home on November the second and let this same gang get control of the government, I won't have any sympathy with you."

Truman's informality was often startling; no other President within memory could so readily shed the dignity of office before a crowd. He frequently ended his exhortation on a personal note. In Provo, Utah,[14] he urged the crowd to exercise "that God-given right . . . to go to the polls on the second of November and cast your ballot for the Democratic ticket—and then I can stay in the White House for another four years." In Ogden, Utah,[15] he suggested that if the voters did the right thing "that will keep me from suffering from a housing shortage on January 20, 1949." In Colorado Springs,[16] he made a neat equation of public and private interest: "If you go out to the polls . . . and do your duty as you should I won't have to worry about moving out of the White House; and you won't have to worry about what happens to the welfare of the West. Those two things go together."

The frequent reference to his housing situation dismayed Truman's staff. "I cannot help feeling that it is a pitifully weak statement," Bill Batt wrote Clifford on September 24. "People are always more interested in what you can do for them than in what they can do for you. Remarks like this do not help create a picture of strength and confidence . . ." Elsey agreed. "We wince every time this is said," he wrote Batt, "and every time that point approaches in a platform speech, we pray and cross ourselves and hope it won't come out." [17]

Truman was full of surprises. Sometimes an odd braggadocio emerged. At Truckee, California, on September 22, he announced, "I am glad that so many people at this place deemed it advisable to come out and take a look at the next President of the United States." In Denver,[18] at a luncheon of the Colorado Truman-Barkley Club, he startled his audience by reminding them of the dump-Truman movement of the previous spring. Occasionally, he indulged in reminiscences about his family. In Salt Lake City,[19] he recalled how his grandfather Young, a freight forwarder, had driven an ox-train load of merchandise to Salt Lake City and had difficulty disposing of it. He went to see Brigham Young, who advised him "to rent space down on the main street here in Salt Lake City, place his goods on display, and he would guarantee that my grandfather would lose no money, and he didn't."

Toward the end of his trip, in Shelbyville, Kentucky,[20] Truman delighted the crowd with a story of how his grandfather Truman had eloped with a local farm girl. Fearing her father's wrath, they moved to Missouri after the marriage; not until three or four years later, when the in-laws wanted to see their first grandchild, was a reconciliation effected. When he finished with family history, Truman turned to political matters. He then introduced Mrs. Truman and Miss Margaret. "You all know my daughter Margaret," the President said jovially. "She was down here several years ago, looking up the records to see if my grandparents were legally married." The train then pulled away. Soon afterward, press secretary Ross hastened back to the press car with assurances that the President had been speaking facetiously.[21]

It all made for an entertaining show, but most reporters present had no reason to believe that Truman was gaining votes. Crowds were large, curious, good-natured, but not especially enthusiastic. As Earl Richert wrote in the Scripps-Howard papers, "The President . . . has called the Republican congressional leaders just about everything but horse thieves. But his epithets do not stir his audiences. They're the kind of words that need to be roared or snarled to bring crowd responses. But the President just says them in his dry, matter-of-fact way." On the other hand, Richert reported that the phrase, the "do-nothing Congress," had become widely known as Truman's campaign theme. "The people come to the railroad stations expecting to hear him say these words. And, whether they agree or not, they chuckle or applaud when he says them." [22]

Summarizing his impressions of Truman's tour up to Los Angeles, Richard H. Rovere wrote in *The New Yorker:* "Nobody stomps, shouts or whistles for Truman. Everybody claps. I should say that the decibel count would be about the same as it would be for a missionary who had just delivered a mildly encouraging report on the inroads being made against heathenism in Northern Rhodesia. This does not necessarily mean that the people who come out to hear him intend to vote against him—though my personal feeling is that most of them intend to do exactly that." [23]

Midway in the Truman trip there was also a good deal of press criticism of the mechanical arrangements aboard the train, which worked a disservice both on the candidate and on the fifty-member press party. Truman's prepared texts were often available only an hour or so before delivery; this meant that for the principal evening speech delivered on the West Coast, text would be available too late to be printed verbatim in the first editions of the morning papers in the East, where it was three hours later. Reporters were dismayed at the lack of a loudspeaker in the press car, which compelled them to dash back to the end of the train to catch the President's words at a brief whistle-stop. They were also not allowed in the last three cars of the train, where the Presidential staff worked and local politicians were received; a useful news source was thus cut off. The same lack of forethought also extended to such housekeeping details as laundry arrangements and baggage pickups; when the Truman train stopped overnight in a city, it was every man for himself.[24]

Dewey set off from Albany on his first tour of the campaign late on Sunday afternoon, September 19, two days after Truman began his travels. Only six weeks remained before the election, which led the *New York Times* to comment that Dewey's campaign would be "the shortest undertaken in recent years by the Presidential candidate of the major party out of power." [25] The brevity of Dewey's campaign reflected a transference of roles already widely noted: the incumbent President, rather than the opposition candidate, had become the challenger. As the expected victor, Dewey was the object of far more press attention than Truman. By the time his "Victory Special" reached California, there were 98 journalists aboard, nearly twice the number who traveled with Truman. Some 35 newspapermen, who had applied too late, could not be accommodated. Dewey's train, like Truman's, contained 17 cars—the maximum length allowed in most states—but his personal staff numbered 43, compared with Truman's 20-odd. Dewey had two physicians aboard, five speech writers, one researcher, a large secretarial staff and various expediters and odd-chore men. Paul Lockwood was in charge of the train arrangements and at each whistle-stop would signal railroad officials when to pull out of the station. James C. Hagerty handled the press and was a model of crisp efficiency. Ed Jaeckle shepherded local politicians in and out of the Governor's presence.

Newspapermen were impressed by the smooth professionalism of the Dewey operation. Prepared texts for speeches were usually available twenty-four hours before delivery, giving reporters plenty of time to mull over their stories. The press car and the two dining cars were equipped with loudspeakers, enabling newspapermen to hear Dewey's back-platform comments without stirring from their air-conditioned quarters. (Many reporters, of course, scrambled to the rear of the train to observe crowd reactions.) No housekeeping detail was overlooked, down to laundry which was dispatched and retrieved within a few hours.[26]

When the train left Albany, the press was given a fourteen-page schedule outlining the program in minute detail for the next several days. At Albuquerque on September 22, for example, the train was due to arrive at 7:50 P.M. A reception committee would then come aboard. At 8:10 P.M., Governor and Mrs. Dewey would leave the train and enter an automobile. Ten minutes later they were due in the University of New Mexico gymnasium. They would appear on the platform at 8:30. Albert K. Mitchell, the state's national committeeman, would introduce the candidate, who would speak until 9:00. Fifteen minutes later, they would leave the university, returning to the railroad station at 9:30.[27] The train kept to such timetables with remarkable fidelity. During the first six days on the road it was not more than twenty minutes late anywhere.[28]

The "Victory Special" was to cover much the same territory as the Truman train, except for a loop through Oregon, Washington, Montana and Idaho, which substituted for Truman's swing through the Southwest, Texas and Oklahoma. At some points, in the Midwest and California, the two candidates would only be a day or two apart. Geographic proximity, however, did not encourage Dewey to start a debate. In keeping with his carefully calculated strategy, he rarely even acknowledged Truman's existence; when he did so, he avoided use of his name.

Dewey's opening speech, in Des Moines, Iowa, was on Monday, September 20, two days after Truman's "pitchfork in the back" speech in Dexter. Dewey addressed an overflow crowd of 9,500 in the Drake University field house; the meeting, originally scheduled in the stadium, which seated 30,000, had to be moved indoors because of rain.[29] Although he was appearing in a farm state, Dewey made only passing references to agricultural problems. Instead, in a speech entitled "The Challenge of Tomorrow," he enunciated the main themes of his campaign.

"Tonight we enter upon a campaign to unite America," Dewey announced. "On January 20, we will enter upon a new era. We propose to install in Washington an administration which has faith in the American people, a warm understanding of their needs and the competence to meet them. We will rediscover the essential unity of our people and the spiritual strength which makes our country great. We will begin to move forward again shoulder to shoulder toward an even greater America and a better life for every American, in a nation working effectively for the peace of the world."

The speech was full of such ringing declarations of high-minded intent. Dewey pledged that as President his every act "will be determined by one principle above all others: is this good for our country?" His administration would be made up of men and women whose love of country would take precedence over all other considerations. They would be "really qualified" and would operate as a team "without loose talk, factional quarreling or appeals to group prejudice." They would also know how to get on with the Congress; Washington would enjoy the same glow of unity that would suffuse the rest of the country. Dewey added, in what was to become a favorite phrase of his, that on January 20 there would begin in Washington "the biggest unraveling, unsnarling, untangling operation in our nation's history."

The Governor acknowledged that serious problems confronted the nation—strife and tyranny abroad; inflation, a shortage of decent housing, racial and religious discrimination at home. He offered no specific proposals to deal with these problems but promised them later in the campaign. His proposals, however, would not be the product of "wishful thinking." "I have no trick answers and no easy solutions," he declared. "I will not offer one solution to one group and another solution to another group."

At times the speech took on that tone of sober reconciliation

more appropriate to a victory statement than a campaign manifesto. "I will not contend," said Dewey, "that all our difficulties
today have been brought about by the present national administration. Some of these unhappy conditions are the result of circumstances beyond the control of any government. Any fair-minded
person would agree that others are merely the result of the administration's lack of judgment, or of faith in our people. Only part are
deliberately caused for political purposes."

Only once in the course of his speech did Dewey himself indulge
in a sharp political thrust. That occurred when he made a passing
reference to the American people being told "that the exposure of
communism in our government is a 'red herring.' " He was alluding
to Truman's characterization of the congressional investigations of
communism in government which had begun in Washington several
weeks before. Truman regarded the investigations as a calculated
diversion from the real problems facing the country; his epithet
inadvertently provided the Republicans with a taunt which they were
to throw back at the Democrats for years. Dewey, however, did
not dwell on the issue. He clearly preferred the spongy rhetoric of
spiritual affirmation: "We have sometimes failed in our faith and
often fallen short of it. But in our hearts we believe and know that
every man has some of the Divine in him, that every single individual is of priceless importance. . . ."

The audience was generous in its applause, but did not stream
out of the hall with the glint of combat in its eye. Unity had perhaps been purchased at the price of boredom. In one sense at least
Dewey had proven the viability of his strategy: it was possible to
deliver a lengthy campaign speech without arousing controversy or
making enemies. With his generous treatment of the Democrats, he
might even have calculated that he had made some new friends.

As he moved west, Dewey's prepared speeches got down to some
specifics: in Denver on the 21st, he talked largely about conservation of natural resources and reclamation projects, as Truman had
the day before; in Albuquerque on the 22nd, he discussed both
his anti-inflation program and his aspiration for a federation of
Western Europe; in Phoenix on the 23rd, he addressed himself to
"America's Future in the Atomic Age."

Throughout, Dewey continued the same tone of quiet reasonableness which he had displayed in Des Moines. Thus he by no means completely blamed the Democrats for the inflation which had victimized the country since the end of the war. "The immediate causes of the present high prices," he pointed out, "are rooted in the heavy government spending of the war. That, of course, was unavoidable, and we do not begrudge a cent of it." Inflation was further stimulated by the huge backlog of consumer demand, which had developed during the war, and by large postwar appropriations for foreign aid. The Democrats, however, had "greatly aggravated" a deplorable situation by their poor judgment and incompetence, as well as by a calculated desire to bring on inflation.[30] In a campaign speech, this could only be regarded as a balanced statement.

When Dewey came to enunciate his own program, his specifics often sounded like generalizations. He devoted several paragraphs in his Denver speech to the deplorable fact that the nation's oil reserves were running down. What to do about it? "I propose to you," said Dewey, "that we get an administration which will devote itself seriously to a wise and intelligent use of oil reserves in this country, in the closest cooperation with the states of the union." He was also disturbed by dwindling supplies of critical metals. His solution: "Government must help industry and industry must cooperate with government . . . we must encourage the development of superior technical skills as well as new investment. . . ."

At times, the Denver speech had the tone of a grade school primer: "By adequate soil conservation we can do much to preserve our own future. We must also use the water we have wisely and well. We need the water from our rivers for power as well as agriculture. . . . The mighty rivers of the West should be developed with a view to the widest possible use for conservation, power, navigation, flood control, reclamation, and irrigation." Who could possibly disagree? The only contentious statement he made on this subject was a claim that the Republican Eightieth Congress had appropriated more money for the Bureau of Reclamation than did the prior Democratic Congress. The Seventy-ninth Congress, he pointed out, had appropriated $247 million; the Eightieth Congress had increased the figure to $389 million—an increase of more than

50 percent. Dewey did not address himself to the fact, however, that Truman had asked for considerably more money than Congress had been willing to grant.

When he discussed the problem of inflation in his Albuquerque speech, Dewey's proposals were as platitudinous as they were vague. He advocated a reduction in government expenditures, the creation of a budgetary surplus to retire some of the national debt, as well as a reduction in taxation "to encourage savings and stimulate production." He assured his audience that "National income is now at such high levels that we can build up our military strength, reduce our debt, and still see to it that taxes are less of a burden on our people and less of a throttle to their enterprise." This was a prescription for a miracle; the arithmetic calculation on which it was based was not to be found in his speech.

Perhaps one unintended consequence of Dewey's determination to say as little as possible was a flaccid prose style distinguished by an extraordinary array of clichés. Having traveled for two days cross country, Dewey spoke appreciatively in Denver of the nation's "teeming cities," "soft, rolling wooded country," "fertile plains" of the Midwest, and "incredible beauty" of the Rocky Mountains, all of which left him impressed with the "sheer majesty" of the United States. In Denver and points west, he frequently celebrated the "creative genius" of a free people, deplored the "prophets of gloom," sought a "just and lasting" peace and inveighed against the "dead hand" of government. In Phoenix, he announced that "America's future—like yours in Arizona—is still ahead of us."

Dewey's speeches sounded somewhat better than they read the next morning. He was, after all, an accomplished speaker, with a thorough mastery of pace and modulation. With his silken baritone and artful phrasing, he was especially good at infusing lofty significance into a banality. When he came to his punch lines—such as the biggest "unraveling, unsnarling, untangling operation" in Washington—his timing was superb.

On the way to each evening's speech, Dewey's train would stop at intervals for him to make short back-platform talks. He made about half the number of whistle-stops that Truman did and expended far less energy in these efforts. His manner was more relaxed and informal than when he delivered a prepared speech, but there was always something a bit forced and awkward about Dewey when he was being folksy with the voters. He was visibly trying hard, however; some reporters suggested, as they had during the Oregon primary campaign, that a "new Dewey" had emerged. Among the items of evidence: when a woman in Rock Island, Illinois, squealed "Hi, Tom!" in the middle of his talk, he rewarded her with a smile, a wave of the hand and a genial "Hi!" [31] But in other matters, he stood on his dignity. During the Oregon primary, when he was desperate, he had been willing to frolic with the cavemen at Grant's Pass, but now he would not even try on an Indian headdress or a ten-gallon hat when it was offered to him.

The principal purpose of Dewey's whistle-stops was to boost the candidacy of the party's congressional or senatorial nominee in each area. Dewey always got the name straight, usually appended the proper nickname, and would add a genial flourish of commendation; he was adept at suggesting a lifelong regard for a man whose acquaintance he had made ten minutes before. Unlike Truman, he did not feel the need to favor every trainside audience with a new speech. He used no speech outlines and delivered the same basic speech—a plea for unity, a commitment to honest and competent government and a promise of that grand "unsnarling" operation after he got to Washington. Often, he would also interpolate a paragraph or two of new material from the speech which he was planning to deliver that night.[32] When his talk was over, he would introduce Mrs. Dewey, who would smile and wave at the crowd.

It was Dewey's custom, in the manner of a nightclub comedian, to polish and reuse the lines which drew applause and discard those that bombed. Apart from the "unsnarling" operation, the crowds responded loudly to his assurance that "In my cabinet we'll have people who are competent to do a job, and people who will do it without petty bickering and squabbling among themselves." They approved of his declaration that "We must get rid of sectionalism, of attempts to divide one group from another, to set group against group." The biggest crowd favorite, however, was his statement about Communists in government: "This administration asked Congress for $25,000,000 to spot and fire the Communists whom they themselves put in the government. I have a better way to handle the Communists—and a cheaper one. We won't put any Communists in the government in the first place." [33]

The statement was a superb bit of demagogy, for it was so artfully contrived that it implied far more than it asserted. It implied that the Democrats had consciously "put" Communists into government—certainly an inaccurate and unfair accusation—and yet it did not actually say this. It could also be read as merely implying that the Democrats had *unwittingly* given employment to Communists, and that a Dewey administration would not repeat the error. Such ambiguity is of the essence of respectable demagogy. Yet Dewey's delinquency was mild, compared to the demagogic assaults in which Truman was to indulge before November 2—or compared to the exploitation of the Communist issue which was to occur in the Presidential campaign four years later.

Dewey never made much of the Communist issue in the 1948 campaign. This was not for lack of material. During the summer, two ex-Communists—Elizabeth Bentley and Whittaker Chambers—had testified in vast detail before congressional investigating committees about Communist penetration of federal agencies throughout the New Deal period and the war years. They named many individuals as undercover Communists, some of whom were alleged to have been involved in espionage activities. In August, Chambers' testimony before the House Committee on Un-American Activities first brought to light the Communist past of Alger Hiss, a prominent former State Department official who was now president of the prestigious Carnegie Endowment for International Peace. Hiss denied the charge and had a dramatic confrontation with Chambers before the House Committee. A few months later, Chambers was to produce documentation that Hiss had been involved in espionage and Hiss was ultimately to go to jail for perjury. Even in September, however, the Hiss-Chambers affair, plus the other revelations of Chambers and Bentley, had made Communists-in-government a combustible political issue.

Dewey's treatment of the issue was never inflammatory. He had no need to stir popular passions, for he felt certain of victory. Moreover, in this area, the temperate tone of his campaign was clearly in accord with his private views. In his Oregon debate with Stassen, he had enunciated the traditional civil libertarian attitude toward domestic communism: punish deeds, not words. It was an attitude which one might have expected of a sophisticated lawyer; there was no reason to question his sincerity. During the autumn campaign, he consistently expressed the same attitude; only in his intermittent jibes at Truman did he play for the roar of the crowd.

Dewey made his principal speech on communism at the Hollywood Bowl, in Los Angeles, on September 24. It was a dazzling evening, part political rally and part vaudeville show, the theatrical elements being directed by actor George Murphy. Before Dewey came on, the crowd of 20,000 was entertained by a marimba band and a line of chorus girls; Jeannette MacDonald sang the "Star Spangled Banner" and a procession of Hollywood actors—among them Gary Cooper, Ginger Rogers, Frank Morgan—extolled the New York Governor in brief talks.[34]

Dewey devoted much of his speech to the failures of communism in Russia, largely as measured by the impoverishment of its citizens. He deplored the fact that in the United States "Communists and fellow travelers had risen to positions of trust in our government, in some labor unions, in some places in our arts, sciences, and professions." He spoke scornfully of Truman's "red herring" remark, without however referring to Truman by name. He then addressed himself to the problem of how to handle our domestic Communists.

"We must neither ignore the Communists nor outlaw them," he said. "If they—or if anyone else—break our law against treason, they'll get traitors' treatment. If they engage in sabotage or break any other laws we'll jail them. If our laws aren't adequate, we'll get ones which are. But in this country we'll have no thought police. We will not jail anybody for what he thinks or believes. So long as we keep the Communists among us out in the open . . . the United States of America has nothing to fear from them within its own borders." Truman had said much the same sort of thing in his Chicago speech in June.

The moderation of Dewey's approach was even more apparent when contrasted with the intemperate statements on the Communist issue being made by party chairman Hugh Scott. Addressing the Massachusetts convention of the Republican party on September 25, the day after Dewey's Los Angeles speech, Scott charged that Truman's "indifference to Communist penetration at home" could be traced back to the Communists' endorsement of his Vice-Presidential candidacy in 1944. (The Communists were then in a phase of uncritical admiration of the Roosevelt administration, because of the wartime alliance with the Soviet Union.) In support of his bizarre accusation, Scott quoted two excerpts from a statement by Communist leader Eugene Dennis in the *Daily Worker* of August 12, 1944. One read: "The question is put whether or not labor and the people, the cause of progress, suffered by Wallace's defeat for the Vice-Presidential nomination. The answer to this question is a categoric denial." The other: "It is a ticket representative not only of the Democratic party but of important and wider sections of the camp of national unity." Scott also discerned sinister implications in a letter signed by Senator Truman which appeared in the *Daily Worker* of August 14, 1944. Addressed to the paper's public relations director, the letter was a routine thank-you note acknowledging receipt of a copy of a flattering article which the *Worker* had printed about Truman. About all it proved was the naïveté of Truman's office staff.[35] Hugh Scott, since 1959 a senator from Pennsylvania, years later conceded that he had overplayed the Communist issue in 1948.[36]

Like Dewey, Truman held to the convention of not mentioning his opponent's name. But he increasingly began to respond to Dewey's elevated rhetoric, dropping such comments into his whistle-stop speeches as "You know where I stand. I would like you to try to find out where the opposition stands. You'll get a lot of double talk if they ever tell you anything."[37] In Los Angeles, on September 23, he announced, "This is a championship fight . . . the American people are sold on the idea that nobody deserves to win a championship fight by running away . . . or ducking the issues." He charged that the Republicans "are trying to lull you to sleep with 'high-level' platitudes."

Truman's Los Angeles speech was largely devoted to Republican derelictions in the fields of housing, social security, medical care. At the end, Truman delivered an extended plea to liberals not to vote for Wallace. Los Angeles was the obvious site for this appeal because the third party was expected to poll a large vote in California; indeed, only professional Democratic optimists gave Truman any chance of winning the state. Truman urged that the third party be rejected not only because it was Communist-controlled but because it had no chance of achieving power. "The simple fact is that the third party cannot achieve peace, because it is powerless. It cannot achieve better conditions at home, because it is powerless. . . . I say to those disturbed liberals who have been sitting uncertainly on the outskirts of the third party: think again. Don't waste your vote."

Truman only drew between 10,000 and 16,000 people to his rally in Gilmore Stadium, considerably less than the number Dewey attracted the following night at the Hollywood Bowl.[38] Truman's street crowds were larger than Dewey's but reporters thought this might have been because his motorcade arrived at 5 P.M. when there were more people on the streets than at 4 P.M., the hour when Dewey arrived.[39] The following day in San Diego, however, Truman's curbside crowd numbered 40,000 and he faced his most enthusiastic audience thus far in the tour when he spoke to 10,000 people at the local ball park.[40]

On Saturday the 25th, Truman quickly covered New Mexico, speaking twice and offering generous endorsements of Clinton Anderson, who had resigned as Secretary of Agriculture to run for the Senate against General Patrick J. Hurley. Anderson was regarded as the front-runner. By 11 A.M., Truman was in El Paso for the start of an intensive four-day tour of Texas, the first state he visited where the Dixiecrats were on the ballot. He made a speech on public power in El Paso, then addressed five more whistle-stop audiences in the next ten hours. He was in jolly humor. "It has been an education to see these bright and shiny faces," he told the crowd in Valentine. "Everybody seems to be happy and everybody seems to be interested in the welfare of the United States because you have come out to meet your Chief Executive and look him over and see what you think of him." A new note of optimism appeared in his comments. The Republicans, he twice exclaimed, "are on the run now! We've got them scared and we want to keep them that way."

He arrived in Uvalde at daybreak on Sunday the 26th to have breakfast with seventy-nine-year-old John Nance Garner, F.D.R.'s first Vice-President. Garner, the high school band, and some 4,000 citizens were on hand at the railway station. So was an angora goat, clothed in a gold blanket with red lettering bearing the legend "Dewey's Goat." Truman posed for pictures with the animal, telling the press, "I'm going to clip it and make a rug. Then I'm going to let it graze on the White House lawn for the next four years." (He was forced, however, to leave the goat behind, there being no facilities on the train for it.)

Truman's visit to Uvalde was billed as purely a social affair, but it represented a small political coup: if old "Cactus Jack" Garner, a very conservative gentleman, found Truman palatable, he was clearly no threat to the Texas Democracy. Garner served Truman an enormous breakfast, lovingly detailed in the press: white-wing dove and mourning dove, bacon, ham, fried chicken, scrambled eggs, rice and gravy, hot biscuits, Uvalde honey, peach preserves, grape jelly and coffee. When the feast was over, Garner introduced Truman to the crowd waiting outside as an "old and very good friend." Truman responded: "Mr. President—that's the way I used to address him in the Senate—I haven't had such a breakfast in forty years. . . . John Garner and I have been friends for a long time and we are going to be friends as long as we live. I'm coming back for another visit sometime. I fished around for another invitation and got it." At this point Mrs. Truman broke her long-standing rule against speaking in public and told the throng: "Good morning and thank you for this wonderful greeting." Garner then urged everyone to go to church.[41]

On Monday, traveling north through Texas, Truman opened a new attack on Dewey's unity theme. "Republican candidates," he said in Dallas, "are apparently trying to sing the American voters to sleep with a lullaby about unity in domestic affairs. . . . They want the kind of unity that benefits the National Association of Manufacturers. . . . They don't want unity. They want surrender." In Bonham, he charged that under the Republicans the country would have "the unity of the Martins and the Tabers and the Wherrys and the Tafts. Then it would be unity in giving tax relief to the rich . . . unity in letting prices go sky high . . . unity in whittling away all the benefits of the New Deal . . ."[42]

Large and friendly crowds greeted Truman everywhere—15,000

at Waco, another 15,000 outside the railroad station in Fort Worth, 20,000 or more at the Rebel Stadium in Dallas.[43] Initially, advance man Donald Dawson had wanted to hold the Dallas rally at the railway station, fearing that Rebel Stadium would look empty.[44] He was wrong. At Dallas, before Truman spoke, Attorney General Tom Clark introduced him at some length, winding up with the declaration, "And I was with him when he stopped Joe Louis in the courts." Truman was still laughing when he got to the microphone. "Tom, you gave me too much credit," he said. "It wasn't Joe Louis I stopped—it was John. I haven't quite that much muscle." Texas was altogether a triumph. In Fort Worth,[45] Governor Beauford Jester, who had bitterly opposed Truman's civil rights program, took a prominent part in the festivities, promising that Texas would again go Democratic in November. Truman had the discretion not to mention civil rights once during his tour of the state.

Next on Truman's schedule was Oklahoma, where he was again met with large crowds for his back-platform talks; at most stops he boosted the candidacy of Robert S. Kerr, a former governor now running for a Senate seat being vacated by a Republican. At Oklahoma City[46] Truman delivered a major speech on communism and national security, seeking to answer Republican charges that he had "coddled" Communists in government. He made much of his administration's record in combating communism abroad and argued that the FBI was doing an effective job eradicating domestic subversion. He denounced the Republican congressional committees, maintaining that they were more interested in political propaganda than national security.

"I charge that the Republicans have impeded and made more difficult our efforts to cope with communism in this country. . . . I charge that they have not produced any significant information about Communist espionage which the FBI did not already have. . . . I charge them with having recklessly cast a cloud of suspicion over the most loyal civil service in the world. . . . I charge that in all this they have not hurt the Communist party one bit. They have helped it."

It was a strong speech, more crisply written than most of Truman's orations. Its impact was difficult to gauge, but it was agreeably received by the 20,000 persons in the state fair grounds; scattered applause interrupted Truman eighteen times. The speech was regarded as sufficiently important for the Democratic National Committee to pay for a "live" radio broadcast for the first time on this tour.[47] Considerable thought had also been given to the setting for the speech, with Oklahoma finally being selected because Truman's strategists had the impression that the Republicans were exploiting the Communist issue most effectively in the Midwest.[48]

The Oklahoma City speech on September 28 was the high point of the second week of Truman's tour. On the following day, he finished his tour of Oklahoma and crossed into southwest Missouri, delivering sixteen speeches between 7:35 A.M. and 11:15 P.M., most of them from the rear platform of the train. He arrived in Mount Vernon, Illinois, early on the morning of September 30, made a 7:40 A.M. speech, and then switched from the train to a motor caravan for a 141-mile trip through southern Illinois; in five and a half hours he spoke nine times. This was farming and coal country, largely Republican in its politics, but there was a great outpouring of spectators. The *New York Times* estimated that at least 75,000 people saw the President; he put the figure at half a million. He delivered his familiar message, but in Carbondale, where he spoke at the University of Southern Illinois, he made a brief comment about civil rights; he was in the North again. A new metaphor also appeared in the Carbondale speech. The Republicans, he said, "have begun to nail the American consumer to the wall with spikes of greed." [49] By late afternoon, Truman was whistle-stopping through Kentucky; that evening in Louisville, he gave a prepared speech in large part devoted to an attack on the National Association of Manufacturers.

The following morning, in Lexington,[50] Truman's public show of optimism took the immodest form of likening himself to the famous horse Citation, a frequent winner despite being a slow starter. "It doesn't matter which horse is ahead or behind at any given moment," he assured his admirers. "It's the horse that comes out ahead at the finish that counts. I am trying to do in politics what Citation has done in the horse races." The first lap of the race was over that night after three appearances in West Virginia. His last major speech of the tour, broadcast over nationwide radio from

Charleston, West Virginia, was a recitation of most of his stock themes, enlivened by the prediction of "a headlong dash toward another depression" if a Republican President as well as a Republican Congress was elected.

By the time Truman returned to Washington on Saturday morning, October 2, he had covered 8,300 miles and delivered 140 speeches; he estimated that he had been seen by 3,000,000 people.[51] The journalists who had accompanied him had difficulty assessing the impact of the tour. However inflated Truman's estimate might be, there was no question that large crowds had turned out to hear him; but was this an indication of political preference? As Robert J. Donovan wrote in the *New York Herald-Tribune*, "The American people have a very high regard for the office of President of the United States and a very great curiosity about the man who occupies it. When he comes to town they turn out in droves, tack up the welcome signs, bring out the bands, and drag all the children out of school to see the President and, if possible, to shake hands with him. But does that mean they are going to vote for him?"[52] The reporters agreed, however, that the President appeared confident of victory wherever he appeared. To his advisers, he never expressed anything but optimism about the final outcome. Clark Clifford's testimony is emphatic: "From the beginning of the campaign until election day I never heard him express a doubt about his winning. I don't know, of course, whether this was a deep conviction or his idea of the attitude a leader should take. But he certainly had no patience with gloomy reports. I've seen him ashen with fatigue, but never discouraged."[53]

Despite the lively show that Truman put on, there were increasing complaints in the press that the campaign was a dull one. The problem was not only that Dewey was so far ahead that it was difficult to develop any suspense. (On September 24 Gallup gave him 46½ percent to 39 percent for Truman.)[54] Dewey's lofty rhetoric and his refusal to respond to Truman's taunts suppressed the natural excitement of an election contest. Dewey's campaign increasingly came to resemble an elaborate lecture tour. As he continued his travels, up the west coast to Seattle, then east to Montana and Utah, he delivered a number of set speeches notable for their dignity and responsibility. *Time* observed that "He seemed less like a candidate bidding for votes and more like a statesman speaking not only for his party but for his country." [55] In Portland, Oregon,[56] and Great Falls, Montana,[57] he warned our foreign adversaries not to be misled by the divisiveness of a political campaign; on fundamentals, Americans were united. "The totalitarian states must not misunderstand what is happening here," he said in Great Falls. "They must not make the error of believing that because we are exercising our constitutional right to change our government this nation is at all split or divided."

When not addressing the world, Dewey devoted a good deal of attention to regional concerns—notably power and reclamation projects, soil conservation, development of forests. He was now a bit more specific than he had been before; the cliché count in his speeches also seemed to have decreased somewhat. His speech in Portland, expressing his pleasure at being back in Oregon and cataloguing the agricultural wonders of the state, had the ring of genuine feeling. There was no question that he was grateful to the voters of Oregon.

He delivered his major foreign policy speech of the campaign at the Mormon Tabernacle in Salt Lake City on September 30. The speech, the subject of continuous exchanges with John Foster Dulles in Paris, had been written by Elliott Bell during the two days prior to its delivery. Bell consciously set out to compose not a campaign manifesto but a sober pronouncement by the next President of the United States.[58] The speech thus scored no debating points against the Truman administration; its only partisan flavor came in its brief disavowal of postmortems, such as "It does not advance our purpose to discuss the manner in which the Soviet has been able to pick up the fruits of diplomatic victories that were yielded up at that series of secret conferences culminating in Potsdam."

Throughout, the tone was firm, temperate, realistic. Appeasement was rejected; the errors of Munich recalled. At the same time, Dewey avoided any suggestion of belligerency. He offered a detailed outline of his foreign policy: "unstinting support" to the United Nations; "all reasonable aid" to restore the economies of "friendly and like-minded nations"; the use of the European-aid program "as the means for pushing, prodding, and encouraging the nations of Western Europe toward the goal of European union"; the transformation of the Ruhr into a "workshop for peace" by keeping it demilitarized and under international control; more generous aid to China; closer and more cordial cooperation with Latin America; the creation of an American military establishment "so strong that no nation will again risk attacking us"; and the maintenance of a productive economy at home rid of the danger of depression and mass unemployment. ("Military strength alone is not enough.") In essence, Dewey was advocating the continuance of the present bipartisan foreign policy, with certain shifts of emphasis—such as greater concern for Nationalist China (which had not yet been ejected from the mainland) and the use of economic aid to "prod" Western Europe into political union.

Some 8,000 people filled the tabernacle; every seat was taken an hour before Dewey arrived. An overflow crowd of 4,000 heard the speech on television in adjoining auditoriums. Applause interrupted Dewey twenty-four times.[59] The street crowds, however, were slimmer than those which had turned out for Truman nine days before. That afternoon, Elliott Bell became aware for the first time of public apathy toward Dewey. "We hit Salt Lake City around five P.M.," he has recalled. "I was struck by the fact that there were very few people on the sidewalks—and a good many people walking hardly bothered to look at the motorcade." He was puzzled, but hardly worried.[60]

Dewey covered Wyoming the following day and on October 2 made a series of talks in Kansas and Missouri, where he drew the biggest and most enthusiastic back-platform crowds of his tour. Late at night, in St. Louis, where no speech was scheduled, the crush of people was so great in the station that Dewey left his train and stood on a bench to address the crowd. Several times during the course of the day he made a brief defense of the Eightieth Congress, stating that it "gave us the first long-range farm price support program in the history of the country and I am for it one thousand percent." [61] This was similar to his defense of the Congress, in the West, for its record on reclamation. He was incapable of saying much more in behalf of the Eightieth Congress, without doing violence to his own well-publicized views. Truman had already attacked Dewey for saying a kind word about the Eightieth Congress on the reclamation issue and Dewey now responded indirectly. "Your next national administration," he said, "will want to and know how to work with your elected representatives in Congress, and will not go around the country blackguarding the Congress. The present administration, by its quarreling and bickering, has presented us to the world as a nation incapable of governing itself." [62] In light of what Truman was saying, this was a mild reproof.

By the time Dewey returned to Albany on October 3, he had covered 8,862 miles and delivered sixty speeches, forty-seven of which were extemporaneous. He had traveled a few hundred miles more than Truman but spoke less than half as many times; he rarely made a speech before 10 A.M. As for his crowds, the *New York Times* summed up the common impression: "In many cases the audiences were not as large as those which turned out to hear him in 1944 and generally were not as demonstrative as they were then, but they accorded to him the utmost of respect." The *Times* reported that a poll of forty-seven journalists on the Dewey train found them unanimous in believing he would win. Dewey's admirers were equally confident. Ed Jaeckle told reporters that Dewey would carry every one of the fourteen states he visited, including Truman's own state of Missouri. Less confidence was expressed about the senatorial elections to be held in nine of the fourteen states. Dewey's people believed that the Republicans were well ahead in Kansas, Idaho, Oregon and Illinois; the elections were expected to be close in Iowa, Colorado, New Mexico, Montana and Wyoming.[63]


While Dewey and Truman were relaxing after their first campaign tours, their running mates were still bounding around the country. As is usually the case, the Vice-Presidential candidates made little news, for they did little more than echo the themes enunciated by their principals. The tradition has always been that Vice-Presidential nominees are to be seen and heard, but are not to say much.

Senator Alben Barkley, who had urged Truman to "mow 'em

down," kept up an unceasing fusillade of his own throughout the campaign. He was a far better speaker than Truman; on merit he did not deserve to be relegated to the second-run houses while Truman was playing the big time. Barkley traveled with a small staff, including two speech writers, on a chartered DC3, and in the course of the campaign covered thirty-six states and made over 250 speeches. There were occasions when he addressed several thousand people, but his audiences were as small as 350 people, which led *Time* to call him "the poor man's candidate." For a seventy-year-old, his energy was astonishing; at any hour of the day or night he was ready with several thousand improvised words about the sins of the Eightieth Congress and the great achievements of sixteen years of Democratic rule. He was as confident as he was loquacious. Early in the campaign, reporters in New Haven asked whether he thought the Democrats would win. "Certainly," he responded jovially. "What do you think I'm running around for?" [64]

The Republicans were sufficiently affluent to provide Governor Earl Warren with a fourteen-car train, almost as elaborately fitted out as that of a Presidential candidate. He set off on September 15 from Sacramento on a thirty-one-day transcontinental tour which took him across the Rocky Mountains to Utah, south to New Mexico, thence through Texas, Oklahoma, Missouri, and Kentucky, north to Ohio and Michigan, east to the New England and Middle Atlantic states, a brief dip into the South, after which he traveled through the Midwest on his way back to California. He generally made one set speech in the evening and a few whistle-stops during the day.

Warren's campaign style was more relaxed than Dewey's. A big, genial man, he was as engagingly folksy as Truman and gave the impression of being equally sincere. His appeals for "unity" were even loftier and less controversial than Dewey's. In a speech in Salt Lake City on September 16, he set the tone of his campaign: "The vast majority of Americans know . . . that good Americans are to be found in both parties. They realize that there are progressives and conservatives in the ranks of both. . . . No party has a patent on progress, a copyright on governmental principles or a proprietary interest in the advances made in former days." Nonetheless, there was a good reason for voting Republican: "Is the present national administration displaying the unity, the competence, and the leadership to warrant extending its tenure to twenty years? Or has the time come for better housekeeping methods that can only be supplied by new leadership and a new broom?" [65]

Wherever he went, Warren brought genial reassurance. In Philadelphia on October 1, he assessed the international situation and found the outlook for peace reasonably good: "If we meet the realities of each day neither with appeasement nor bluff, without coddling communism one day and scolding it the next—if we keep our national defenses strong—if we faithfully fulfill our commitments to the world—if we keep our own national life sound and wholesome, no nation on earth is going to be misled to the mistake of believing that any good could come to it from starting a war with the United States." [66]

In Charleston, West Virginia, on October 5, he came out for both big and little business: "The little jeeps of small business should have a chance to keep moving, just as well as the ten-ton trucks of big business." On the other hand, he warned that "We have got to be on the watch for the appearance of the economic road hog," by which he meant monopoly. [67] The following day, in Chicago, he advocated a straightforward foreign policy: "There will be no vacillation or appeasement. . . . Just sound, practical American determination based upon the realities of the day." [68] Moving on to Madison, Wisconsin, he had a few harsh words for "the jealous, watchful eye of a paternal federal government" and spoke warmly of the need for more local initiative. [69]

Little wonder that the Governor's campaign became known as the "Warren goodwill tour."

# CHAPTER 10
# The Home Stretch

After his transcontinental trip, Truman took only a four-day rest before he resumed his campaign. On Wednesday morning, October 6, he entrained once again for a three-day tour of Delaware, Pennsylvania, New Jersey and upstate New York. There were no surprises. Truman had no need to vary his routine, for his audiences could hardly have been more approving. Everywhere he traveled the crowds were abundant and enthusiastic; the press duly reported that fact, but expressed doubt as to what it meant. *Time* attributed the turnout to Truman's "growing entertainment value."

In Philadelphia, 12,000 cheering, feet-stomping partisans nearly filled the huge auditorium where the conventions had been held; 500,000 people thronged the streets to watch Truman's motorcade. Some 35,000 welcomed him to Elizabeth, New Jersey, and another 100,000 lined the route to Newark. From Newark to Jersey City, around 10 P.M., the motorcade was cheered by an estimated 300,-000 people. An enormous fireworks display entertained the crowd, with three fifteen-foot portraits of Truman and a forty-foot Niagara Falls lighting up the sky. The next day, on his train ride from Albany to Buffalo, Truman had crowds of from 5,000 to 10,000 at each stop, despite intermittent rain. At Auburn, New York, there was a sudden downpour just before he began to speak, but most of the 7,000 people in the station square stayed until he finished.[1]

Throughout, the President was in good form. In Wilmington,[2] Delaware, he talked about the Republican refusal to pass housing legislation. He recalled Herbert Hoover's campaign slogan of "Two cars in every garage" and quipped that the present Republican candidate apparently "is running on a slogan of two families in every garage." In Philadelphia,[3] he charged that the Republicans wanted to roll up all the people in the country "into one big company union and run it for the benefit of the National Association of Manufacturers." In Auburn,[4] he topped all prior denunciations of the local congressman, John Taber, chairman of the House Appropriations Committee, by charging him with having "used a butcher knife and a saber and a meat axe on . . . every forward-looking program that had come before the Congress." Truman called the legislative butchery "the Taber dance."

The President returned to Washington on Saturday morning, October 9, and soon afterward went to the airport to welcome Secretary of State Marshall, who was returning from Paris for consultations. By this time the newspapers were full of the abortive "Vinson mission"—a plan of the President, vetoed by Marshall, to send Chief Justice Fred M. Vinson to Moscow for private conversations with Stalin. Though the mission had been canceled, Truman was soon to be widely criticized for playing politics with foreign affairs and for making a blunder as rash as his endorsement of Henry Wallace's Madison Square Garden speech in September 1946. The serious basis of the criticism, apart from its partisan motivation, was that the President's gambit might have destroyed confidence in the consistency of U.S. foreign policy, for the State Department had recently won the British and French to the view that no further direct negotiations should be held with the Soviet Union until they ended the Berlin blockade. The Chief Justice's trip, it was feared, would also have undercut the UN, which was then trying to grapple with the Berlin crisis.

The Vinson mission was one of the most curious episodes of the campaign. At the time, Clark Clifford was mistakenly credited with having inspired the idea.[5] Its actual authors were speech writers David Noyes and Albert Carr, who believed that a direct approach to Stalin by the eminent Chief Justice might moderate some of the tensions of the Cold War and at the same time be of considerable political benefit to Truman, by way of stopping the leakage of Democratic votes to Wallace because of the "peace" issue.[6] Noyes and Carr readily sold the plan to Truman, who in his memoirs speaks of his hope that "Vinson's mission, as an off-channel approach to Stalin, might expose the Russian dictator to a better understanding of our attitude as a people and of our nation's peaceful aspirations for the whole world. I had a feeling that Stalin might get over some of his inhibitions if he were to talk with our own Chief Justice." [7]

Truman relates that he conferred with Vinson on Sunday, October 3, the day after his return from his transcontinental train tour. Vinson was initially reluctant to accept the assignment—he thought it inappropriate for a Supreme Court Justice to engage in nonjudicial activities—but finally agreed.[8] Truman then instructed his press secretary to ask the radio networks for a half hour's free time for a Presidential speech. On Tuesday morning, October 5, Charles Ross met in his office with representatives of the four networks. When he requested free time for a nonpolitical speech (political time of course had to be paid for), they asked what the President would talk about. In strict confidence, Ross told them about the Vinson mission. At the same time, elsewhere in the White House, Truman was conversing by teletype with General Marshall in Paris. Marshall was firmly opposed to the whole project and Truman canceled it on the spot. He then asked Marshall to come to Washington for a conference. Ross subsequently telephoned the radio networks to withdraw the request for free time; once again, he asked them to keep the matter confidential. But there was a leak and the story broke on Friday morning, October 8, while Truman was campaigning in upstate New York.[9]

On Saturday, after Truman conferred with Marshall, he issued a statement in which he sought to explain the bungled affair. Alluding to his "continuing great desire to see peace firmly established" and his "particular concern at this time over the attitude taken by the Soviet representatives regarding the atomic problem," he said that he had asked Marshall on Tuesday "whether he felt that a useful purpose would be served" by sending Vinson to Moscow. Marshall told him of the "possibilities of misunderstanding" to which unilateral action could give rise and so Truman "decided not to take this step."

Truman's explanation did not restrain his critics. *Time*'s comment was typical: "His attempted action was shocking because it showed that he had no conception whatever of the difference between the President of the United States and a U.S. politician." [10] Dewey, however, did not join in the attack. He was reported as believing that Truman's blunder was too serious to be exploited for political purposes; instead Dewey took it upon himself to reassure the world that there had been no shift in the direction of American foreign policy. After discussing the matter with Vandenberg and Dulles, the Governor issued a brief statement in which he said that "The people of America wholeheartedly and vigorously support the labors of our bipartisan delegation at Paris and specifically its insistence on a prompt lifting of the blockade of Berlin. The nations of the world can rest assured that the American people are in fact united in their foreign policy . . ." [11]

Once again, Dewey's admirers could applaud his statesmanship. The *New York Times* reported that Dewey's entourage regarded Truman's scheme as "an error of judgment of such proportions that it could alone be sufficient to swing the election, if the contest were in doubt. . . . There is no feeling, however, among the Governor's counselors that victory is in question. The effect on the election result from their point of view will be to increase the size of the victory." [12] That being the case, Dewey did little more than make an occasional veiled allusion to the Vinson mission in his later campaign speeches.

Truman did not share the same view of the impact of the aborted mission. At a meeting of his speech writers in the Cabinet Room, at which Clifford, Murphy, Noyes, Carr and a few others were present, Truman went around the room asking everyone's opinion of the affair. All expressed dismay. With a twinkle in his eye, Truman remarked, "I don't think it's that bad." His implication was clear: whatever embarrassment had been caused, he had demonstrated to the American people that he was a man of peace. [13]

Truman emphasized that point in his October 18 speech before the American Legion convention in Miami. After explaining how much he detested war, he deplored the "dark fog of distrust" which had arisen between the Soviet Union and the West. "In recently considering sending a special emissary to Moscow," he said, "my purpose was to ask Premier Stalin's cooperation in dispelling the present poisonous atmosphere . . . This proposal had no relation to existing negotiations within the scope of the United Nations or the Council of Foreign Ministers. Far from cutting across these negotiations, the purpose of this mission was to improve the atmosphere in which they must take place and so help in producing fruit-ful and peaceful results. . . . I want to make it perfectly clear that I have not departed one step from my determination to utilize every opportunity to work for peace."


While the Vinson affair was still in the headlines, both Truman and Dewey set out on train tours of the Midwest. Truman left on October 10 for a trip through Ohio, Illinois, Minnesota, Wisconsin and West Virginia. The following night, Dewey departed from Albany to cover Pennsylvania, Kentucky, southern Illinois, Oklahoma, Missouri and Michigan.

The first day of Dewey's trip was notable as the only occasion when he departed from the consistently temperate tone of his campaign. On the night of October 10, shortly after his train left Albany, Dewey dropped by the compartment of his press secretary for a private chat. It was just three days after Truman had made his tour of upstate New York, drawing enormous crowds wherever he appeared. Dewey asked Jim Hagerty how he thought Truman was doing. "I think he's been doing pretty well," said Hagerty. "I think so too," said Dewey. From what followed, Hagerty had the impression that Truman's jibes had aroused Dewey's normal combativeness; the high-level campaign was not in character for him. Dewey asked Hagerty to plant a question in the crowd when the train reached Erie the next morning. After he had been speaking for two or three minutes, he wanted to be interrupted by a demand for his views on the Taft-Hartley Act.[14]

The following morning, Hagerty jumped off the train and quickly accomplished his mission.[15] When the question came, Dewey responded with a vigor and asperity that recalled the 1944 campaign. Truman's message vetoing the Taft-Hartley Act, he said, had been "the wrongest, most incompetent, most inaccurate document ever put out of the White House in 160 years." The President had predicted increased strikes under Taft-Hartley; instead they had almost been cut in half. There had been fewer rather than more jurisdictional strikes; discharges, instead of increasing, had been reduced by 25 percent. It was altogether an effective polemical thrust.[16]

After the train left Erie, Hagerty walked into the press car and was met with questions as to whether Dewey was switching his pace in the final three weeks of the campaign. Hagerty replied that they had heard the speech and could judge for themselves. He then entered the candidate's car, where several staff members expressed surprise at Dewey's unexpected combativeness. Hagerty said he favored the change, but no one else agreed.[17]

Dewey continued his aggressive thrusts at his three remaining back-platform appearances in Sharon, New Castle, and Rochester, Pennsylvania. But his experiment did not outlast the day; according to Hagerty, the candidate bowed to his staff's disapproval. "For a few brief hours after his tour left Albany, Dewey acted as though he were in a campaign," the Chicago *Daily News'* Edwin A. Lahey wrote. "But he soon got himself in hand, and is back on a high road of rich baritone homilies."[18]

On the evening of October 11, in Pittsburgh, Dewey delivered his principal labor speech of the campaign. It cast the Republican party as the champion of collective bargaining, spoke warmly of the Wagner Act, defended the Taft-Hartley Act, though conceding that it was not perfect and promising unspecified changes where necessary. In listing the goals of "your next administration" (a favorite phrase), Dewey's most specific commitments involved a rise in the statutory minimum wage and increases in social security benefits and coverage. (Dollar figures were not mentioned, however.) He also promised vigorous enforcement of the antitrust laws, a break in the "log jam in housing," an end to inflation, a solution to "the problems of race relations and discrimination," and much more. He did not, however, discuss the mechanisms for achieving these goals.

As he continued his tour, Dewey delivered a major speech each evening (the subject was "peace" in Louisville and Oklahoma City, "good government" in Kansas City, Missouri), which were not notably more specific than his Pittsburgh speech. In his back-platform appearances, he campaigned less for himself than for the local senatorial candidates—John Sherman Cooper in Kentucky, Ross Rizley in Oklahoma, Senator Joseph Ball in Minnesota. "Don't worry about me, but vote for Ross Rizley," he would say. "We need him on our team in Washington." In Oklahoma, Dewey rivaled Truman by making thirteen speeches. There was logic to his exertions, for Rizley was regarded as trailing ex-Governor Robert Kerr. In Minnesota, Ball faced an equally serious threat from Hubert Humphrey. It was impossible to gauge how effective Dewey's appeals were. Correspondents noted that his crowds were not impressive, except in strongly Republican Tulsa and in his birthplace of Owosso, Michigan. Owosso gave him an elaborate homecoming celebration, featuring a parade with nine floats illustrating various periods of his life, from birth to installation in the White House.[19]

Dewey's public display of confidence never faltered, even when faced with such a poor turnout as the one in St. Paul on October 15, when half the 12,500 seats in the Municipal Auditorium were unfilled. Staff men explained to the press, as *Newsweek* put it, "that in every campaign Governor Dewey had entered he had lost when the crowds were big and won when the crowds were small." [20]

Midway in the tour, however, Dewey and some of his advisers were beginning to have doubts about the way their campaign was going. Dewey felt the first tremors of anxiety in Kansas City, on October 14, when he had a conversation with Roy Roberts, the politically astute editor of the Kansas City *Star*, which was almost as disconcerting as the painful attack of bursitis that had hit his right shoulder. Roberts told Dewey that the farmers in the Midwest were defecting from the ticket and advised him to make a farm speech which would promise abundant federal help. Dewey respected Roberts' appraisal, but bridled at the prescription, for he was opposed to making promises which he believed could not be fulfilled.[21] The speech he gave the following night in St. Paul did no more than restate his previously expressed views on agricultural policy.

When he was in St. Paul, Dewey talked by telephone with Harold E. Keller, his Commissioner of Commerce, who was in Albany. When they finished their main business, Dewey asked Keller how he felt the campaign was going. Keller thought things looked good, at which point Dewey told him that some of the state leaders were getting "restive" and were urging a few "fighting" speeches. Keller advised Dewey to step up his tempo a bit, but not to start swinging hard. Dewey was pleased with his comment and said that his staff on the train were of the same opinion.[22]

Dewey's concern was also shared by Elliott Bell, who had first become aware of public apathy in Salt Lake City. Increasingly he was hearing complaints from such of the common citizenry as one encounters on a political tour—policemen, elevator operators—that Dewey was running a disappointingly lackluster campaign. Bell remembers several conversations with Dewey in the latter half of October about the wisdom of going on the offensive to engender some enthusiasm. The decision was always made, however, to continue on the present course. The polls still showed Dewey to be far ahead; virtually all journalistic observers thought he was going to win. The ineffectiveness of Dewey's aggressive tactics in 1944 was frequently recalled and there was some fear that if he began to hit hard, Truman would be able to exploit his role of underdog even more dramatically. In general, according to Bell, "the view was that the die was probably cast—that if you hadn't won the election by this point, you wouldn't win it at all." [23]

Dewey, however, was eager to have a sampling of opinion broader than that of his personal staff. After the Midwest tour was over, Herbert Brownell set up a series of conference telephone calls around the country with about ninety of the ninety-six state committeemen and women. They were asked their opinions on how the campaign was progressing and specifically whether Dewey's strategy should be changed. With one exception, all agreed that the present strategy should be continued. The dissident was Harry Darby, national committeeman from Kansas, who was troubled by disaffection in the farm belt and advised that Dewey go over to the offensive.[24]

Apart from these private stirrings of doubt, Dewey's mid-October tour was notable for two public embarrassments. On October 12, in his Louisville speech, he took credit for introducing the bipartisan foreign policy, stating that "I first proposed to Secretary Hull during the election campaign four years ago that we have cooperation between our two parties to win the peace." [25] The following day, James Reston published a sharp piece in the *New York Times* in which he disputed Dewey's version by quoting Cordell Hull's memoirs. According to this account, Hull had publicly proposed a conference with Dewey "to straighten out any points connected with the postwar organization and a nonpartisan approach to it." Dewey then accepted Hull's invitation and sent John Foster Dulles to talk with him.[26]

Two days after Reston's article appeared, Hull issued a statement from his hospital room deploring Dewey's revision of history and suggesting that he consult the newspapers of August and September 1944.[27] Dewey's reply, inserted that night into his St. Paul speech,[28] was feeble. He said that in 1944 "I appointed a representative to work in the creation of the great new organization for peace. . . . Secretary Hull accepted his cooperation handsomely and we succeeded in lifting the whole problem of the United Nations out of the partisanship of a political campaign." All this was true enough, but Dewey skirted the point of whether he or Hull first proposed the cooperative effort.

The dispute over Dewey's boast did not have the impact, however, of the incident at Beaucoup, Illinois, on October 12. As Dewey began to speak from the rear platform, the train suddenly moved backward into the crowd. It stopped after a few feet and no one was hurt. Dewey momentarily lost his poise. "That's the first lunatic I've had for an engineer," he told the crowd. "He probably ought to be shot at sunrise but I guess we can let him off because no one was hurt." [29] The flash of temper was forgivable under the circumstances, but it was to cost Dewey dearly. Before the campaign was over, the Democrats inflated the remark to the dimensions of a *cause célèbre,* charging that it proved that Dewey was unfeeling and hostile to the workingman.

Truman had a good deal of fun with the incident at Beaucoup. Three days later, he told a rear platform audience in Logansport,[30] Indiana, "I was highly pleased when I found out . . . that the train crew on this train are all Democrats. . . . We have had wonderful train crews all around the country and they've been just as kind to us as they could possibly be." In a nationwide radio broadcast on October 21, sponsored by the International Ladies' Garment Workers' Union, he remarked, "We have been hearing about engineers again recently from the Republican candidate. He objects to having engineers back up. He doesn't mention, however, that under the 'Great Engineer' we backed up into the worst depression in our history."

Truman's Midwest tour was marked by the same outpouring of

crowds that attended his procession a few days before through Pennsylvania, New Jersey and upstate New York. In Ohio, 100,-000 people lined the streets in Akron, 50,000 in Dayton. In Springfield, Illinois, he drew a capacity crowd in the 6,000-seat state armory; in St. Paul, 15,000 filled the civic theater and three adjacent auditoriums; in Indiana, he attracted enormous audiences in small communities—25,000 in Kokomo, 20,000 at Hammond, 12,000 at Logansport, 9,000 in Tipton. Indianapolis was the triumph of the week—a crowd of 45,000 at the War Memorial.[31]

Both politicians and reporters were impressed. In his memoirs, Truman recalled that Frank Lausche, the Democratic candidate for governor of Ohio, got on the train for a short ride. There was a crowd of 6,000 to 8,000 at the station where Lausche climbed aboard and larger crowds at the next two stops. "Is this the way all the crowds have been?" Truman quoted Lausche as asking. "Yes, but this is smaller than in most states," Truman replied. "Well," said Lausche, "this is the biggest crowd I ever saw in Ohio." He stayed on the train beyond his planned departure.[32]

The traveling press party reported in detail about the size of the crowds, but the one possibility which they were unwilling to credit was that Truman might be winning votes. Minnesota was the only state he was given a hope of carrying. The October 15 story of Charles T. Lucey, a Scripps-Howard writer, was typical: "The polls and the pundits say Harry Truman hasn't a chance to be returned to the White House, but you'd never guess it from the way people come out to see him. . . . Mr. Truman attracted crowds reminiscent of the 1940 Roosevelt-Willkie campaign. Republican parade crowds this fall often have been only thin lines along the curb . . ." Yet Lucey agreed with the polls and the pundits, once again pointing out that crowds did not necessarily represent votes and that "The local Democratic officials often talk, not of whether Mr. Truman or Mr. Dewey will be elected, but of Mr. Dewey's margin. If it is not too great, they think they may elect some local or state candidates." [33] In a long analysis in the *New York Herald-Tribune* of October 16, Bert Andrews made many of the same points. He had an additional reason for believing that Truman was doomed: whereas Dewey's staff was confident to the point of cockiness, Truman's people were "a bit grim," making only *pro forma* predictions of victory. Andrews was impressed, however, with Truman's buoyancy: "He either honestly believes he will win on November 2 or he is putting on the most magnificent and fighting front of optimism that any doubtful candidate ever did."

There is one piece of evidence which indicates that Truman, by this time, believed his own victory claims. On the afternoon of October 13, after the train pulled out from Duluth on its way to St. Paul, George Elsey went to the rear car to confer with the President. He found him alone. They sat down at the dining table and Truman suddenly proposed to give Elsey a state-by-state rundown of his election predictions. Elsey wrote the figures on the back of a mimeographed transcript of the President's remarks at Duluth. Elsey still has the document among his papers.[34]

Truman's overall forecast showed 340 votes for him, 108 for Dewey, 42 for Thurmond, with 37 labeled "doubtful." (Four electoral votes were accidentally left out of the calculation.) Truman correctly predicted that he would win Massachusetts, Rhode Island, West Virginia, Kentucky, North Carolina, Tennessee, Georgia, Arkansas, Oklahoma, Texas, New Mexico, Arizona, Nevada, Washington, Montana, Wyoming, Illinois, Missouri, Iowa, Minnesota, Ohio; he also thought he would get half of Florida's 8 electoral votes. He mistakenly laid claim to New Hampshire, Pennsylvania, New Jersey, Maryland, Michigan and Indiana, all of which Dewey won. On the other hand, he erred in conceding to Dewey Colorado, Virginia, Idaho; he was wrong in giving Thurmond 4 Florida votes (Truman took all 8) and did not foresee that one Tennessee elector would go for the Dixiecrats. The President labeled California and Wisconsin as doubtful and in the end won both states; he also took the 4 votes of Utah, about which he had forgotten. Thus, Truman's state-by-state forecasts were only partially accurate; his overall forecast also erred on the optimistic side, for he ultimately polled 303 rather than 340 electoral votes and Dewey's total stood at 189 rather than 108.

The exercise certainly proved that Truman's private calculations were in line with his public exuberance. On October 16, three days after his session with Elsey, he told reporters at a press conference on the train: "Never felt better in my life. I have been very highly pleased with the trip. I was agreeably surprised in Ohio, Minnesota, Wisconsin, Illinois, and Indiana. . . . In fact, I don't think we have had a dud on the trip." Asked whether he thought that "your stock has gone up as a result of this trip," he replied, "Well now, that's what you're along for. That's your job. I am the candidate. The candidate is not going to comment. He's optimistic!"

Few Democratic supporters were willing to parade their optimism. One of the few who did was Jack Kroll, the head of the CIO's Political Action Committee, who in the last week of the campaign predicted Truman's victory. After the election, much was made of labor's contribution, but it received relatively little attention during the campaign. This was in part by labor's own design. During the 1944 campaign, when CIO–PAC made its debut, its lavishly publicized activities in behalf of Roosevelt in itself became an issue. The Republicans picked up a phrase attributed to Roosevelt—"Clear it with Sidney"—and repeated it insistently to imply that Sidney Hillman, the veteran labor leader who was CIO–PAC's first director, had taken over the entire Roosevelt campaign. In 1948, labor's electoral efforts never created much of a flurry in the press. For one thing, the Republicans had no need to make an issue of it; for another, labor did not mount a flamboyant campaign for the head of the ticket but concentrated on the undramatic chores of registering its supporters and getting them to the polls on election day.

The AFL and the railway brotherhoods were involved in this effort, as well as the CIO. In 1947, the AFL had created Labor's League for Political Education to parallel the CIO–PAC; it was headed by Joseph Keenan, a little-known official of the International Brotherhood of Electrical Workers. Never before had the AFL felt the need for a national organization to coordinate the political efforts of its constituent unions. Its establishment was directly related to the passage of the Taft-Hartley Act, for it was self-evident that the only way the act could be repealed was by a change in the complexion of the Congress. Throughout the campaign, LLPE, CIO–PAC, and the railway brotherhoods, as previously suggested, concentrated on the election of pro-labor congressmen and senators. Far less attention was paid to Truman's candidacy, be-

cause of the general expectation of his defeat. But as the head of
the ticket, Truman obviously stood to gain from the labor effort in
behalf of state and local candidates.

There was little national coordination of the activities of different
labor groups, but liaison was often close on the local level. CIO–
PAC made by far the largest effort; one of Kroll's associates could
fairly boast that "We're running an honest Tammany Hall on a national scale." Throughout the campaign, PAC had about 100,000
volunteers in the field, organized on a precinct and block basis like
the old-style Tammany operation. On election day, some 250,000
block workers were on the job.[35]

Local organization was often surprisingly professional. Philadelphia, for example, had a city-wide CIO–PAC committee, which
coordinated the operations of subordinate units in congressional
districts, wards, precincts and voting districts. Each congressional
district was generally the responsibility of the CIO union with the
largest membership in the area; thus the Amalgamated Clothing
Workers supplied most of the PAC workers in the First, Second,
and Fourth Congressional districts. Close liaison was maintained
with the Democratic party. The party was so weak that it had precinct workers in only 800 of the 1,343 voting districts in the city.
CIO–PAC provided workers for the remaining 543 districts and
paid part of their $15-a-day stipend. PAC also loaned money to the
party to keep it afloat until election day.[36]

In Detroit, CIO–PAC—which largely meant the United Automobile Workers—undertook a massive effort to get its membership
to register and vote. Leaflets were printed in press runs of 500,000.
A series of eight colored posters were turned out in editions of
5,000 each for display in union halls and factory bulletin boards.
("Depression is coming if you don't vote.") Spot advertisements
were bought on two Detroit radio stations during registration week;
sound trucks toured the streets reminding the workers of their civic
duty. Throughout the week the union offered free transportation
from factory or home to registration points.[37]

The Taft-Hartley Act had prohibited the expenditure of union
funds in federal election campaigns, but this restriction was cir-
cumvented by the solicitation of voluntary donations from members. The LLPE disbursed $319,000 during the course of the cam-

paign, spending $139,000 on operating expenses and on important senatorial races, and giving its state affiliates $180,000 to help finance congressional races.[38] The national CIO–PAC spent $513,-000; of this sum, over $300,000 represented campaign contributions to individual candidates. The national committee also printed 10,-000,000 pieces of literature, made several short films, and produced 423 records for use over radio. Local affiliates of PAC spent another $500,000. In a year when the Democrats had to stretch every dollar, labor's financial contribution was as welcome as its manpower.[39]

While the unions' election drive received scant attention, political observers were well aware by mid-October that both the Wallace and Dixiecrat efforts were losing momentum. Both movements had "peaked," as the politicians say, months before; for each of them, the campaign proper was an anticlimax.

The Progressive party had expected that its July convention would reinspire the faithful and attract substantial new support. Instead, potential supporters were alienated, for the abundant press coverage highlighted allegations that the party was Communist-dominated. Nothing that occurred after the convention seemed to obscure the red taint. On August 24, Wallace made some further statements on the Communist issue, which only seemed to envelop him in fresh absurdities. After denying that he was a Communist or that his party was controlled by the Communists, he declared that "Communism and progressive capitalism differ fundamentally although we share many social objectives. I welcome the support of those who believe in such social objectives," which seemed to indicate that he welcomed the support of Communists. He went on to tell reporters that "I don't know what percentage of Communists really believe as persons in the violent overthrow of the government. There is as much variation in the beliefs of Communists as in the beliefs of Democrats and Republicans"—which certainly ranked as a novel political insight.[40]

These rhetorical exercises only increased the dismay of many liberals who had initially been sympathetic to Wallace. In the weeks after the convention, his only new liberal support of any consequence came from Ted O. Thackrey, copublisher and coeditor of the *New York Post,* who late in August declared for Wallace.[41] Thackrey, however, had been sympathetic to Wallace's cause for some time. His endorsement meant that Wallace would be the beneficiary of a series of signed editorials. Thackrey could not enlist the support of his newspaper, for the other copublisher and coeditor, his wife Dorothy Schiff, differed with his views on Wallace and also wrote a series of signed editorials, eventually backing Dewey. This unusual debate went on for twelve weeks.

While Thackrey was rallying to the cause, Wallace's most prominent New Deal supporter, Rexford Guy Tugwell, was quietly defecting. He did not publicly repudiate Wallace, though he had been disillusioned by the Communist operation in Philadelphia.[42] In August, he told the *New York Post* that he had an "open mind" about the Progressive party and was waiting to see whether the left-wingers "are going to get the upper hand." He said, "I certainly don't know whether they are Communists, but they act as though they are." [43] In the end, although he welcomed Wallace's statement of August 24, Tugwell's doubts were not allayed and he kept a discreet distance from the campaign.

In the labor movement, where Wallace had once hoped to gain considerable support, his candidacy made no further progress. Not even every union controlled by the Communists went all the way with him. Mike Quill, the flamboyant president of the Transport Workers Union, had already broken with the Communists and kept his union from endorsing Wallace. The largest Communist-dominated union, the United Electrical Workers (most of whose 500,000 members were of course not Communists), welcomed Wallace to its September convention but did not endorse him, preferring to avoid the internal ructions which endorsement would have caused.

While Gideon's Army was not visibly increasing in numbers, Wallace did not fade from the headlines. His eight-day tour of the South, beginning on August 29, was clearly designed not to attract southern votes but to publicize his crusade. Wallace had announced in advance that he would not address segregated audiences; he also refused to sleep in segregated hotels.[44] Even if he was not arrested, as Glen Taylor had been in Birmingham earlier in the year, all sorts of dramatic confrontations were likely to occur.

In Virginia, his first stop, Wallace's rallies went off smoothly, for they were described as "private parties," with admission by ticket only, thereby circumventing the segregation laws. (Anyone who arrived at the door was given a ticket.) The first disorder occurred in Durham, North Carolina, where his meeting in the armory was disrupted by an invasion of pickets, fist fights, tossed eggs, and firecrackers. A police escort was necessary to get Wallace into the hall. Hecklers continually interrupted his speech and most of what he said was inaudible. The next day, Wallace was pelted by eggs and tomatoes at open-air meetings in Burlington, Greensboro, and High Point, North Carolina. "I would like to see some indication that I am in the United States," he kept saying to the heedless throng in Burlington. In three days in North Carolina he was hit by missiles at least five times and splattered by the debris of five near-misses. Governor R. Gregg Cherry denounced the mob and promised better police protection; President Truman deplored the "violation of the American concept of fair play."

Moving on to Alabama, Wallace spoke without incident to small crowds in Decatur, Huntsville, and Guntersville, but he canceled his rallies in Gadsden, Birmingham, and Bessemer because the police had insisted on segregating the open-air meeting places. He passed swiftly through Mississippi, suffered intermittent displays of hostility in Louisiana, and finally had an enthusiastic audience of 1,500 on the steps of the War Memorial Building in Nashville, Tennessee. He told the unsegregated crowd that he now had "a pretty good idea of what it must have felt like to have been an early Christian martyr." He also said that he understood that 700,000 southern Negroes would be eligible to vote in the November elections; he was sure that his southern journey would have a "profound effect" on their political preferences. It was to prove a vain hope.[45]

"What had he achieved?" *Time* editorialized. "He had thrown a harsh light on the problem of racial segregation—a problem which the U.S. as a whole cannot continue to shrug off. He had shown that there are a few hooligans in the South, and also responsible statesmen who deplore hooliganism. He had found material for future demagogic campaign speeches, although it was unlikely that he had changed many votes." [46]

On September 10, in New York's Yankee Stadium, Wallace addressed 48,000 people who paid between $.50 and $3.60 each to hear him. It was by far his largest rally of the campaign, and proved that whatever was happening elsewhere in the country, he retained a devoted following in New York. Saying that he had "tested fascism," he blamed big business and the great plantation owners for the violence he had encountered. "They don't personally engage in lynching either free speech or human beings, just as they don't personally engage in fighting the wars from which they profit. But they inflame the passions of others." [47]

On September 21, just prior to Wallace's last major tour, campaign manager C. B. Baldwin announced a significant policy change: the party was withdrawing its candidates in a number of congressional and senatorial races where liberal Democrats were running. Previously, the Progressives had taken the position that any Democratic candidate who supported Truman's foreign policy warranted opposition, even if there were no differences of opinion in domestic policy. This inflexible doctrine created great hostility to Wallace's candidacy, for it threatened the tenure of many liberal officeholders. Baldwin's move was clearly designed to deflect this criticism. He announced the new policy at a $100-a-plate dinner in New York of Businessmen for Wallace. Wallace was also present and he initially demurred, arguing that it was impossible to build a new party if it supported candidates standing for conflicting policies. "We've got to build a party, Beanie, we've got to build a party," said Wallace. But he went along with the new approach.[48]

At the end of the month, Baldwin announced that the Progressives had withdrawn thirteen congressional candidates and would not field candidates in a number of other races; in all the Progressives would be represented in only one hundred congressional and eleven senatorial contests. Hubert Humphrey in Minnesota, gubernatorial aspirant Chester Bowles in Connecticut, Representatives Helen Gahagan Douglas and Chet Holifield of California were among the beneficiaries of the Progressives' withdrawal.[49] Baldwin argued that his party's action "discloses the false and malicious nature of the charge made by many labor and liberal sources that the Progressive party was a 'red plot' to defeat every liberal that supported the Marshall Plan." He maintained that "if Henry Wallace were not in the race, chances for a progressive Congress would be hopeless," arguing that Wallace's candidacy "is ensuring that millions of American voters will come to the polls." [50] Baldwin's announcement, however, led to no great expressions of approval for his party's sense of responsibility but was interpreted as a confession of weakness.[51]

Wallace's final speaking tour began on September 23 in Toledo, Ohio. Traveling by chartered plane, with a small party of aides and newspaper reporters, he addressed several rallies in the Midwest, dipped south for meetings in Dallas, Houston, and El Paso, then spent nearly a week in California, after which he worked Oregon and Washington, returned to the Midwest for appearances in Minnesota, Wisconsin, Chicago, and Michigan. In late October, he campaigned intensively in Pennsylvania and New Jersey, made a foray into Connecticut, and wound up with several days in New York. In all, he covered some ten thousand miles. It was an exhausting trip, but except in New York, it was generally below expectations in crowd turnout and enthusiasm. He had visited many of the same cities earlier in the year; this time around, fewer customers were putting down their money to hear him. In Los Angeles, he attracted 19,000 to Gilmore Stadium—quite a respectable figure—but he had 31,000 the previous May. In Bakersfield, only 372 paid to hear him in a baseball park which seated 3,000. In Minneapolis, he drew only 2,500 to the armory, compared to 8,000 on a cold night the previous winter.[52]

Part of the difficulty may have been that Wallace's novelty appeal had worn off; he had been campaigning since January and was hardly a fresh face. The polling evidence suggests that he had also suffered a gradual erosion of support. By the third week of October, the Gallup poll credited him with only 4 percent of the popular vote; he had 5 percent in August, 6 percent in June, 7 percent the previous January.[53]

Writing from California on October 7, the *New York Post*'s James A. Wechsler attributed the chief causes of Wallace's West Coast slump to "the conspicuous role of left-wingers in the third party, widespread liberal and labor support for the Marshall Plan, and entrance of Progressive party Congressional candidates against liberal Democrats—a policy that was belatedly modified. It was highly uncertain whether his last-ditch journey had changed the picture. Present opinion now is that he would receive between

300,000 and 400,000 California votes in contrast with springtime hopes of 800,000." (In the end Wallace got 190,000.)

At times, Wallace indicated that he knew that the political tides had turned against him. He was occasionally bitter, denouncing the "misleaders of labor" who would not join his crusade.[54] But he also could appear sad and bewildered. At a small luncheon in St. Louis, the chairman had remarked that so many former Wallace supporters were no longer present. Wallace took up the theme. "I can't help feeling that their chief governing motive is that they hate Henry Wallace," he remarked. "I don't know why they hate me. I'm still holding the door open for them. I used to say they'd come along after Truman was nominated. But they didn't come flocking to us the way I hoped. They've made a lot of extreme statements. I just ask now that they not make statements so extreme that it will be impossible for us to get together after the election." [55]

There was always New York, however, to restore Wallace's spirits. There the crowds still poured out to greet him; 19,000 people filled Madison Square Garden on the evening of October 26 for a "Get Out the Vote" rally;[56] a few days later Wallace attracted large audiences at street rallies in Manhattan and Brooklyn. In Brooklyn, on October 31, he spoke to an estimated 100,000 people at sixteen meetings; at least 500,000 residents lined the route of his motorcade.[57] It was an extraordinary expression of both curiosity and support, which found some reflection in the voting figures two days later.

Wallace's Madison Square Garden speech was a curious paean to victory—not to electoral victory but to equally remarkable accomplishments in foreign and domestic affairs. As a consequence of the Progressive party campaign, Wallace announced, "We have stopped the cold war in its tracks. We have delayed its progress. We have thrown it out of gear. . . . There shall be no war." This was by no means all. "Because of us," said Wallace, "the gallant patriots of Israel . . . have not been betrayed by Wall Street and its oil . . . the Bill of Rights was not murdered by those infamous agents of reaction, Mundt and Nixon . . . the big brass has halted in its attempt to saddle American youth with Universal Military Training . . . millions of Americans in the South, black Americans and white, stand on the threshold of a new and richer freedom." [58] Rarely have the fantasies of a doomed candidate been expressed with such abandon.

By mid-October, it was equally clear that the States' Rights campaign was running downhill. The announced Dixiecrat goal, it will be recalled, was to throw the election into the House of Representatives, in the hope that a coalition behind J. Strom Thurmond would somehow be created. In October, Governor Thurmond was still predicting that the southern states would give him 100 electoral votes[59]—a figure which seemed adequate to force the election into the House—but dispassionate observers had difficulty following his arithmetic. For Thurmond to win 100 electoral votes meant taking all but three or four of the southern states—clearly an impossible task.

Thurmond was the favorite in Alabama, Louisiana, Mississippi, and South Carolina, which had a combined electoral vote of 38. In each of those states, the Dixiecrats were in control of the Democratic party machinery and Thurmond and Wright had been named as the official party candidates in place of Truman and Barkley, who had to seek another place on the ballot. (In Alabama, because of a quirk in the state law, Truman and Barkley did not appear at all.) In other states of the South, however, the Dixiecrat candidates failed to win the Democratic designation and had to run on the States' Rights ticket, with considerably reduced chances of victory. The Georgia situation was a particularly bitter blow. In September, young Herman Talmadge won the primary for governor on a white supremacy–states' rights platform almost indistinguishable from that of the Birmingham conference. The Dixiecrats assumed that the Talmadge group would honor ideological affinities and give Thurmond the Democratic nomination, but it never happened. For his own reasons, Talmadge apparently preferred not to break with the national party.

The same reluctance was evident in many places in the South. "Boss" Ed Crump of Memphis spoke up for the Dixiecrats, but his favorite senator, Kenneth D. McKellar, supported the regular ticket. Such leaders as Senator Harry Byrd of Virginia, Senator Richard Russell of Georgia, Governor Ben Laney of Arkansas,

Governor Cherry of North Carolina did nothing to aid the Dixie-crats. Some, like Byrd and Russell, sat out the Presidential race. Others, like Governor Beauford Jester of Texas (and senatorial aspirant Lyndon Johnson) supported Truman.

A variety of reasons accounted for this coolness to the Dixie-crats. In many parts of the South, federal patronage cemented party loyalties; even if the Democrats were about to lose the White House, past favors were remembered. Senators and members of the House of Representatives had reason to fear the loss of committee seniority if they bolted the party—and everyone conceded that there was a reasonable chance that the Democrats would win con-trol of the Senate even if they lost the Presidency. In states such as Virginia and North Carolina, in some sections of which the Repub-licans were strong, Democratic candidates were reluctant to support the Dixiecrats lest the Republicans benefit from the diversion of votes. In other areas, liberal Democrats preferred to remain with the national party, even though they disagreed on civil rights, for the Dixiecrats by and large represented the more conservative ele-ment in the party.

In the end, the Dixiecrat candidates waged a forlorn campaign. They had little newspaper support (most of the prestigious south-ern papers, like the *Atlanta Constitution,* backed Truman) and the slenderest of campaign funds. Rumors occasionally appeared in the press that the oil interests, eager to have the tidelands reserves re-stored to the states, were generously endowing the Dixiecrat treas-ury. Thurmond denied it and he certainly ran a campaign as Spar-tan as that of Norman Thomas.[60] He had neither a campaign train nor a chartered DC3, as Barkley did, and only in Virginia and Texas did a press agent accompany him. Elsewhere, as he hopped about the South, his only companion was his wife. When they ar-rived in a new state, local supporters would drive the Thurmonds to their speaking dates.[61] He made one venture into the North, to address a luncheon of the Overseas Press Club in New York City early in October, slipping in and out of town so quietly that pickets were not alerted to his presence.

In New York Thurmond rested his case on what he declared to be "fundamental" constitutional principle. He had an apt illustra-tion of what states' rights should mean to New Yorkers. "If you people in New York want no segregation, then abolish it and do away with your Harlem. Personally, I think it would be a mistake, but if the people of New York want no segregation, that is their right under the Constitution and no federal law would seek to force segregation upon you. And by the same reasoning, no federal law should attempt to force the South to abandon segregation where we have it and know it as best for both races." He warned that once the precedent of federal intervention was allowed, the Congress would take over state elections, interfere with state crime prosecution, create a national police force which in turn would go "a long step toward a police state in America." [62] It was the same message that he was delivering throughout the South.

On the whole, it was a solemn campaign for Thurmond, but there was one memorable—if inadvertent—light moment. Late in July, Thurmond had sent a form letter to William H. Hastie, governor of the Virgin Islands, expressing regret that they had never met and stating, "It is my earnest hope that, during my term of office, you and your family will honor South Carolina with a visit to Columbia and be our guests at the Mansion." Hastie declined with thanks and invited Thurmond and family to visit the Virgin Islands "and be our guests at Government House." It was only after the two letters were published by Ted Poston in the *New York Post* that Governor Thurmond realized that Governor Hastie was a Negro. Thurmond's reaction was somewhat less than gracious: "I would not have written him if I knew he was a Negro. Of course, it would have been ridiculous to have invited him." [63]

A familiar figure from the past, Socialist leader Norman Thomas, received a surprising amount of attention before the campaign was over. In 1948, Thomas, then sixty-three, was conducting his sixth (and last) campaign for the Presidency. He had made his best showing in 1932, when he polled 884,000 votes. Ever since, his following had dwindled and in 1944 his vote had been a mere 79,000. As he often wryly remarked, the New Deal had stolen his thunder—and much of his platform; even Thomas' eloquence could not compete against the magic of Roosevelt. In 1948, however, the minuscule Socialist party enjoyed a brief sputter of revival. The lack of enthusiasm for Truman among the non-Communist left, their abhorrence of Wallace because of his liaison with the Communists, plus the certainty of Dewey's victory, led to a renewed interest in the quadrennial Socialist candidate. Old admirers of Thomas could indulge their affection and nostalgia without worrying unduly about "wasting" their vote in a futile protest.

Wherever he went, Thomas was heard with respectful attention; he had long since become one of the most popular as well as durable figures on the political scene. The *New York Times* characterized him as "this sane, logical, humanitarian gentleman, this ex-preacher honestly trying to apply New Testament ethics . . ." [64] The *Saturday Evening Post* suggested that "Our advice to those who want to protest against the two major parties is to take either Norman Thomas or the Dixiecrats. Mr. Thomas is the outstanding personality of the campaign and a man of character and wit. . . . He is also vigorously anticommunist. . . . For those who are unhappy outside a lost cause, he would be our selection." [65]

The Denver *Post* hired Thomas to cover the three party conventions, improvising a syndicate of fourteen papers to carry his columns; in Philadelphia, Thomas occasionally stole the show from the performers he was supposed to be chronicling. Throughout the campaign, he addressed his largest meetings in years. Prominent non-Socialists like Max Lerner and Dorothy Thompson endorsed his candidacy, as did *The Progressive,* once the organ of the La Follettes. Euphoric Socialists began to talk of a vote of over 600,-000[66] and Thomas expressed the hope that his campaign would promote "an inevitable realignment of American politics," with the emergence of a mass, non-Communist party of the left.[67] Both hopes were to prove illusory.

In the final week of the campaign, Truman gathered his energies for a climactic oratorical assault on a public already inundated by speeches. Dewey stepped up his tempo a bit, but he maintained to the end the aloof, mildly inspirational tone with which he had begun.

On Saturday, October 23, Truman made a one-day tour of Pennsylvania. His major speech, at a CIO rally in Pittsburgh, included a new item in his routine: a long comic turn ridiculing Dewey's pretensions. "My opponent," said Truman, "has set himself up as some kind of doctor with a magic cure for all the ills of mankind." A little skit followed, with the patient, the American people, going to see the doctor for his quadrennial checkup; Truman read both roles.

"You been bothered much by issues lately?" asks the doctor. The patient allows that he has been concerned with a few—high prices, housing, education, social security. "That's too bad," says the doctor. "You shouldn't think about issues. What you need is my brand of soothing syrup—I call it 'unity.' " Then the doctor suggests that the patient does not look too well; the patient insists that he "never felt stronger, never had more money, and never had a brighter future." But the doctor proposes a major operation. Will it be serious? the patient wonders. "Not so very serious," says the doctor. "It will just mean taking out the complete works and putting in a Republican administration." The audience howled.

After his Pittsburgh speech, Truman returned to Washington for a day's rest. On Sunday evening, October 24, he left on his final campaign tour, with major speeches scheduled in Chicago, Cleveland, Boston, New York, St. Louis, and Independence. Dewey's "Victory Special" departed Albany on October 25 and followed Truman one day later in the Midwest, Boston and New York.

In Chicago, on October 25, the party organization and the unions turned out an enormous crowd for Truman, with 50,000 people marching in a parade from the Blackstone Hotel to the Chicago Stadium and perhaps another 500,000 lining the route. Brass bands, fireworks, roman candles, and aerial bombs added to the festivities. At the stadium, where 23,000 people had gathered,[68] Truman also seemed to be in a festive mood, but the speech he delivered, largely written by Noyes and Carr,[69] was his most intemperate of the campaign. It was a liberal version of McCarthyism, nearly two years before the term was coined, for its main theme was a strident warning that a Republican victory carried the threat of fascism. "The real danger to our democracy . . ." said Truman, "comes mainly from the powerful reactionary forces which are silently undermining our democratic institutions. . . . When a few men get control of the economy of a nation, they find a 'front man' to run the country for them." In Germany, "they put money and influence behind Adolf Hitler. We know the rest of the story. We also know that in Italy, in the 1920's, powerful Italian businessmen backed Mussolini, and that in the 1930's, Japanese financiers helped Tojo's military clique take over Japan." The *New York Times* accurately headlined the speech, "PRESIDENT LIKENS DEWEY TO HITLER AS FASCISTS' TOOL."

The day after the speech, the *Times'* James Reston explained Truman's amazing performance as a final appeal for the support of the racial and religious minorities in the cities. In 1948, three years after the end of the war, invoking the names of Hitler and Mussolini stirred up anxieties that were hardly dormant. Truman made his motive very clear when he inveighed against "a new outcropping of demagogues among us. Dangerous men, who are trying to win followers for their war on democracy, are attacking Catholics and Jews and Negroes and other minority races and religions." But there may have been another motive as well for Truman's invective—an effort to provoke Dewey to some injudicious outburst which Truman could then exploit. Such at least is the recollection of David Noyes, one of the two authors of the speech.[70]

Dewey, however, was not to be provoked. Truman's speech was the subject of long discussion on the Dewey train, heading toward Chicago. The Governor was greatly angered; his impulse was to make a vigorous rebuttal. He stayed up half the night rewriting his Chicago speech, but all his advisers counseled against any dramatic change in the tone of his campaign, fearing that it would be interpreted as a confession of weakness. Jim Hagerty took an informal poll of the press party and reported to Dewey that almost all the newsmen also advised against a slugging match with Truman.[71]

When he finally came to deliver his speech, in the same arena where Truman had spoken, Dewey limited his reply to two cautious paragraphs in which he deplored the fact that the Democratic candidates "have spread fantastic fears among our people. They are openly sneering at the ancient American ideal of a free and united people. They have attempted to promote antagonism and prejudice. They have scattered reckless abuse along the entire right of way from coast to coast and have now, I am sorry to say, reached a new low of mudslinging. I know that you regret as much as I do that this should have happened. This is the kind of campaign that I refuse to wage. . . ."

Truman did not revert to the theme of his Chicago speech, but he kept hitting out in all directions. In Cleveland, on the 26th, he charged that the Republicans had rigged the polls "to prevent a big vote on November 2 by convincing you that it makes no difference whether you vote or not." That same day, in South Bend, Indiana, and Sandusky, Ohio, he criticized the press, charging that 90 percent of the newspapers were against him. (*Editor and Publisher,* the trade weekly, reported a few days later that Dewey was supported by 65 percent of the dailies and Truman by 15 percent.[72])

In Boston, on the 27th, he managed in the course of one speech to link the Communists and the Republicans (arguing that the former wanted the latter to win) and to invoke in his behalf the memory of Alfred E. Smith, long a hero to the Boston Irish, whose defeat in the Presidential election of 1928 could partly be attributed to anti-Catholic prejudice. "There are some Republicans who have been trying to make you believe that your government is endangered by Communist infiltration," said Truman. "That is just a plain malicious lie. . . . All of this Republican talk about Communism . . . is in the same pattern with their appeals to religious prejudice against Al Smith in 1928. They are afraid to go before the American people on the merits of the policies they believe in. So they try to distract the people's attention with false issues. I want you to get this straight now. I hate communism." In Massachusetts, one of the few northern states Truman was given a chance of winning, this was an appealing argument.

He had enormous crowds in Boston (an estimated 250,000 during the late afternoon rush hour) as well as in the industrial cities of southeastern Massachusetts through which he made a motor tour. On the 28th and 29th, Truman brought his campaign to New York City; he made thirteen speeches during two days in Manhattan, Brooklyn, and Yonkers, just north of New York City. The crowds were large, but for some reason were friendlier and more demonstrative on the second day of his visit.[73]

In New York, the Democratic party had long since written off Truman; the only substantial activity in his behalf was done by the Liberal party, an organization of trade unionists and independents in large part financed by the International Ladies' Garment Workers' Union. It was the Liberal party, rather than the Democratic party, which rented Madison Square Garden for the traditional campaign windup on the 28th. "When we hired the Garden, we didn't think that Truman had a chance," Alex Rose, the veteran party strategist, has said, "but we thought we owed it to him." [74] Donald Dawson, who did the advance work for Truman's New York visit, was appreciative of the Liberals' efforts, but feared that they might not fill the Garden (which had been packed for Wallace's appearance the night before). The Liberals had sold large blocks of tickets to various trade unions, but this was no guarantee that their members would appear. Dawson had a contingency plan if the Garden seemed slow in filling up. An hour or so before the President arrived, Dawson was alerted that the hall was only 10 percent full. He rushed over and immediately ordered that the lights be extinguished in the topmost tier of seats. He then ordered that the doors be thrown open to the public; tickets would no longer be required. Not long afterward, the President's motorcade reached the Garden, followed by a large crowd on foot; they were all urged to enter the hall. In the end, Truman had an audience of 16,000, compared with Wallace's 19,000.[75]

In his Garden speech, Truman made an undisguised appeal to Jewish voters with his strongest statement on Israel—"It is my desire to help build in Palestine a strong, prosperous, free and independent democratic state. It must be large enough, free enough, and strong enough to make its people self-supporting and secure." His chronicle of events made him sound like a consistent Zionist, going back to 1945; and he pointed out that the United States had been the first country "to give full and complete recognition" to Israel the previous April. For the rest, the Garden speech was a repetition of his familiar themes, enlivened by the humor which had first appeared, in his set speeches, in Pittsburgh. He had occasion to complain to his physician, he said, that for the past two or three weeks "everywhere I go there's somebody following behind me. The White House physician told me not to worry. He said: 'You keep right on your way. There is one place where that fellow is not going to follow you—and that's in the White House.'" Truman referred several times to his persistent shadow: "He can follow me into Framingham, Mass., but he won't follow me in raising the minimum wage to at least seventy-five cents an hour. . . . He can follow me into Cleveland, but he won't follow me and broaden the coverage of our social security insurance laws . . ."

On his second day in New York, Truman went into the Negro ghetto of Harlem to deliver his only civil rights speech of the campaign. It was one of the oddities of the 1948 election that while civil rights significantly affected the outcome, Truman said very little about the issue. He clearly wanted to avoid further southern defections, while relying on the record—and the oratorical efforts of lesser candidates—to rally the Negro vote. The Harlem speech of October 29 was hardly one of Truman's major efforts; it was brief and largely consisted of a tribute to the work of the President's Committee on Civil Rights, whose historic report had been published just one year before. Truman reaffirmed his civil rights message of February 2 and declared that "Our determination to attain the goal of equal rights and equal opportunity must be resolute and unswerving." In 1948, this was regarded as adequate rhetorical recognition of Negro aspirations. The speech was written by Philleo Nash, an assistant to David K. Niles, the White House expert on minority affairs.[76]

After New York, Truman's train headed west to Missouri. On Saturday night, October 30, he appeared before an enthusiastic audience in St. Louis' Kiel Auditorium for his final campaign rally. It was perhaps his angriest performance of the campaign, largely delivered extemporaneously. "Of all the fake campaigns," Truman said, "this is tops so far as the Republican candidate is concerned. He has been following me and making speeches about home, mother, unity and efficiency. . . . He won't talk about the issues, but he did let his foot slip when he endorsed the Eightieth Congress."

Once again, he predicted his victory: "I have been all over the United States from one end to another, and when I started out the song was—well, you can't win—the Democrats can't win. Ninety percent of the press is against us, but that didn't discourage me one little bit. You know, I had four campaigns here in the great state of Missouri, and I never had a metropolitan paper for me that whole time. And I licked them every time!"

Meantime, the man who was following Truman around continued his dignified victory tour. Never once did Dewey betray anger. He still viewed the opposition's crass appeals with sorrow tinged with contempt, but his responses got a bit sharper as the campaign neared its close. In Cleveland, on the 27th, he declared that he and Governor Warren had "not been guilty of using our high responsibility to rip our country apart or to arouse fear and prejudices." He suggested that Democratic warnings of another Republican depression echoed "the worldwide Communist propaganda that America was heading from boom to bust." On the other hand, he was generous enough to say that the Cassandras "are not Communists. They are not even Communist sympathizers. . . . Perhaps, being in office, they are acting from the human urge to stay in office at all costs."

The following day, in Boston, Dewey derided Truman for stating "that the head of the Soviet Union was really 'good old Joe' and that the exposure of Communists in our government was just a 'red herring' . . ." Much of the Boston speech, however, was devoted to his welfare program—expanded social security benefits, increased minimum wages, an improved public health service to provide medical care for the poor.

On Saturday night, October 30, in his last major speech of the campaign in Madison Square Garden, Dewey delighted the crowd by ridiculing the opposition's tactics; it was the first time he allowed himself any extensive levity. "Tomorrow night is Halloween . . . I mention the date because since this campaign began, some people have been trying to give the impression that every night is Halloween. Grown men have been going around the country threatening: 'Vote our way or the goblins will get you!' . . . Members of Congress . . . are described as 'predatory animals.' Each has a 'mossback.' They do their dreadful work with 'meat axes, butcher knives and sabers,' and what do these monsters eat? Why, 'Red Herring,' of course."

For the rest, Dewey restated his campaign themes and soon lifted his rhetoric into the clouds. "We will wage the peace patiently and firmly, with intense labor and new devotion. . . . Tonight we are called, not to pride and boasting, but to humility. In this momentous time our country is called to renew its faith so that the world can begin to have hope again. . . ." He was cheered by an overflow audience; the Republicans had no difficulty filling the Garden. Elsewhere during the final week, Dewey had drawn impressive crowds in Chicago and Boston, though Truman seemed to have the edge in numbers.

As always, both candidates had ended their campaigns with predictions of victory. Truman's shrill insistence could be charitably attributed to exhaustion: he had put on an amazing show, traveling 21,928 miles and delivering 275 speeches.[77] Even retrospectively, few members of his entourage have been willing to say that they thought he would win. Senator McGrath, whose post as national chairman compelled him to issue optimistic forecasts, said years later that he became confident of victory only in the latter part of October, because of the tremendous crowds which Truman was attracting.[78] But such a sense of confidence was unusual. More typically, Clark Clifford had the impression that Truman was picking up strength in the final weeks—and that he might have a chance of winning if the campaign could last a fortnight longer.[79]

The polls showed a narrowing of the gap, but still gave Dewey a long lead. On the eve of the election, Gallup credited Dewey with 49.5 percent of the vote to 44.5 percent for Truman; the Crossley poll gave Dewey 49.9 percent and Truman 44.8 (the remainder going to Thurmond and Wallace).[80] Roper, it will be recalled, had announced on September 9 that he had stopped polling, because of the certainty of Dewey's victory. Journalistic impressions were in line with the polls. *Newsweek* periodically questioned fifty of the country's leading political reporters and found that all of them predicted Dewey's election. The final *New York Times* survey, published on October 31 and based on reports of correspondents in 48 states, credited Dewey with 345 electoral votes to 105 for Truman and 38 for Thurmond. Dewey was expected to carry 29 states; Truman, 11; Thurmond, 4. Four states with 44 electoral votes were regarded as doubtful. The Senate outcome was seen as close, but the *Times* predicted that the Republicans would keep control of the House of Representatives.

On election day, Dewey awoke at 9:30 A.M. in his suite in New York's Roosevelt Hotel, had breakfast with Mrs. Dewey, and spent a leisurely morning. Around noon, to the accompaniment of police sirens and crowd cheers, his limousine drew up before a school building on East 51st Street where the Deweys were to vote. Office workers in a nearby skyscraper displayed signs reading, "Good luck, Mr. President." The demands of cameramen prolonged the voting process for half an hour; the Governor voted first, followed by his wife. He then linked his arm in hers and told the press, "Well, I know of two votes we got anyway." They returned to their car, drove north to Madison Avenue and 55th Street, where they unexpectedly got out to walk half a mile to their hotel. Followed by policemen and a small crowd, the Deweys stepped smartly down the avenue, the Governor doffing his hat to startled pedestrians and cabdrivers who yelled, "Good luck, Mr. Dewey."

After a light lunch, the Governor read the papers and chatted with staff members. That evening, as he had on the eve of every election in which he had run, Dewey dined at the home of his friend Roger Straus; his wife, two sons and his mother, who had arrived from Owosso, accompanied him. As with a ceremonial state function, the menu was released to the press: consommé, roast duck, cauliflower, peas, fried apples, deep dish blueberry pie, coffee and milk.

While still at the Strauses', Dewey was surprised at the returns from the first New Hampshire towns to report: he was not doing as well as a Republican candidate might expect. Back at his hotel suite, with his family, Elliott Bell and Paul Lockwood at his side, Dewey sat with a scratch pad listening to the returns and reading wire service bulletins. Jim Hagerty told the press, "We may be out of the trenches by midnight," but long before that it was apparent that Dewey was in trouble. He was not pulling enough votes in the populous eastern states that came in first. In the New York returns, Hagerty always watched the upstate cities of Syracuse and Rome; Dewey was carrying them, but his margin was too slender for comfort. Not until after 1 A.M. was it certain that Dewey would take his home state, but by a margin of only about 60,000. In the Dewey suite, the atmosphere was tense and somber; the shock inhibited any memorable comments.

Down in the mezzanine ballroom, where campaign workers had

gathered to follow the returns, swallow whiskey and cheer the victory, the festive air had dimmed by midnight. Herbert Brownell appeared at 11:30 P.M. and again at 1:45 A.M., both times claiming victory, but by the latter hour the room was less than half full and it was difficult to raise a cheer. An hour or two later, it was apparent that the election hung on the returns from Ohio, Illinois, and California. At 4:20, after conferring with Dewey, Hagerty told reporters, "We're in there fighting. The returns are still coming in but it looks as if we won't know definitely until midmorning." At 4:55, he said, "We are not making any predictions or claims." Sometime after dawn, with the outcome still in doubt, the Governor went to bed.[81]

Out in Independence, the Trumans voted at 10 A.M. in the town's Memorial Hall. To accommodate photographers, the President twice went through the ritual of marking and folding his ballot; all three Trumans then posed for a family picture. "It can't be anything but a victory," the President announced, but he later told reporters that he doubted that he would sit up for the returns. "I think I'll go to bed. I don't expect final results until tomorrow," he said.[82]

At lunchtime he appeared at the Rockwood Country Club to attend a party given by the mayor of Independence, Roger T. Sermon. The guests were some thirty old friends, whom Truman regaled with reminiscences of his political career in Missouri. Later that afternoon he drove with two Secret Service men to the Elms Hotel in Excelsior Springs, some thirty miles from Kansas City. He had a Turkish bath, ate a sandwich and a glass of milk, and went to bed early in the evening. At midnight, he recalls in his memoirs, he woke up and listened to radio commentator H. V. Kaltenborn, who reported that Truman was 1,200,000 votes ahead but destined to lose. He went back to sleep. He was awake again at 4 A.M., at which point Kaltenborn had Truman 2,000,000 votes ahead but still a likely loser. (Several weeks later, Truman was to impersonate Kaltenborn's staccato commentary in an hilarious speech before the Electoral College dinner.) By 6 A.M., suspecting that Kaltenborn was wrong, Truman had motored to the Muehlebach Hotel in Kansas City and went up to the eleventh floor penthouse where his staff was installed.[83] All night, newsmen had wondered where he had disappeared, but he was on hand, freshly barbered and turned out in a natty blue suit, when Dewey's concession came.[84]

In New York, Dewey had awakened at 10:30 A.M. to discover that Truman had taken Ohio as well as Illinois and California. He conferred with his aides, and at 11:14 A.M.—four minutes after McGrath had issued a victory statement—he had a telegram on the wires to Truman: "My heartiest congratulations to you on your election and every good wish for a successful administration. I urge all Americans to unite behind you in support of every effort to keep our nation strong and free and establish peace in the world."

At 1 P.M., Dewey met the press. He looked weary, but he managed an occasional smile and his voice had lost none of its resonance. "Anything I can tell anybody here that they don't already know?" he asked.

"What happened, Governor?"

"I was just as surprised as you are," he said, "and I gather that is shared by everybody in the room, as I read your stories before the election." He did not believe that there had been any error of strategy or tactics—"We waged a clean and constructive campaign and I have no regrets whatsoever." Further postmortems would have to await a closer study of the election returns. Would he consider running a third time? "No," said Dewey. And a moment later, "It has been grand fun, boys and girls. I enjoyed it immensely." [85]

He was dignified and self-possessed to the end. That post-election press conference was perhaps Dewey's finest hour.

## CHAPTER 11

# What Happened

On the evening of the day after the election, Truman attended a victory celebration in the courthouse square at Independence, where some 40,000 people gathered on a few hours' notice. Thanking the crowd, Truman announced that "Protocol goes out the window when I am in Independence. I am a citizen of this town and a taxpayer and I want to be treated just like the rest of the taxpayers . . ." The next day he set out on his "Victory Special" to return to Washington. When the train reached Union Station in St. Louis, the waiting crowds pushed aside police barriers and scrambled over the tracks. Truman delighted his admirers by holding aloft the previous day's early edition of the Chicago *Tribune,* with the memorable headline "DEWEY DEFEATS TRUMAN." The President also made a little speech. "The reason I am so happy," he said, "is because my home state stood by me so well. You must continue to stand by me, because I have got the biggest job in the world now." The next day, when he reached Washington, he was greeted by an estimated 750,000 people massed along the route from the railway station to the White House. Bands blared, schoolchildren cheered, confetti spiraled through the air, fire trucks made triumphal arches with their ladders, the parade passing underneath. Few wartime heroes have received a more ardent welcome.[1]

For the journalists and the pollsters, the shock of the election lingered after the disbelief had worn off. Some adopted a bantering tone to cover their embarrassment; thus, the Alsop brothers: "There is only one question on which professional politicians, polltakers, political reporters and other wiseacres and prognosticators can any longer speak with much authority. That is how they want their crow cooked. These particular reporters prefer their crow fricasseed." [2] The pollsters were even more dismayed. On every side, they were ridiculed and abused, an inevitable development given the omniscience to which they had laid claim. In his first post-election column, Elmo Roper sounded completely deflated: "I could not have been more wrong. The thing that bothers me most is that at this moment I don't know why I was wrong." He promised to find out.[3] A few newspapers canceled their subscriptions to the Gallup Poll. Many people recalled how the *Literary Digest* had gone out of business after the 1936 election, when its celebrated poll had predicted Alfred M. Landon's victory, only to have Franklin D. Roosevelt carry every state in the union but Maine and Vermont. The *New York Times* asked Wilfred J. Funk, the last editor of the *Literary Digest,* for a comment on the current plight of the pollsters. "I do not want to seem to be malicious," said Funk, "but I can't help but get a good chuckle out of this." [4]

The postmortems began the day after the election and continued for years afterward. The figures told a paradoxical story: Truman had won by a decisive majority and yet the election had been close. In popular votes, the President had polled 24,179,345 to Dewey's 21,991,291—a plurality of 2,188,054. In electoral votes, the score was Truman, 303; Dewey, 189; Thurmond, 39. The minority candidates had done poorly, with Wallace polling a mere 1,157,326 votes; Thurmond, 1,176,125; Norman Thomas, 139,572; and all the other fringe parties, including the Prohibition party, 150,167. The Wallace and Thurmond candidacies, however, had attracted enough Democratic votes to deny Truman an absolute majority; the final tally showed him with 49.6 percent of the popular vote to Dewey's 45.1 percent. The total vote had been low, with only 51.2 percent of the electorate going to the polls.

A plurality of over 2,000,000 votes was substantial, but Truman's lead in three states was so slender that the outcome might easily have been reversed in the Electoral College. Truman carried Ohio by only 7,107 votes, California by 17,865, Illinois by 33,-612; his total plurality in the three states came to 58,584 votes. The arithmetic irony was clear: a swing to Dewey of less than 30,-000 votes, appropriately distributed in the three states, would have given him an additional 78 electoral votes and the Presidency; the electoral vote would then have been 267 for Dewey to 225 for Truman and 39 for Thurmond. A switch of any two of these three states to Dewey (Ohio and California each had 25 electoral votes and Illinois 28) would have left Truman with the lead in the Electoral College but without the majority of 266 necessary to win, thereby throwing the election into the House of Representatives. All of which explained, of course, why Dewey waited until Wednesday morning before conceding.

There were other paradoxes. Truman had won despite the loss of four of the largest industrial states—New York (47 electoral votes), Pennsylvania (35), Michigan (19), New Jersey (16), all of which (with the exception of Michigan in 1940) had been carried by Roosevelt in the two preceding Presidential elections. On the other hand, Truman won three Midwest states—Iowa, Ohio, and Wisconsin—in which the farm vote was important and which Roosevelt had lost to Dewey in 1944.

Equally surprising was the impact of the Wallaceite and Dixiecrat defections. Truman was hurt, but not as badly as anticipated. His loss in the South was limited to the four states in which the Dixiecrats took over the Democratic party label—Alabama, Louisiana, Mississippi and South Carolina—whose electoral vote totaled 38. (Thurmond's 39th electoral vote came from a Democratic elector in Tennessee who could not abide Truman.) Wallace was responsible for Truman's defeat in three states—New York, Maryland and Michigan; in New York, for example, Wallace polled 509,559 votes—nearly half his national total—and Dewey won the state by 60,959. On the other hand, Wallace's vote in California—190,381—was far short of expectations and he was not on the ballot in Illinois. Had Wallace done just a trifle better in California and had he not been kept off the ballot in Illinois, Truman would have lost both states and the election of the President would have been decided by the House of Representatives. The Constitution provides that when the House elects a President, during January of the following year, each state delegation has but one vote; and the winning candidate must win a majority—which would have been 25 votes in 1948. One can assume that each state delegation would vote along party lines. On that assumption, Truman would have won, for the Democrats controlled 25 state delegations after the 1948 election; the Republicans had 20; three were evenly split.

As things turned out, Truman's winning coalition of states bore a remarkable resemblance to the design sketched by Clark Clifford in his memorandum of November 1947. The President took every state in the West but Oregon, won seven of the eleven states of the old Confederacy, the four border states of Kentucky, Oklahoma, Missouri, and West Virginia, and five states in the Midwest—Illinois, Iowa, Minnesota, Ohio, and Wisconsin; his only victories in the Northeast were in Massachusetts and Rhode Island.

Not only had the experts failed to anticipate the specific design of Truman's victory, but neither the pollsters nor the journalists foresaw that Truman would poll over 2,000,000 more votes than Dewey. The New York *Star* had the rare distinction of being able to boast that two of its writers, columnists Jennings Perry and Gerald Johnson, had predicted that the election would be close.[5] In September, Robert Bendiner had also published an article in *The Nation* entitled "Don't Count Truman Out." [6] It was largely a review of a book by Louis Bean, *How to Predict Elections,* which described the rise and fall of the Democratic and Republican electoral "tides," over long spans of years, and argued that the Republican tide had begun to ebb by 1947. Bean foresaw the possibility of Truman's victory, but did not predict it.

How had almost all the experts been so wrong? As regards the journalists, the *New York Times* provided some instructive answers after querying the forty-eight correspondents who had provided the newspaper's state-by-state survey on the Sunday preceding the election. The correspondents reported that in taking their soundings, they had talked with local political leaders, checked with their colleagues, interviewed some rank-and-file voters and, of course, studied the polls, both local and national. An inordinate amount of reliance had been placed on the polls, far more than on "grass roots" reporting. One correspondent confessed: "I was too gutless to put stock in my own personal hunch, based on nothing better than tours of the area, chats with businessmen, union men, miners, ranchers, farmers, political leaders." He felt that he could not "pin down" his hunch, so he followed the trend indicated in the polls. Local political leaders also relied heavily on the polls in assessing the situation in their areas; the consequence was that when a reporter interviewed a politician, he often only picked up an echo of a poll which he had already read.[7]

Newsmen traveling on the campaign trains were at an inevitable disadvantage in reporting the sentiments of the voters, for they lingered so briefly in a town that they had little opportunity to talk either to the voters or the local politicians. They were meticulous, as we have seen, in reporting crowd turnout and in describing the demeanor and attitude of the crowds, but they were usually unwilling to draw conclusions which hindsight showed to be obvious. Thus the great throngs which Truman attracted in the last two weeks of the campaign led almost no one to hazard the guess that he might just conceivably win; the tendency remained to attribute the crowds to idle curiosity or to Truman's "entertainment value" rather than to partisan zeal. The journalists were unwilling to credit the reality of what they saw and heard, so firmly had they accepted the assumption of Dewey's victory. In large part, this was a result of the polls; it was also a consequence of the political diagram of the campaign, with the Dixiecrat and Progressive party breakaways apparently making it impossible for Truman to win a majority in the Electoral College. If the electoral vote were the only error in prediction, it would have been understandable (the outcome in the Electoral College, after all, was narrowly decided). The more grievous error was the complete misreading of the popular vote.

The press had clearly been led astray by the myth of Dewey's invincibility. In a letter to his own paper, the *New York Times'* James Reston wrote: "There were certain factors in this election that were known (and discounted) by almost every political reporter. We knew about the tradition that a defeated candidate had never been nominated and elected after his defeat. We knew that the national income was running at a rate of $210 billions a year, that over 61,000,000 persons were employed at unprecedentedly high wages, and that the people had seldom if ever turned against the administration in power at such a time. . . . In a way our failure was not unlike Mr. Dewey's: we overestimated the tangibles and underestimated the intangibles . . . just as he was too isolated with other politicians, so we were too isolated with other reporters; and we, too, were far too impressed by the tidy statistics of the polls." [8]

*Time*'s judgment on its colleagues was even harsher: "The press was morally guilty on several counts. It was guilty of pride: it had assumed that it knew all the important facts—without sufficiently checking them. It was guilty of laziness and wishful thinking: it had failed to do its own doorbell-ringing and bush-beating; it had delegated its journalist's job to the pollsters." [9]

Everybody's mistakes, in the end, could be attributed to the polls. Eight days after the election, the Social Science Research Council set up a committee of academic experts to analyze what had gone wrong. The Gallup, Roper and Crossley organizations all cooperated in the investigation, making available both their files and their personnel. On December 27, 1948, the committee issued a detailed report and subsequently published the staff studies on which it was based.[10]

The pollsters, the committee concluded, had made many errors. All three national polls had not been alive to the possibility of a decisive swing to Truman in the last two weeks of the campaign. Gallup and Crossley stopped polling too early. Gallup's final prediction, published the day before the election, was actually based on two national samples gathered during mid-October. Crossley's final forecast was derived from a combination of state surveys taken around mid-August, mid-September and mid-October. Roper's final estimate used data he collected in August, which provided the basis for his September 9 column in which he predicted Dewey's victory and announced he was no longer going to publish periodic surveys. (Roper, however, did take a poll in the final week of the campaign, which he did not publish. It showed a slight upswing for Truman, but Dewey was still far in the lead.)

The Gallup and Crossley organizations obviously assumed that the final stages of the campaign would have no significant impact on the preference of voters. As he indicated in his September column, Roper believed that the entire campaign was likely to be irrelevant, given Dewey's enormous lead (44.2 percent to Truman's 31.4 percent). The absurdity of these assumptions was proven when Gallup and Roper conducted post-election surveys. Respondents were asked if they had voted, who they had voted for, and when they had made their decisions. One out of every seven voters claimed to have made up his mind within the last fortnight of the campaign; *three-quarters of these delayed decisions favored Truman.* Other data corroborated these findings. A post-election poll conducted by the Survey Research Center of the University of Michigan[11] reported that 14 percent of the Truman voters recalled making up their minds in the two weeks prior to the election; 3 percent decided on election day. The figures for Dewey voters were 3 and 2 percent, respectively. "Even if one makes allowance for errors in such reports," said the Social Science Research Council analysis, "one must conclude that failure to detect and measure changes of mind about voting during the closing days of the campaign account for a considerable part of the total error of the prediction." [12]

Some of the voters who made up their minds toward the end of the campaign had previously been undecided; others switched candidates. The Michigan survey showed that, on balance, the last-minute vote changes favored Truman. Thus, of the voters who said they were for Dewey in October, 14 percent switched to Truman and 13 percent did not vote. Of the Truman supporters in October, more failed to vote—25 percent—but only 5 percent switched to Dewey. Thus Truman benefited; as a report on the Michigan survey pointed out, "To lose a vote because of non-voting is only half as penalizing as to lose a vote through its going to one's opponent." [13]

Gallup, Crossley, and Roper made equally grievous errors in handling the undecided vote. Voters who would express no choice, but said they planned to vote, were nearly twice as numerous in 1948 as in 1944; in the Gallup figures, they accounted for 15 percent of the total. The pollsters either disregarded the undecided, on the grounds that they were unlikely to vote, or divided them among the candidates in the same proportions as the decided voters. In past elections going back to 1936, such simple solutions had created no embarrassing distortions, because of Roosevelt's substantial lead, but in 1948 not only did the undecided bulk large, but over half of them voted—and they voted for Truman in the ratio of about two to one, according to the post-election surveys.

The pollsters also failed accurately to gauge intent to vote. "The error in predicting the actual vote from expressed intention to vote was undoubtedly an important, although not precisely measurable, part of the over-all error of the forecast," the SSRC report stated. "The prediction of human behavior from an expression of intent is, in the present state of knowledge, and particularly with the actual methods used, a hazardous venture. This is a central problem for research, which has been largely ignored in pre-election poll predictions." [14]

The polls' difficulties were further compounded by errors in sampling and interviewing techniques, which resulted in too few interviews with people of grade school education. The Democratic vote thus tended to be underestimated. Finally, the polls added to their own problems by an exuberant desire to make flat predictions, not distracting the reader with qualifications or "technicalities." The reader was not taken behind the scenes and shown how the forecast was put together. Instead of merely trying to indicate the state of public opinion at some particular point of time and within stated margins of error, the polls insisted on picking the winner. The polls had made many of the same errors in the three previous Presidential elections, but they did not result in the wrong choice of the winner, given Roosevelt's large lead over his opponents. And, in the past, luck had enabled some of the pollsters' errors to cancel each other out. For example, underestimation of the northern Democratic vote had been compensated for by overrepresentation of the South, which had been solidly Democratic until 1948. After 1948 the poll-takers became a more modest and chastened lot, and their techniques improved considerably.

Dissecting the errors of the polls did not demonstrate, however, how Truman had managed to assemble his plurality out of the diverse elements in the electorate that have to coalesce to elect any President. Where had the voters come from?

They came from the same sources that F.D.R. had tapped. On an electoral-vote basis, as previously mentioned, Truman did not recreate the old Roosevelt coalition, for he lost New York, Pennsylvania, New Jersey, and Michigan as well as four states in the previously Solid South. When the constituents of the popular vote are analyzed, however, it is apparent that Truman retained the basic elements of the old Roosevelt coalition. That is to say, he held most of the South; he ran well in the urban North though not as well as Roosevelt; he successfully appealed to the conservation-minded West, where he won more states than Roosevelt had in 1940 and 1944; and he also had considerable success in the Mid-west farm belt, where Roosevelt's support had begun to erode in 1940.

Throughout the campaign, it had been widely assumed that the Roosevelt coalition had been shattered, largely because of expected defections in the South to the Dixiecrats and in the metropolitan centers of the North and West to the Wallaceites. Such defections did of course occur, but, as we have seen, they were marginal, in terms of both the popular and electoral votes. Samuel Lubell, in his brilliant 1952 volume, *The Future of American Politics,* persuasively argued that the States' Rights and Progressive campaigns actually strengthened Truman. While they siphoned off some votes, they simultaneously solidified support for Truman among certain groups of traditionally Democratic voters, who had either defected in 1944 or were likely to defect in 1948. Thus, Henry Wallace's campaign took the Communist curse off Truman. With the Wallace movement being openly supported (as well as covertly manipulated) by the Communists, and with Truman denouncing him for the liaison, the President was much less vulnerable than he might otherwise have been to charges of being "soft" on communism. His strength went up among Catholic voters.

Lubell provided considerable data to support this contention. His research method was to collate the county returns in successive Presidential elections, determine which geographic areas typified the shifting voting patterns of various economic or ethnic groups, and then go out and talk to the voters to determine why they had voted as they had; it was a new technique that combined scientific opinion-sampling with journalistic interrogation.

In Boston, for example, Lubell found that the heavily Irish Catholic wards voted more overwhelmingly for Truman than they had for any Democratic Presidential candidate since Al Smith, in 1928. In Massachusetts, to be sure, a birth-control amendment was on the ballot and there were other referendum proposals which the unions opposed, all of which brought out a heavy Catholic vote, but had there been a measure of Catholic hostility to Truman on the Communist issue, Dewey might have been the beneficiary of some normally Democratic votes. (It will be recalled that Truman, in his Boston speech late in the campaign, had emphasized his anti-Communist credentials.) Moreover, Lubell described the same pattern elsewhere in the country. St. Paul, Minnesota, which had a large Catholic population, gave Truman 10 percent more votes than Roosevelt received four years before, whereas in nearby Minneapolis, which was predominantly non-Catholic, Truman's vote was 6 percent under Roosevelt's. In East Pittsburgh, the local leadership of the United Electrical Workers put on a strong drive for Wallace. The result was a record Democratic Presidential vote from the predominantly Catholic union members; Truman polled nearly 25 percent more votes in East Pittsburgh than Roosevelt had in 1944.[15]

Similarly, the Dixiecrat rebellion against Truman's civil rights program assured him of the loyalty of the great bulk of Negro voters, many more of whom might otherwise have been attracted to Wallace or even to Dewey, under whose administration New York had been the first state to enact a law against discrimination in employment.[16] Wallace held some appeal for Negroes, but far less than his managers had expected. In the Negro ghettos of the North, Lubell found that Wallace did best in Harlem, where he polled 20,000 votes to 108,000 for Truman and 34,000 for Dewey.[17] Throughout the country, according to the Michigan post-election poll, nearly twice as many Negroes voted for Truman as for Dewey. The figures showed that 18 percent of the Negro respondents voted for Truman, 10 percent for Dewey, less than one-half of one percent for Wallace; the great bulk of Negroes did not vote at all (many said they could not, apparently because of southern election customs). The irony, of course, is that if the administration's civil rights plank had been adopted by the Democratic convention, the President's appeal to Negroes would have been considerably undercut.

As in the Roosevelt years, the less affluent citizens, the trade union members, the ethnic minorities remained steadfastly Democratic. Such was the common impression at the time, validated by what studies we have of the socioeconomic characteristics of the 1948 voter. The Michigan survey showed that 57 percent of the

Truman voters had annual incomes of under $3,000, as compared with 33 percent of the Dewey voters; 53 percent of the Truman voters came from working-class homes, as did only 21 percent of the Dewey voters; a mere 9 percent of the Truman voters, or their head of family, held managerial or professional positions, as against 37 percent of the Dewey voters; 39 percent of the Truman voters were members of trade-union families (the figure for Dewey voters was 11 percent). Lubell's researches led to similar findings, though he generally did not deal in percentage figures; so did the exhaustive study of the voting habits in 1948 of the citizens of Elmira, New York. "The higher the socioeconomic status, the more Republican the vote," said the Elmira study; "put crudely, richer people vote Republican more than poorer people." [18] Lubell also detected an interesting wrinkle in ethnic preferences: a marginal decline in the predominantly Democratic sentiments of Jewish voters, with some defecting to Wallace and others to Dewey. Lubell attributed the movement to the fact that Jews had been the most pro-Roosevelt sector of the electorate and hence were proportionately more disillusioned by Truman's performance.[19]

The rallying of the blue-collar vote and the ethnic minorities allowed Truman to maintain the normally Democratic hold on the cities, though declines occurred in most places. In the twelve biggest cities in the nation (New York, Chicago, Philadelphia, Pittsburgh, Detroit, Cleveland, Baltimore, St. Louis, Boston, Milwaukee, San Francisco, Los Angeles), Truman's plurality was one-third below that of Roosevelt in 1944, but his margin of victory was still substantial—1,443,000 votes—nearly three-quarters of his countrywide plurality.[20]

"Labor did it," Truman was quoted as saying the day after the election,[21] and many commentators attributed his victory, in large part, to the efforts of the unions to get their members to the polls. It was observed that in many states, such as Illinois, Minnesota, Michigan, Truman had run behind the state tickets, leading to the obvious—though unprovable—conclusion that the "coattail" effect had been reversed in this election; that is to say, that Truman had benefited from the greater popularity of lesser candidates. Whether that had in fact occurred, it was certainly reasonable to assume that the union drive had helped Truman simply by bringing out a larger

Democratic vote, even if the intended beneficiaries were liberal congressmen and senators.

A major surprise of the election, however, was Truman's showing in farm areas. His victory in Iowa was the great shocker; and it was apparent that he had done well in the farm country of Wisconsin, Ohio, Illinois, Minnesota. These facts were duly commented upon immediately after the election; after a while a theory developed that the farm vote had been the crucial element in Truman's victory. Professor Arthur Holcombe, for example, argued that "the losses to Dewey in the industrial states of the northeast would have cost Truman the election but for his extraordinary gains in the grain-growing and stock-raising states. His ability to recapture Wisconsin, Iowa, Colorado and Wyoming, which Dewey had carried in 1944, and to hold Minnesota and Washington, which had voted for Roosevelt at the earlier election, secured his victory. . . . The grain-growing and stock-raising interests . . . held the balance of power." [22] In a memorandum to Elliott V. Bell,[23] dated March 2, 1949, Gabriel Hauge argued that "The margin for the Truman victory came, not from labor, but from the turnabout of farm votes in the midwest, a fact which appears to be closely allied with the drop in corn prices before election." He pointed out that of the "eight leading corn states"—Illinois, Iowa, Indiana, Minnesota, Nebraska, Ohio, Wisconsin, and Missouri—Truman carried all but Indiana and Nebraska; in those two states, Dewey's plurality dropped sharply from 1944.

The theory that the farmer elected Truman attained a certain vogue, probably because of its ironical overtones: the Democratic leader loses strength in his city strongholds while suddenly blossoming forth as the farmer's friend. But the theory cannot be sustained merely by showing that certain farm or stock-growing states went to Truman. The relevant question is what segment of the electorate caused the state to shift—the farm areas, the small towns, the big cities, or perhaps some combination of these areas. Conclusive proof that a shift in the farm vote caused a state to go Democratic would be a demonstration that while the Democratic vote in the cities, normally the party's largest source of strength except in the South, remained stable or declined, a swing in the farm areas put the state in the Democratic column. A majority of farmers would not have had to vote Democratic, only a large enough number to tip the balance.

A detailed analysis prepared for this book by Victor A. Soland of Louis Harris & Associates proves that there was a significant shift in the farm vote to Truman, but that it by no means won him the election. The county returns were analyzed in twelve Midwest and Western states where the farm vote could have been significant. In each state the counties were grouped according to percentage of persons employed in agriculture, the spectrum being divided into segments of 10 percentage points each—less than 10 percent, 10 to 19.9 percent, and so on. For purposes of analysis, any county with more than 30 percent of the working population engaged in agriculture was regarded as a farm county, inasmuch as census data indicated that in such areas the number of people engaged in manufacturing was generally 10 percent or less. The remainder of the employed—people working in commerce and the service trades —could fairly be assumed to share the economic interests of their farm customers. Those counties with between 10 and 30 percent employed in agriculture contained small and medium-sized towns and were not especially dependent on farming. The counties with less than 10 percent employed in agriculture basically represented the cities. The division of the two-party vote, in 1944 and 1948, was then compared for each group of counties in each state studied. This made it possible to determine just where the vote-swing occurred and what its magnitude was.

Only in Wisconsin and in Iowa was the farm swing the crucial element in Truman's victory. In 1944, Dewey won Wisconsin with a plurality of 24,119 votes; in 1948, Truman's plurality was 56,351 votes. In the cities, Truman had a plurality of 61,581 votes —a decline of 14,347 from Roosevelt's plurality in 1944. In the small towns, on the other hand, the Republican plurality of 25,716 in 1944 was transformed into a Democratic plurality of 3,070 in 1948—a swing to the Democrats which negated their losses in the cities and wiped out much but not all of Dewey's 1944 plurality. Thus, if the remainder of the state had voted the way it had in 1944, Dewey would have won again with a small plurality. In the farm areas, however, Truman cut Dewey's 1944 plurality of 74,331 to 8,300. This swing gave Truman the state.

Similarly in Iowa. Had there been no Republican defections in the farm belt, Dewey would have won the state with a plurality of about half the 47,000 which he had in 1944, for Truman ran better than Roosevelt did in 1944 in both Iowa's cities and small towns. In addition, however, Dewey's 1944 plurality in the farm belt was cut by 52,030, which was more than enough to give the state to Truman. (Truman's statewide plurality was 28,362.) Moreover, even if Truman had not improved on Roosevelt's showing in the cities and small towns, the swing in the farm country would have been sufficient to bring him victory by a scant 4,639 votes.

In Ohio, Truman's performance in agricultural districts occasioned considerable comment, but it was not sufficient to win the state for him, even though his plurality was a mere 7,107 votes out of more than 2,800,000 cast. Truman had a plurality of 100,332 in the cities, a decline of 89,971 from Roosevelt's 1944 plurality. The farm areas showed a decline in the Republican plurality of 22,375 —far less than needed to compensate for the decline in the Democratic urban plurality and to overcome Dewey's statewide plurality of 11,530 in 1944. However, in the small towns the Republican plurality declined 85,233 from the 1944 figure—almost but not quite canceling out the decline in the Democratic city plurality. This development, together with the Republican losses in the farm areas, moved the state into the Truman column. The farmers alone did not do it. Had there not been defections from Dewey in the normally Republican small towns, Truman would have lost Ohio.

In Illinois the farm swing was not decisive, in view of Truman's small-town vote. In 1944, Roosevelt won Illinois with a plurality of 140,165; in 1948, Truman won by 33,612. Truman had an urban plurality of 169,883, a decline of 155,979 from 1944. If the Republican vote had remained stable elsewhere in the state, Truman would have lost. In the farm areas, however, the Republican plurality declined in 1948 by 20,433 votes—enough to have put Truman over. But the same phenomenon occurred in the small towns, where the Republican 1944 plurality declined by 28,993. Thus Truman was not dependent on the farm swing for his victory; it merely increased the size of his slender plurality. But there was one other crucial factor: Henry Wallace was not on the ballot in Illinois. Had his name appeared, there is no doubt that he would have attracted enough support to have wiped out Truman's plurality of 33,612. In New York State, after all, Wallace polled over 500,000 votes, and in California, 190,000.

In Minnesota, there was a substantial swing in the farm areas; it accounted for the largest proportion of the increase in the Democratic plurality from 62,448 in 1944 to 209,349 in 1948, but even without the farm swing Truman would have improved on Roosevelt's victory. In California, where the Democratic Presidential plurality dropped in every area, the farm vote had no effect on the outcome. Truman's plurality decreased less (1.2 percent) in agricultural than in other areas, but even if the decline had been as great as in the cities (7.1 percent), Truman would still have carried the state by a tiny margin.

While it was only in Wisconsin and in Iowa that the farm vote meant victory for Truman, his appeal to farmers throughout the Midwest was one of the remarkable features of the election and certainly swelled his popular vote. Lubell's interviews in Guthrie County, Iowa, showed that Truman's popularity basically derived from apprehensions that the Republicans would not continue the agricultural policies of the New Deal. The farmers had prospered under the Democrats and feared change under the Republicans; their very conservatism, Lubell pointed out, led them to discard their traditional Republican loyalties.[24]

One voter, a lifelong Republican, explained to Lubell that he was fearful of the great "house cleaning" which Dewey promised in Washington. "What would be swept out with the house cleaning?" he asked. "Price supports and other agricultural aids? If another depression comes, what will the farmer do?" Another citizen told Lubell, "I talked about voting for Dewey all summer, but when the time came I just couldn't do it. I remembered the depression and all the good things that had come to me under the Democrats." [25]

Truman's harangues in the farm country apparently had their effect, though it is impossible to tell which issue was most important—the shortage of grain storage bins, the doubts cast on the Republican commitment to the price-support system, the failure of Congress to ratify the International Wheat Agreement, the taxes which some Republicans sought to impose on agricultural cooperatives. The sharp decline in farm prices, as a consequence of bumper crops, doubtless added to the sense of anxiety. Corn, for example, fell from \$2.25 a bushel in July to \$1.26 a bushel at the end of October, well below the support level of \$1.53. The price drop, combined with the inability of many farmers to store the crop and get a government loan at the support level, lent reality to Truman's charge that the Eightieth Congress had betrayed the farmer. The consequence was apparent, among other places, in the corn country of northern Iowa, where Truman won 20 counties to Dewey's 7.

There may well have been other factors, of a less tangible nature, that contributed to Truman's victory. Clearly the Republicans suffered from excessive overconfidence and let most of the arguments go to Truman by default. Somewhat less clearly, depending on one's personal preferences, Truman was a more appealing candidate than Dewey. In the retrospective wave of admiration for Truman that followed his victory, his zest, combativeness, and informality were favorably contrasted with Dewey's somewhat prim dignity and aloofness; a temporary amnesia seemed to overtake the country in regard to those other qualities of Truman (such as his lack of dignity or seeming lack of competence) which had formerly brought him disparagement. What evidence we have suggests that the voters were more critical of Dewey than of Truman; the Michigan survey reported that Dewey's personal qualities came in for twice as much unfavorable comment as Truman's. "The criticism of Dewey made most frequently was that he had too high an opinion of his own abilities. 'Patronizing,' 'superior,' 'cold' were adjectives associated only with Dewey." [26] On the other hand, the study could not estimate what effect such personal evaluations had on the vote.

It became a commonplace to blame Dewey's defeat on overconfidence. Typically, Leverett Saltonstall, a Republican senator from Massachusetts, argued that overconfidence had "led the Republicans to put on a campaign of generalities rather than interesting the people in what a Republican administration could and would do for them if elected and, contrariwise, it led Republicans to fail to answer in sound, forceful speeches the charges of the Democrats concerning . . . the Eightieth Congress." [27]

Might Dewey have won if he had conducted a different kind of campaign? In an election as close as this one, it is impossible to answer in the negative. A campaign less devoted to high-minded platitudes, a campaign style less suggestive of the inevitability of victory, might have made enough of a difference to have swung the three states which in the end proved decisive. The more relevant question is whether Dewey could have bested Truman in the popular vote. It hardly seems likely, given the mood and the dominant political attitudes of the country and the impact of the Wallace and Dixiecrat campaigns. From the analysis thus far presented, one can plausibly conclude that the only way Dewey might have won the popular vote would have been to campaign on Truman's platform. In no other fashion could he have cut into the big-city vote which contained the bulk of Truman's plurality. No searching analysis of voter motivation is necessary to prove that Truman's supporters reaffirmed their loyalty to the New Deal and endorsed the more ambitious program of governmental intervention in the private sector which Truman offered. But Dewey could hardly have run as a New Deal candidate. Without committing himself to specifics, he did in fact endorse much of Truman's program, as in his Pittsburgh speech. For Dewey to have sought to outflank Truman on the left would have meant the repudiation of the Eightieth Congress and the denial of support for a host of conservative Republican candidates for the House and Senate. Even with the relaxed degree of party discipline prevailing in the United States, such a course would have been unthinkable.

After the election, some prominent Republicans—among them New York's Senator Irving Ives and Representative Jacob K. Javits—did attribute Dewey's defeat to the burdens imposed on him by the record of the Congress. Javits also argued that the party had been hurt by departing "from its origins as the party of the worker and producer, and as the party of reform." The right wing of the party had a different view of why Dewey had lost and how he might have won.[28] Immediately after the election, the Chicago *Tribune* editorialized: "For the third time, a Republican convention fell under vicious influences and nominated a 'me-too' candidate who conducted a 'me-too' campaign. For the third time the strategy failed. That is why Mr. Truman was elected and with him a Democratic House and Senate.

"After this experience, we may hope the Republicans have

learned their lesson. If the same forces control the next Republican convention the party is finished and the millions of patriotic men and women who have looked to it for leadership will have to look elsewhere." [29]

This became the dominant conservative diagnosis. Dewey was defeated because he offered a pale version of the New Deal; if he had conducted a vigorous campaign providing a clear-cut conservative alternative, he would have swept the country. In his postmortem, Senator Taft stated, "It was necessary in 1948 to run on the record of the Republican Congress," a record which he insisted would have been an asset to a candidate who championed it. Senator-elect Karl E. Mundt of South Dakota criticized the Republican failure "to focus attention on the mistakes of Yalta and Potsdam. Very little was made even of the Vinson-to-Moscow travesty. Americans apparently like both their candidates and their baseball players to be of the hard-hitting variety." [30]

Had Dewey assaulted Truman from the right, the result would unquestionably have been a livelier campaign, but he would probably have suffered a greater defeat. To have defended the domestic record of the Eightieth Congress (its foreign policy record was not basically controversial) would have involved a defense of tax legislation which favored the more affluent sector of the population, anti-inflation measures that were inadequate, the Taft-Hartley Act (to which the whole of the labor movement was hostile), failure to pass even the housing bill which bore Taft's name, and an equal lack of action in the fields of federal aid to education and health insurance. If Dewey had mounted such a campaign, he would have provided an even easier target for Truman and the latter's urban majorities would have been much larger. The country was in no mood for the policies of governmental restraint typified by the Hoover administration; that issue had been settled in 1936, when Alfred Landon, in anything but a "me-too" campaign, carried only Maine and Vermont. Nor does it seem likely that Dewey could have picked up much support had he emphasized Democratic failings at Yalta and Potsdam; by the autumn of 1948, Truman's foreign policy was consistently anti-Communist and the existence of the Progressive party, as already noted, tended to reinforce Truman's anti-Communist *bona fides*.

The one alteration in strategy which Dewey might have adopted, also suggested by Mundt among others, would have been a fuller discussion of farm issues. In this area, the Republican record was by no means as deplorable as Truman suggested and the Democrats were not without their own vulnerabilities. On the grain storage issue, for example, the Democrats had not raised any great cry in Congress when the Commodity Credit Corporation charter had been extended in June. Dewey might well have picked up some more votes in the Midwest had he made a determined effort to assure farmers that the Republicans favored the federal-aid policies instituted by the New Deal. But it is doubtful that Dewey could have denied Truman all his gains in the farm belt.

In long-range terms, Truman's success in holding together the old Roosevelt coalition proved that the Democratic party was truly the majority party in the country. Throughout the Roosevelt era, it had been possible for Republicans to attribute their long eclipse to the accidents of depression and the Second World War and to the astonishing personal popularity of F.D.R. It had been possible to hope that once Roosevelt had passed from the scene and once the country had reverted to a peacetime economy, the political pattern that prevailed prior to 1932 would reassert itself. The Republican victory in the congressional election of 1946, keyed to the slogan of "Had enough?", seemed to confirm that hypothesis. It seemed further confirmed by the fissiparous tendencies at work in the Democratic party in the early months of 1948.

Then came the victory of Harry Truman, a candidate whose prospects had seemed so dim that many of his party's leaders had sought to repudiate him just a few months before. If Truman could win, there could no longer be any doubt that a basic and irreversible alteration had occurred in the political loyalties of the American electorate (irreversibility being measured in quadrennia, not eternity). The New Deal revolution had passed beyond the stage of meaningful debate and the Republicans could not readily replace the Democrats as the majority party. As Walter Lippmann put it two days after the election, "Mr. Truman's own victory, the Democratic majorities in both houses of Congress, the Democratic victories in so many states, attest the enormous vitality of the Democratic party as Roosevelt led it and developed it from 1932 to 1944 . . . the party that Roosevelt formed has survived his death, and is without question the dominant force in American politics."[31]

The concept of majority and minority party does not imply that the minority never wins a national election. It implies, rather, that the majority party expresses the predominant political sentiment of the nation, that over a long span of years it wins more often than it loses. Only under extraordinary conditions does the minority party attain the Presidency. From 1896 to 1932, the Republican party was the majority party, winning the Presidency by decisive majorities at every election except in 1912 and 1916; Wilson's victory in 1912 occurred after Theodore Roosevelt split the Republicans and ran as a third-party candidate.

Lubell has argued persuasively that "two population currents" ultimately cracked the long Republican ascendancy: "Between 1910 and 1930 for the first time a majority of the American people came to live in cities. The second population shift might be described as the triumph of the birth rates of the poor and underprivileged over those of the rich and wellborn." The cities filled up with immigrants and displaced farmers whose offspring were numerous, whose conditions of life were bleak, and whose politics (and whose children's politics) were Democratic. "The human potential for a revolutionary political change had thus been brought together in our larger cities when the economic skies caved in," Lubell writes.[32] He points out that the urban shift to the Democrats actually began, in a small way, in 1928. In the country's twelve largest cities, the Republicans had a plurality of 1,638,000 votes in 1920; nearly 400,000 votes less four years later; by 1928 there was a Democratic plurality of 38,000, which rose to 1,910,000 in 1932 and reached its peak of 3,608,000 in 1936. By 1948, the Democrats had controlled the twelve largest cities through six Presidential elections.[33] There resided the key ingredient of its majority status, in terms of both popular and electoral votes. Those twelve cities were in states controlling 231 electoral votes; in most elections in the '30s and '40s, as Samuel J. Eldersveld demonstrated in a significant article in 1949, the pluralities in the twelve cities won the states for the Democrats. Without them, the Democrats would have lost the Presidency in 1940, 1944 and 1948.[34]

Truman not only perpetuated the old Roosevelt coalition but moved it several degrees to the left, both rhetorically and programmatically. As the Alsop brothers wrote soon after the election, "His campaign speeches were consistently more aggressive and more radical than any Franklin Delano Roosevelt ever uttered. At his hottest and angriest, Roosevelt never laid it into big business as Truman did. Nor did Roosevelt ever promise specific reforms, well beyond any currently popular with other politicians, as Truman did." [35] Indeed, the Truman program—especially such items as civil rights legislation, compulsory medical insurance, federal aid to education—constituted an agenda of unfinished business most of which was not completed until the Johnson administration. Some items have not yet been enacted, such as the repeal of the Taft-Hartley Act or the provision of medical insurance for all citizens, not merely the aged or the indigent.

The pale pink glow which the election seemed to cast over the country owed much to the Democratic successes in the congressional and gubernatorial contests. Not only did the Democrats win sizable majorities in the House (263 to 171) and Senate (54 to 42), but many liberals, and most of the candidates favored by labor, were elected. The CIO's Political Action Committee supported 215 House and 21 senatorial aspirants, of whom the winners totaled 144 and 17.[36] The AFL's Labor's League for Political Education could boast that 86 of its 105 congressional candidates had been elected and 14 of its 16 senatorial choices.[37] In most instances, of course, the two labor groups endorsed the same men.

The Democratic class of 1948 contained an abundance of attractive liberal talent. In Illinois, both Adlai Stevenson and Paul Douglas won instant celebrity in the national press because of the astonishing margins by which they defeated the Chicago *Tribune*'s candidates. Stevenson, a former delegate to the United Nations, won the governorship by a plurality of over 570,000. Douglas, whose only previous elected office was that of alderman in Chicago, was elected U.S. senator with a plurality of more than 400,000, defeating C. Wayland ("Curly") Brooks, one of the least prepossessing relics of the old isolationist bloc in the Midwest. In Minnesota, Hubert Humphrey, whose dazzling oratorical gifts had so impressed the Democratic convention in July, trounced the incumbent senator, Joseph Ball, by 729,494 to 485,801 votes. In Tennessee, Estes Kefauver won an easy election to the Senate over B. Carroll Reece, the former chairman of the Republican National Committee. Kefauver, with his coonskin cap and shambling, folksy manner, had already received a measure of national attention when he had won a difficult primary race against the candidate of the Crump machine. In Connecticut, Chester Bowles, the former price-control administrator, surprised everyone, possibly including himself, by getting elected governor by a mere 1,400 votes. Bowles was not to win another election, but his single, unexpected triumph laid the base for an energetic career in high appointive office. Another startling upset occurred in Michigan, where thirty-seven-year-old G. Mennen Williams, a little-known lawyer who had never held elective office, defeated the incumbent Republican, the flamboyant Kim Sigler, by a decisive 163,854 votes while Harry Truman lost the state by 35,147 votes.

All the ironies of the 1948 election were not to be apparent until a few years later. Despite the great liberal victory, Truman was able to win congressional acceptance for few of the major items in his domestic program. Before long, the old coalition of conservative Republicans and conservative southern Democrats reasserted itself, winning effective control of the Congress and becoming almost as obdurate as the "do-nothing" Eightieth Congress. By the time Truman's term was up, it was possible to speculate that more might have been accomplished had that switch of some 30,000 votes occurred in Ohio, Illinois, and California and had Dewey been elected. What would have been the likely consequences? There would certainly have been no change in the direction of American foreign policy, which continued to enjoy bipartisan support throughout the Truman years. Dewey would have been quite as inclined as Truman to respond with alacrity to the Communist invasion of South Korea in 1950, a response that was properly celebrated as one of Truman's finest hours. In domestic affairs, one can plausibly argue that Dewey might have won the enactment of more liberal measures than Truman did, assuming that Dewey confronted the same Congress (as indeed he would have, had he won in a photo finish).

The reasoning is simple: a Republican President, at least in the opening stages of his administration, could be far more persuasive with the Republican members of Congress. Dewey might well have thwarted a new Republican–Southern Democratic coalition, at least for a time, appealing for a chance to make a domestic record. Another coalition might have been created—between the congressional Republicans who were indulgent to Dewey's leadership and the bulk of the Democrats, who favored his program, which in many particulars was similar to Truman's.

This thesis is of course open to dispute, but what seems unarguable is that a Dewey victory would have spared the country the vast trauma of the McCarthy era. Senator McCarthy, it will be recalled, did not become a McCarthyite until his Wheeling, West Virginia, speech in February 1950, in which he claimed to have the names of a sizable number of Communists in the State Department. McCarthy's discovery of the Communist issue had been fortuitous. Richard Rovere, in his biography of the Senator, relates how he was casting about for a usable issue early in 1950; he was up for reelection in 1952 and he felt that he needed a new sales pitch to impress the voters. One acquaintance suggested the issue of Communist subversion, which had created abundant headlines ever since the Chambers and Bentley testimony in 1948. McCarthy enthusiastically agreed and soon found within himself a fabulous talent for distortion and demagogy.[38] By the 1952 campaign, he was filling the airwaves with denunciations of "twenty years of treason."

McCarthy's crusade could hardly have been launched had Dewey been elected President. The Senator would have lacked either the target or the impulse. He could not have blamed the sins of the prior Democratic administration on the Republicans in control of the executive department. Any raking up of the past would have been of purely historical interest. Moreover, with his own party in power, McCarthy would not have obtained the (often covert) support of other Republicans who were happy seeing him belabor the Democrats. McCarthy would have had to find another issue for his reelection campaign.

Truman's success in 1948 had another ironical consequence: the

Eisenhower boom in 1952. Many Republicans were not slow in appreciating the fact that the Democrats had solidified their position as the majority party. Truman's legislative initiatives could be frustrated, but clearly more voters preferred the Democrats to the Republicans when they got into the polling booth. To the moderate Republicans, at least, it became apparent that if they could not win in the favorable circumstances of 1948 with a politician of Dewey's ability, the best solution was to present a candidate who transcended party differences, a candidate who could make an effective nonpolitical appeal.

No search was required to find the man. World War II had produced two great American wartime heroes—General Dwight D. Eisenhower and General Douglas MacArthur. From the outset, MacArthur had been hopelessly compromised by involvement with right-wing Republicans; after his defeat in the Wisconsin primary of 1948, he lost what little appeal he had previously possessed to professional politicians. General Eisenhower, however, came through 1948 with his reputation intact. His popularity remained buoyant throughout the second Truman administration, during which he left his duties as president of Columbia University to organize the military machine of the newly created North Atlantic Treaty Organization. Long before the 1952 conventions, the prospect of Eisenhower's candidacy was as dazzling to liberal Republicans as it had been to the Democratic rebels who had sought to dump Truman in 1948. Eisenhower had everything—the glow of wartime military triumphs, a radiant and attractive personality, an identification with the magnanimity and military realism of America's postwar foreign policy, a total lack of identification with divisive domestic squabbles. "The chant of 'We like Ike' was more nearly a hymn of praise and entreaty to a demigod than a political war cry," Marquis Childs has written. "Eisenhower represented strength, triumph, unswerving confidence. Millions were happy to take him on faith, on his face, on his smile, on the image of American manhood, on the happy virtue of his family life." [39]

The alternative to Eisenhower, at the Republican convention, was Taft. He had the virtue of representing the true Republican faith and of being able to inspire the party zealots. The major case against him was that his appeal would be too narrowly partisan;

and, indeed, it is quite possible that Taft, had he been nominated, would have been defeated by Stevenson. Instead, Eisenhower won by a large plurality. The General put together a winning coalition by attracting two-thirds of the voters who considered themselves independents (they constituted sixteen percent of the electorate) and by cutting deeply into such traditional sources of Democratic strength as the families of union members and voters of German, Irish, and Polish descent. Eisenhower also ran especially well in the new suburban areas, he reasserted the Republican hold over the farm vote, and he won four southern states.[40] He repeated his massive victory in 1956. But these were clearly personal triumphs, which did not dislodge the Democrats' status as majority party. The Republicans only managed to win a narrow control of the Congress in 1952; thereafter, in the elections of 1954, 1956, and 1958, the Democrats won control. They remain the majority party to this day, with roughly a five to three ratio of registered voters.

A second consequence of Truman's victory, so far as the Republicans were concerned, was further to embitter the conservative wing of the party whose hero was Senator Taft. In the view of his admirers, Taft had been unfairly denied the nomination in every convention going back to 1940. When the liberal Dewey, against all expectations, managed to lose in 1948, the Republican right felt confirmed in its judgment, previously quoted from the Chicago *Tribune,* that a "me-too" candidate could not defeat the Democrats. The conviction gradually grew—eventually becoming almost an article of religious faith—that if the voters had been offered a clear-cut choice between an aggressive conservative and a liberal Democrat, the conservative would have won.

Eisenhower's two victories by no means eradicated this conservative dogma; it reemerged in full force after Nixon's close defeat by Kennedy in 1960. Shortly after that election, Senator Barry Goldwater declared, "We who are conservatives will stoutly maintain that 1960 was a repeat performance of 1944 and 1948, when we offered the voters insufficient choice with a me-too candidate." [41] Goldwater's admirers believed that there was truly a conservative majority in the country, which had long remained submerged because it had always been denied a Presidential candidate to rally around. In *The Winning Side: The Case for Goldwater Conserva-*

*tism,* published in 1963, Ralph de Toledano wrote: "Whatever the election results of the past decades may seem to indicate—or the Gallup Poll proclaim—the Republican party has represented a real or potential majority of the electorate. The battle for America must therefore first be fought to recapture the Republican party from those whose heart's desire seems to be to make it a pallid twin of the Democratic party. Once this battle has been won, the confrontation of Left and Right can take place. In 1940, 1944, 1948, 1952, 1956 and 1960, clear-cut distinctions were obscured. The voter seeking a Liberal candidate settled for the real article and not for the Republocratic imitation. The conservative voter knew that he was not being given a significant choice." [42]

The following year, the Republican party was "recaptured" and the voter was finally offered "a choice, not an echo," as Phyllis Schlafy put it in her best-selling paperback book in 1964.[43] In July, Barry Goldwater was the overwhelming choice of the Republican convention. In November, he led his party to its greatest Presidential defeat since 1912. Had Truman not won in 1948, the Republican party would have been spared the Goldwater disaster, as well as Eisenhower's successive triumphs.

The impact of the 1948 election has been felt in other ways as well. The election undermined a theory, widely favored by many politicians, that voters made up their minds soon after the party conventions and were not greatly influenced by the campaign. Truman's mounting appeal in the latter stages of the 1948 campaign, as well as postelection analysis of what happened to the undecided voters, certainly suggested that the campaign proper was far more than an unavoidable ritual. It may well have been decisive.

The 1948 election also demonstrated that it was a mistake to take a static view of the way an intra-party coalition works. The belief that Truman was in large part doomed because of the defection of the Dixiecrats and the Wallaceites was based on a simple arithmetic calculation rather than on an understanding of the dynamics of such a coalition. As Lubell has pointed out, the defection of one or two elements in a coalition could result in a countervailing accretion of support elsewhere along the spectrum. Thus, Truman was more appealing to Negro and Catholic voters once he was deserted by the racists and the far left. Indeed, one can speculate

that had the Dixiecrat and Progressive party breakaways not occurred, Truman might have lost the election through defections to
Dewey on the part of other disaffected elements in the Democratic
party. But once the split-offs occurred, other restive elements in the
party had reason to reevaluate their loyalty, for their defection
under these circumstances could be interpreted as playing into the
hands of the Dixiecrats or the Progressives. This interlocking relationship is likely to persist as long as an American political party
remains a broad coalition, containing mutually antagonistic groups.

In the end, the most salutary consequence of 1948 was probably
a renewed awareness of the contingent quality of events, of the
unpredictability of both leadership in a democracy and of the
choices that voters make in the privacy of the polling booth. Not
for a long time afterward were politicians likely to take the American voter for granted.

# Notes

Texts of President Truman's major speeches, whistle-stop talks, legislative messages, and other statements, as well as transcripts of his press conferences, are published in full in the annual volumes of the *Public Papers of the Presidents of the United States,* issued by the Government Printing Office. I have not thought it necessary to give specific page citations to these volumes, inasmuch as the material is arranged chronologically and it is easy to locate an item once the date is known. The relevant dates are provided in my text or notes. I have followed the same procedure with Governor Dewey's principal campaign addresses, which are published in the *Public Papers of Governor Thomas E. Dewey— 1948.* This volume, however, does not include his whistle-stop talks, which survive in news accounts.

## CHAPTER 1

1. Interview with Donald S. Dawson on December 28, 1965.
2. Interview with Senator Paul Douglas on March 30, 1966.
3. *New York Times,* June 21, 1948.
4. *Washington Post,* July 7, 1948.
5. *Ibid.,* July 13, 1948.
6. *The New Yorker,* October 9, 1948.
7. *Saturday Evening Post,* October 30, 1948.
8. *New York Herald-Tribune,* September 9, 1948.
9. *Life,* November 1, 1948.
10. *Ibid.*
11. New York *Daily Mirror,* November 3, 1948.
12. *New York Herald-Tribune,* November 3, 1948.
13. Detroit *Free-Press,* November 3, 1948.

## CHAPTER 2

1. Interview with Clark M. Clifford on September 14, 1965.
2. *New York Times,* November 7, 1946.

3. *Christian Science Monitor*, December 12, 1946.
4. Harry S. Truman, *Memoirs* (Garden City, N.Y., 1955) I, 186.
5. The visit to Caruthersville is described in Cabell Phillips, *The Truman Presidency* (New York, 1966) p. 141. Phillips provided the Folliard quotation.
6. *New York Times*, September 13, 1946.
7. James S. Byrnes, *Speaking Frankly* (New York, 1947) pp. 239–243.
8. *New York Times*, September 14, 1946.
9. *Ibid.*, September 15, 1946.
10. Byrnes, *Speaking Frankly*, p. 240.
11. Leigh White, "Truman's One-Man Brain Trust," *Saturday Evening Post*, October 4, 1947, and cover story on Clark Clifford, *Time*, March 15, 1948.
12. New York *World-Telegram*, July 14, 1947.
13. Interview with Clifford, September 22, 1965.
14. Phillips, *Truman Presidency*, p. 163.
15. *Ibid.*, p. 164.
16. The biographical data about Clifford from interviews with him on September 14 and 22, 1965.
17. Leigh White article, *Saturday Evening Post*, October 4, 1947, and *Time*, March 15, 1948.
18. *Ibid.*
19. Interview with Clifford, September 29, 1965.
20. A copy of the memorandum, dated November 19, 1947, is in Clifford's files in his Washington law office, where I consulted it.
21. The information on Truman's reaction to the memorandum is derived from an interview with Clifford on September 29, 1965.

## CHAPTER 3

1. John Kord Lagemann, "Governor Dewey," *Collier's*, May 1, 1948.
2. Interview with Elliott V. Bell on December 8, 1965.
3. Interview with Paul E. Lockwood on November 10, 1965.
4. *Time*, November 17, 1947.
5. *Newsweek*, July 21, 1947, has an amusing account of Dewey's "non-political" trip.
6. *Time*, September 22, 1947.
7. Richard H. Rovere, "Taft: Is This the Best We've Got?", *Harper's Magazine*, April 1948.
8. *Ibid.*
9. Cabell Phillips, "With Stassen on the Hustings," the *New York Times Magazine*, April 4, 1948.
10. *Time*, August 25, 1947.
11. New York *World-Telegram*, July 16, 1947.
12. New York *World-Telegram*, February 2, 1948.
13. *New York Times*, March 10, 1948.
14. Miles McMillin, "Wisconsin—Anybody's Guess," *The Nation*, April 3, 1948.
15. *Time*, April 8, 1948, and Phillips, *New York Times Magazine*, April 4, 1948.
16. *New York Times*, April 6, 1948.

17. *New York Herald-Tribune*, April 8, 1948.
18. The quoted reactions to the Wisconsin primary were published in the *Washington Post*, April 8, 1948.
19. *New York Times*, April 8, 1948.
20. *New York Herald-Tribune*, April 8, 1948. Dewey actually got ninety-six delegates in New York State.
21. *Newsweek*, April 5, 1948.
22. *Washington Post*, April 19, 1948.
23. New York *World-Telegram*, June 14, 1948.
24. *New York Times*, May 6, 1948.
25. *Ibid.*
26. *New York Times*, May 2, 1948.
27. Interview with Lockwood on December 3, 1965. He provided the details of his activities during the Oregon primary.
28. Details of Dewey's campaigning in Oregon in the *New York Times*, May 5, 6, and 10, 1948; the *New York Herald-Tribune*, May 16, 1948; and *Time*, May 24 and 31, 1948.
29. *Time*, May 31, 1948.
30. *New York Times*, May 20, 1948.
31. The incident is described in the *New York Herald-Tribune*, May 15, 1948, and *Time*, May 24, 1948.
32. *New York Times*, May 16, 1948.
33. Interview with Lockwood on December 3, 1965.
34. *New York Herald-Tribune*, May 18, 1948.
35. The full text of the Dewey-Stassen debate is published in the *Public Papers of Governor Thomas E. Dewey* for 1948 (Albany, New York, 1949) pp. 620–632.
36. Interview with Bell on November 23, 1965.

## CHAPTER 4

1. From notes which George M. Elsey wrote, dated August 1947, after his conversation with Clifford. Elsey frequently recorded the details of important conferences, for use in a journal which he never wrote. The memorandum is in Elsey's private papers, in his possession, in Washington, D.C.
2. Interview with Elsey on September 16, 1965.
3. *New York Times*, January 8, 1948.
4. Republican reactions in *New York Herald-Tribune*, January 8, 1948, and *Time*, January 19, 1948.
5. *New York Herald-Tribune*, January 8, 1948.
6. *PM*, January 8, 1948.
7. Interview with Elsey on September 16, 1965.
8. Memorandum to Truman by Charles S. Murphy, January 12, 1948, in Elsey Papers.
9. *New York Times*, February 8, 1948.
10. An account of the incident is in the *New York Herald-Tribune*, February 20, 1948.
11. *New York Herald-Tribune*, February 20, 1948, describes the events of the dinner.
12. Jack Redding, *Inside the Democratic Party* (Indianapolis and New

York, 1958) pp. 135–137 provides the details of McGrath's meeting with the southern governors. McGrath confirmed Redding's account in an interview on November 16, 1965.

13. *New York Times*, February 24, 1948.
14. Handwritten memorandum by George M. Elsey, dated February 4, 1948, in Elsey Papers.
15. Elsey Papers.
16. *Time*, March 1, 1948; and Karl M. Schmidt, *Henry Wallace: Quixotic Crusade 1948* (Syracuse, N.Y., 1960) pp. 67–71, for details of the Bronx by-election.
17. Ernest Lindley, "Competition in Blunders," *Newsweeks*, February 9, 1948, was typical of the comment.
18. *Ibid.*
19. *New York Times*, January 10, 1948.
20. *Ibid.*, January 12, 1948.
21. Graham's testimony in *New York Times*, January 14 and 15, 1948, and *Time*, January 26, 1948.
22. *New York Times*, January 14, 1948.
23. As quoted in *Time*, January 26, 1948.
24. Lindley, *Newsweek*, February 9, 1948.
25. Interview with McGrath on November 16, 1965.
26. *Time*, March 29, 1948.
27. *The Nation*, March 27, 1948.
28. *Time*, March 29, 1948.
29. Truman, *Memoirs*, II, 162.
30. Frank Gervasi, "Truman's Troubles," *Collier's*, July 3, 1948.
31. *Time*, April 19, 1948.
32. *Washington Post*, June 11, 1948.
33. Clifton Brock, *Americans for Democratic Action* (Washington, D.C., 1962) p. 88.
34. *Time*, March 15, 1948. The magazine appeared on the newsstands a few days before the date of issue.
35. *The Nation*, March 13, 1948.
36. *PM*, March 29, 1948.
37. *Ibid.*
38. *New York Times*, March 25, 1948.
39. *Ibid.*, March 26, 1948.
40. *Time*, April 26, 1948.
41. *Ibid.*, April 19, 1948.
42. Truman, *Memoirs*, II, p. 179.
43. In folder labeled "Speech—April 17, 1948," Files of Charles S. Murphy, Box 1, Truman Library.
44. Transcript of Truman's extemporaneous remarks before the ASNE are in the same folder, referred to in Note 43.
45. Memorandum written by George Elsey, dated May 3, 1948, in Elsey Papers.
46. Unsigned memorandum, which Elsey recognizes as his handiwork, in Murphy Files, Box 1, folder labeled "Speech—May 6, 1948," Truman Library.
47. *New York Times*, May 15, 1948.
48. Truman, *Memoirs*, II, 178.

49. The account of how Truman was invited to Berkeley is drawn from an interview with Oscar L. Chapman on September 15, 1965, and from a memorandum written by Chapman, dated February 17, 1948, which is in the Chapman Papers, Box 85, Truman Library.
50. Interviews with George Elsey on September 16, 1965, and with Charles S. Murphy on September 22, 1965.
51. Interview with Elsey on September 16, 1965.
52. Interview with William L. Batt, Jr., on September 17, 1965.
53. Interview with Murphy on September 22, 1965.
54. Interview with Chapman on September 15, 1965.
55. The description of the train is drawn from the *Washington Post*, June 4, 1948, and the Kansas City *Star*, June 6, 1948.
56. *Washington Post,* June 4, 1948.
57. *Washington Post*, June 5, 1948, and the *New York Herald-Tribune*, June 5, 1948.
58. *Time*, June 14, 1948.
59. *New York Times*, June 6, 1948, has a good account of Truman's participation in the parade. Another in *New York Herald-Tribune*, June 6.
60. *New York Post*, June 7, 1948.
61. *Time*, June 14, 1948.
62. New York *World-Telegram*, June 8, 1948.
63. The airport incident is described in the *Washington Post*, June 9, 1948, and in *Time*, June 21, 1948.
64. On June 7, 1948.
65. *New York Times*, June 7, 1948.
66. On June 6, 1948.
67. Memorandum by Elsey to Clifford, with hand-written annotations by Elsey, June 14, 1948, in Elsey Papers.
68. New York *Sun*, June 9, 1948.
69. The incident is covered in *Time*, June 28, 1948, and in Robert J. Donovan, "Presidential Reporter," *The Washington Spectator*, July 1952.
70. *New York Herald-Tribune*, June 10, 1948.
71. *Ibid.*, June 11, 1948.
72. *Time*, June 28, 1948.
73. *Christian Science Monitor*, June 16, 1948.
74. *New York Times*, June 10, 1948.
75. *Ibid.*, June 11, 1948.
76. *New York Herald-Tribune*, June 13, 1948.
77. *Time*, June 21, 1948.
78. *New York Times*, June 15, 1948, and *Washington Post*, June 15, 1948.
79. *New York Herald-Tribune*, June 19, 1948.

## CHAPTER 5

1. *New York Times*, June 21, 1948, and *New York Herald-Tribune*, June 20, 1948.
2. *New York Times*, June 20, 1948.
3. *Ibid.*
4. *Ibid.*
5. *Ibid.*, June 21, 1948.

6. *New York Times,* June 25, 1948, and *Time,* July 5, 1948.
7. *New York Times,* June 20, 1948.
8. *Ibid.,* June 23, 1948.
9. *Washington Post,* June 21, 1948.
10. For description of convention arrangements, *New York Herald-Tribune,* June 13, 1948.
11. Details of candidates' headquarters from *New York Times,* June 21, 1948, and *New York Herald-Tribune,* June 20 and 21, 1948.
12. Details of Taft press conference from *Washington Post,* June 21, 1948.
13. Details of Dewey press conference, *Washington Post,* June 21, 1948, and *New York Herald-Tribune,* June 21, 1948.
14. *New York Times,* June 22, 1948.
15. *New York Times,* June 23, 1948, and *Christian Science Monitor,* June 24, 1948, for the response to Hoover.
16. For the wooing of delegate Gillespie, *Time,* July 5, 1948.
17. For the Martin *démarche, New York Times,* June 23, 1948.
18. For the Dewey press conference, *New York Times,* June 23, 1948, and *Time,* July 5, 1948.
19. For the Stassen press conference, *New York Times,* June 23, 1948.
20. For the Halleck, Driscoll, Bradford, and Kem announcements, *New York Times,* June 24, 1948, and *New York Herald-Tribune,* June 24, 1948.
21. Interview with Charles A. Halleck on January 12, 1966.
22. Dewey not only made this disavowal in his Tuesday press conference but also in his acceptance speech.
23. Interview with Halleck on January 12, 1966.
24. *Ibid.*
25. My source is someone in an excellent position to know of Dewey's private denials.
26. Interview with Brownell on June 3, 1966.
27. Interview with Edwin F. Jaeckle on May 9, 1966.
28. *New York Herald-Tribune,* June 24, 1948.
29. The meeting is covered in the *New York Herald-Tribune,* June 24, 1948, and *Time,* July 5, 1948.
30. The morning meeting and the chase are covered in the *New York Herald-Tribune,* June 24, 1948.
31. Story by James Reston, *New York Times,* June 24, 1948.
32. *New York Herald-Tribune,* June 24, 1948.
33. For the details involving the Martin speech, *New York Post,* June 25, 1948, and *Time,* July 5, 1948.
34. For the floor demonstrations and the balloting, *New York Times,* June 25, 1948; *New York Herald-Tribune,* June 25, 1948; and *Time,* July 5, 1948.
35. Interview with Jaeckle on May 9, 1966.
36. For Taft and Brown remarks, *New York Times,* June 25, 1948, and *New York Herald-Tribune,* June 25, 1948.
37. *Newsweek,* July 5, 1948.
38. For Dewey's movements, *New York Times,* June 25, 1948.
39. My source is someone in an excellent position to know of Dewey's dismay.

40. *New York Times*, June 25, 1948, and *New York Herald-Tribune*, June 25, 1948.
41. My source was a participant in the meeting who insists on remaining anonymous.
42. For Dewey's conversations with Warren, *New York Times*, June 25, 1948.
43. *Ibid.*
44. *Time*, July 5, 1948.

# CHAPTER 6

1. New York *World-Telegram*, July 9, 1948.
2. For the convention atmosphere, *New York Times*, July 13, 1948, and *Time*, July 18, 1948.
3. *New York Times*, July 3, 1948.
4. For the reactions of Eisenhower's supporters, *Christian Science Monitor*, July 7, 1948; *New York Times*, July 9 and 10, 1948; and New York *Daily Mirror*, July 9, 1948.
5. *New York Times*, July 7, 1948.
6. *Ibid.*, July 10, 1948.
7. *New York Herald-Tribune*, July 10, 1948.
8. *New York Times*, July 10, 1948.
9. *Ibid.*, July 11, 1948.
10. *Ibid.*, July 10, 1948.
11. *New York Herald-Tribune*, July 12, 1948.
12. *New York Times*, July 12, 1948; *New York Post*, July 12, 1948, and New York *World-Telegram*, July 12, 1948.
13. *New York Herald-Tribune*, July 14, 1948.
14. For the demonstration in behalf of Barkley, *New York Times*, July 13, 1948, and New York *Sun*, July 13, 1948.
15. Interview with Clifford on October 6, 1965.
16. Truman, *Memoirs*, II, 190.
17. Interview with Clifford on October 6, 1965.
18. Truman, *Memoirs*, II, 190.
19. *Ibid.*, pp. 190–191.
20. Alben Barkley, *That Reminds Me* (Garden City, N. Y., 1954) p. 202.
21. Felix Belair story in *New York Times*, July 13, 1948.
22. *Ibid.*
23. Brock, *Americans for Democratic Action*, p. 96.
24. Interview with Joseph L. Rauh, Jr., on October 1, 1965.
25. Interview with George Elsey on November 15, 1965.
26. *New York Times*, July 12, 1948.
27. Winthrop Griffith, *Humphrey: A Candid Biography* (New York, 1965) pp. 151–152.
28. Interviews with Rauh on October 1, 1965.
29. For the debate on the credentials-committee report, *New York Times*, July 14, 1948, and *Time*, July 26, 1948.
30. Interview with John Shelley on October 13, 1965.
31. Griffith, *Humphrey*, pp. 152–153.
32. Interviews with Rauh on October 1, 1965, with Andrew Biemiller

on November 15, 1965, and with Shelley on October 13, 1965.

33. Griffith, *Humphrey*, pp. 153–154, has a good description of Humphrey's long night of pondering. It accords with what Rauh and Biemiller told me.

34. Griffith, *Humphrey*, p. 154. In an interview on July 19, 1966, Humphrey told me that he had talked at length with Mrs. Anderson, "a very close friend and one I've respected a great deal," but could not recall this specific contribution to his decision. He confirmed that he had taken considerable time to make up his mind.

35. The details of the encounter with Rayburn were related to me by Biemiller in the interview on November 15, 1965.

36. Interview with Rauh on October 1, 1965.

37. *Ibid.*

38. The details of Flynn's intervention came from Biemiller in the interview on November 15, 1965.

39. Griffith, *Humphrey*, p. 159.

40. *Time*, July 26, 1948.

41. Truman, *Memoirs*, II, 182.

42. Telephone interview with Clifford on June 13, 1967.

43. *New York Times*, July 15, 1948.

44. For details of the southern walkout, *New York Times*, July 15, 1948; *New York Herald-Tribune*, July 15, 1948; and *Time*, July 26, 1948.

45. *New York Herald-Tribune*, July 15, 1948.

46. Truman's long wait is described in *New York Times* and *New York Herald-Tribune* for July 15, 1948, and *Time*, July 26, 1948.

47. *Time*, July 26, 1948, has a good description of the pigeon incident.

48. A copy of the outline of Truman's acceptance speech is in the Papers of Charles G. Ross, Box 7, folder labeled "Speech Material," Truman Library.

49. *Time*, July 26, 1948.

50. *New York Times*, July 16, 1948.

51. *Ibid.*

52. *Ibid.*, July 19, 1948.

53. *New York Herald-Tribune*, July 27, 1948.

54. A copy of the Thurmond speech, together with his exchange of correspondence with Truman, is in the Truman Papers, P.P.F. 2873, Truman Library.

55. *Time*, July 26, 1948.

56. Scott, Vandenberg, and Brooks quotations in *New York Times*, July 16, 1948.

57. *Time*, July 26, 1948.

58. R. Alton Lee, *Truman and Taft-Hartley* (Lexington, Ky., 1966) p. 121.

59. Margaret L. Coit, *Mr. Baruch* (Boston, 1957) p. 625.

60. Telephone interview with Rosenman on April 21, 1967.

61. Interview with William L. Batt, Jr., on September 17, 1965.

62. Interview with Clifford on September 22, 1965.

63. Interview with Elsey on November 15, 1965.

64. Rosenman Papers, 1947–49, folder labeled "Campaign 1948—HST Acceptance Speech," Truman Library.

65. Telephone interview with Batt on April 19, 1967.
66. Telephone interview with Rosenman on April 21, 1967.
67. Interview with Clifford on September 22, 1965.
68. *New York Times*, July 21, 1948.
69. The account of Brownell's activities in regard to the special session comes from an interview with him on June 3, 1966.
70. Interview with Scott on March 31, 1966.
71. Note by George Elsey on fifth draft of speech, Elsey Papers, National Archives.

## CHAPTER 7

1. Luther A. Huston in the *New York Times*, July 24, 1948.
2. *Ibid.*
3. *New York Herald-Tribune*, July 26, 1948.
4. *New Republic*, December 4, 1965.
5. *Ibid.*
6. *PM*, December 30, 1946.
7. Brock, *Americans for Democratic Action*, p. 51.
8. Curtis D. MacDougall, *Gideon's Army* (New York, 1965) I, 154–155, 157, for the Wallace quotations and the estimate of his audience.
9. *Ibid.*, p. 156.
10. *Ibid.*, p. 158.
11. *Ibid.*, p. 163.
12. *Ibid.*, p. 199.
13. *New York Times*, May 27, 1946.
14. MacDougall, I, 224 *et seq.*
15. New York *World-Telegram*, January 26, 1948.
16. *PM*, May 18, 1948.
17. *Ibid.*, December 30, 1946.
18. Harry Winston, "For a Fighting Party Rooted Among the Industrial Workers!", in *Political Affairs*, XXVII (September 1948) p. 838, as cited in David Shannon, *The Decline of American Communism* (New York, 1959) p. 97.
19. Congress of Industrial Organizations, *Hearings Before the Committee to Investigate Charges Against the International Longshoremen's and Warehousemen's Union* (transcript), May 17, 18, and 19, 1950, Washington, D.C., pp. 66, 67, 99, as cited in Max Kampelman, *The Communist Party vs. the C.I.O.: A Study in Power Politics* (New York, 1957) pp. 144–145, 147.
20. *Ibid.*, p. 74.
21. *New York Times*, January 23, 1948.
22. *New York Post*, December 17, 1947.
23. *PM*, December 18, 1947.
24. MacDougall, *Gideon's Army*, I, 287.
25. *PM*, December 18, 1947.
26. *Ibid.*, December 23, 1947.
27. *Ibid.*, January 17, 1948.
28. *New York Herald-Tribune*, December 18, 1947.
29. *The Nation*, December 27, 1947.
30. *New York Times*, January 25, 1948.

31. Kampelman, *Communist Party vs. C.I.O.*, p. 141.
32. *New York Times*, April 29, 1948.
33. *Washington Post*, May 2, 1948.
34. *New York Post*, June 4, 1948.
35. "Washington Memo," *New York Post*, April 6, 1948. The article is un-
    signed, but I have established that it was by Wechsler, who cov-
    ered the entire Wallace campaign of 1948 for the *Post*.
36. *New York Herald-Tribune*, March 9, 1948.
37. *New York Times*, February 25, 1948.
38. *Ibid.*, February 28, 1948.
39. *Ibid.*, March 16, 1948.
40. *Ibid.*, March 18, 1948.
41. *Ibid.*, March 16, 1948.
42. *New York Post*, May 25, 1948.
43. *Ibid.*
44. New York *World-Telegram*, July 18, 1948.
45. *New York Times*, July 24, 1948, for Wallace press conference.
46. *Ibid.*, July 23, 1948, for Taylor press conference.
47. *New York Times*, September 13, 1946.
48. *Ibid.*, July 28, 1948, for comparison of the two platforms.
49. Interview with Rexford G. Tugwell on July 11, 1966.
50. *New York Times*, August 28, 1950.
51. *Ibid.*, August 12, 1950.
52. Interview with Tugwell on July 11, 1966.
53. *New York Times*, July 26, 1948. MacDougall, *Gideon's Army*, II, 580–
    581, covers the Macedonia issue in detail.
54. MacDougall, *Gideon's Army*, II, 571–576, has the fullest account of the
    debate over the Vermont resolution.
55. *Time*, August 9, 1948, and MacDougall, *Gideon's Army*, II, 506.

## CHAPTER 8

1. *New York Herald-Tribune*, July 22, 1948.
2. *New York Times*, July 24, 1948.
3. Interview with Brownell on June 3, 1966.
4. Interview with Scott on March 31, 1966.
5. Jules Abels, *Out of the Jaws of Victory* (New York, 1959) p. 142.
6. The source is someone well informed about these nightly conversations.
7. Interview with Elliott V. Bell on November 23, 1965.
8. New York *World-Telegram*, August 2, 1948.
9. *New York Herald-Tribune*, August 12, 1948.
10. Interview with Bell on November 23, 1965.
11. *Ibid.*
12. Interview with Paul E. Lockwood on November 9, 1965.
13. *Ibid.*
14. Interview with Bell on November 23, 1965.
15. *Washington Post*, August 4, 1948.
16. *New York Times*, July 15, 1948; New York *Sun*, August 12, 1948; and
    *New York Herald-Tribune*, August 13, 1948.
17. Interview with Scott on March 31, 1966.
18. *Ibid.*

19. Detail on the Dewey speechwriting process came from interviews with Bell on December 8, 1965, and with Merlyn S. Pitzele on November 22, 1965.
20. Interview with Clark M. Clifford on September 22, 1965.
21. Interview with Elsey on September 16, 1965, and with Batt on September 17, 1965.
22. Biographical data from interview with Elsey on September 16, 1965.
23. Charles S. Murphy Files, Box 1, Truman Library.
24. Interview with Clifford on September 22, 1965.
25. Interview with Charles S. Murphy on September 22, 1965.
26. Interview with Clifford on September 22, 1965.
27. Interview with Elsey on September 16, 1965.
28. Interview with Clifford on September 22, 1965.
29. Interview with Murphy on September 22, 1965.
30. Interviews with Albert Z. Carr on May 5, 1966, and with David Noyes on July 6, 1966.
31. J. Howard McGrath Papers, Box 64, folder labeled "Redding, Jack," Truman Library.
32. *Ibid.*
33. Interview with J. Howard McGrath on November 16, 1965.
34. Truman Papers, OF 200-2-H, Truman Library.
35. Interview with Oscar L. Chapman on September 22, 1965.
36. Crowd estimates from *New York Times*, September 7, 1948.
37. *New York Times*, September 2, 1948.

## CHAPTER 9

1. *New York Times*, September 18, 1948.
2. New York *World-Telegram*, September 18, 1948.
3. Interviews with Carr on May 5, 1966; with Noyes on July 6, 1966; with Clifford on September 14, 1965, and over the telephone on June 13, 1967.
4. *Washington Post*, September 20, 1948.
5. *New York Times*, September 3, 1948.
6. *New York Herald-Tribune*, September 4, 1948.
7. Interview with W. McNeil Lowry on May 9, 1966; also E. W. Kenworthy, "Corn Cribs and Ballot Boxes," *The Progressive*, January 1949.
8. Interview with Lowry on May 9, 1966.
9. In a telephone interview on June 13, 1967, Clark Clifford confirmed the importance of Lowry's researches to the Democratic campaign strategy.
10. On September 22.
11. On September 23.
12. On September 23.
13. On September 24.
14. On September 21.
15. On September 21.
16. On September 20.
17. Memorandum dated September 24, 1948, to Clark Clifford from William L. Batt, Jr. Letter dated September 25, 1948, from George M. Elsey to Batt. Both in Elsey Papers.
18. On September 20.

19. On September 21.

20. On October 1.

21. *New York Herald-Tribune*, October 2, 1948.

22. New York *World-Telegram*, September 22, 1948.

23. *The New Yorker*, October 9, 1948.

24. Kansas City *Star*, September 24, 1948; *New York Times*, September 26, 1948; and Richard H. Rovere, "Letter From a Campaign Train," *The New Yorker*, October 16, 1948.

25. *New York Times*, September 20, 1948.

26. *New York Herald-Tribune*, September 25, 1948; Cleveland *Plain-Dealer*, September 26, 1948; and *The New Yorker*, October 16, 1948, for details about the Dewey train.

27. Details on the Albuquerque schedule from "Washington Memo," *New York Post*, September 20, 1948.

28. Bert Andrews story, *New York Herald-Tribune*, September 25, 1948.

29. *Time*, September 27, 1948.

30. Albuquerque speech, September 22.

31. *Newsweek*, October 4, 1948.

32. Interview with Merlyn S. Pitzele on November 22, 1965.

33. New York *World-Telegram*, September 24, 1948, and *Time*, October 4, 1948, on the Dewey applause lines.

34. *New York Times* and the *New York Herald-Tribune* for September 25, 1948, and *Time*, October 4, 1948.

35. *New York Times*, September 26, 1948.

36. Interview with Scott on March 31, 1966.

37. In speech in Roseville, California, on September 22.

38. *New York Times*, September 24, 1948.

39. *Ibid.*, September 25, 1948, story by Leo Egan.

40. *Ibid.*, September 25, 1948, story by W. H. Lawrence.

41. For the Uvalde visit, *Washington Post* and *New York Herald-Tribune* for September 27, 1948.

42. On September 27.

43. *New York Times* and *New York Herald-Tribune* for September 28, 1948.

44. Interview with Dawson on December 28, 1965.

45. On September 27.

46. On September 28.

47. *New York Times* and *New York Herald-Tribune* for September 29, 1948.

48. Memorandum dated September 14, 1948, to Clark Clifford from William L. Batt, Jr., in Philleo Nash Files, Box 29, "Campaign Folder—1948," Truman Library.

49. *New York Times*, October 1, 1948.

50. On October 1.

51. *Time*, October 11, 1948.

52. *New York Herald-Tribune*, October 3, 1948.

53. Interview with Clifford on September 22, 1965.

54. New York *World-Telegram*, September 24, 1948.

55. *Time*, October 11, 1948.

56. On September 27.

57. On September 29.

58. Interview with Bell on November 23, 1965.
59. *New York Times*, October 1, 1948, and New York *Daily Mirror*, October 2, 1948.
60. Interview with Bell on November 23, 1965.
61. *New York Times*, October 3, 1948.
62. *New York Herald-Tribune*, October 3, 1948.
63. For the evaluation of the Dewey tour, *New York Times* and *New York Herald-Tribune*, October 4, 1948.
64. For Barkley's campaign efforts, William R. Mofield, *The Speaking Role of Alben Barkley in the Campaign of 1948*, unpublished doctoral dissertation, Southern Illinois University, 1964, p. 169; *New York Times*, September 22, 1948; and *Time*, October 4, 1948.
65. For the Warren tour, *Time*, September 27, 1948.
66. San Francisco *Chronicle*, October 2, 1948.
67. *Ibid.*, October 6, 1948.
68. *Ibid.*, October 7, 1948.
69. *Ibid.*, October 8, 1948.

## CHAPTER 10

1. For crowd scenes and crowd estimates, *New York Times*, October 8 and 9, 1948; *New York Herald-Tribune*, October 7, 1948; and *Time* and *Newsweek* for October 18, 1948.
2. On October 6.
3. On October 6.
4. On October 8.
5. *Time*, October 18, 1948.
6. Jonathan Daniels, *The Man of Independence* (Philadelphia, 1950) pp. 360–361. Also, interview with Carr on May 5, 1966, and with Noyes on July 6, 1966.
7. Truman, *Memoirs*, II, 215.
8. *Ibid.*, pp. 213–214.
9. *Newsweek*, October 18, 1948, for the account of how the Vinson mission became public.
10. *Time*, October 18, 1948.
11. *New York Times*, October 11, 1948.
12. *Ibid.*
13. Interview with Carr on May 5, 1966.
14. Interview with James C. Hagerty on December 2, 1965.
15. *Ibid.*
16. *New York Times*, October 12, 1948.
17. Interview with Hagerty on December 2, 1965.
18. Kansas City *Star*, October 13, 1948.
19. *Time* and *Newsweek* for October 25, 1948.
20. *Newsweek*, October 25, 1948.
21. My source is someone well acquainted with the Dewey-Roberts conversation and Dewey's reaction to it.
22. Interview with Harold E. Keller on November 12, 1965.
23. Interview with Bell on November 23, 1965.
24. Interview with Herbert Brownell on June 3, 1966.

25. *New York Times*, October 13, 1948.
26. *Ibid.*, October 14, 1948.
27. *Ibid.*, October 16, 1948.
28. On October 15.
29. *New York Times*, October 13, 1948.
30. On October 15.
31. For crowd estimates, *New York Times*, October 12, 1948, and *Newsweek*, October 25, 1948.
32. Truman, *Memoirs*, II, 210.
33. New York *World-Telegram*, October 15, 1948.
34. Interview with Elsey on September 16, 1965.
35. Hugh Morrow, "CIO's Political Hotshot," *Saturday Evening Post*, March 5, 1949.
36. Delbert D. Arnold, *The C.I.O.'s Role in American Politics*, unpublished doctoral dissertation, University of Maryland, 1952, pp. 305–306.
37. *Newsweek*, October 24, 1948.
38. Morton H. Leeds, *The American Federation of Labor in National Politics, 1938–1948*, unpublished doctoral dissertation, Graduate Faculty of Political and Social Science of the New School for Social Research, January 1950, p. 150.
39. Morrow article, *Saturday Evening Post*, March 5, 1949.
40. *New York Herald-Tribune*, August 25, 1948, and *Daily Worker*, August 26, 1948.
41. *New York Post*, August 29, 1948.
42. Interview with Tugwell on July 11, 1966.
43. *New York Post*, August 20, 1948.
44. *Ibid.*, August 27, 1948.
45. For Wallace's southern tour, *New York Herald-Tribune* for August 30 and 31, 1948; *New York Times* for August 31 and September 1, 1948; and *Time*, September 13, 1948.
46. *Time*, September 13, 1948.
47. *New York Times* and *New York Herald-Tribune* for September 11, 1948.
48. *New York Times*, September 22, 1948.
49. *Ibid.*, October 1, 1948.
50. *Newsweek*, October 11, 1948.
51. Typical was Mark Sullivan's column in the *New York Herald-Tribune*, October 6, 1948.
52. *New York Times*, October 18, 1948, and *Newsweek*, October 18, 1948.
53. *Washington Post*, October 22, 1948.
54. *New York Post*, September 17, 1948.
55. *Ibid.*, September 28, 1948.
56. *New York Times*, October 27, 1948.
57. *Ibid.*, November 1, 1948.
58. *Ibid.*, October 27, 1948.
59. *Ibid.*, October 7, 1948.
60. Interview with Thurmond on January 18, 1966.
61. *Ibid.*
62. *New York Times*, October 7, 1948.
63. *Newsweek*, October 25, 1948.

64. *New York Times*, September 21, 1948.
65. *Saturday Evening Post*, October 23, 1948.
66. Column by Marquis Childs, *Washington Post*, October 14, 1948.
67. *New York Herald-Tribune*, July 29, 1948.
68. For crowd description, *New York Times*, October 26, 1948.
69. Interviews with Carr on May 5, 1966, and with Noyes on July 6, 1966.
70. Interview with Noyes on July 6, 1966.
71. My source is someone in an excellent position to recall Dewey's reaction to Truman's speech.
72. *New York Times*, October 30, 1948.
73. *Ibid.*
74. Interview with Alex Rose on March 25, 1966.
75. Interview with Donald Dawson on December 28, 1965.
76. Interview with Charles S. Murphy on September 22, 1965.
77. Charles G. Ross, "How Truman Did It," *Collier's*, December 25, 1948.
78. Interview with McGrath on November 16, 1965.
79. Interview with Clifford on September 22, 1965.
80. New York *World-Telegram*, November 2, 1948.
81. For Dewey's election day and night, *New York Times* and *New York Herald-Tribune*, November 3, 1948, and *Time*, November 8, 1948. Interviews with Lockwood on November 9, 1965; with Bell on December 8, 1965; and with Hagerty on December 2, 1965.
82. *Washington Post,* November 3, 1948.
83. Truman, Memoirs, II, 220–221.
84. *Time*, November 8, 1948.
85. Text of Dewey's press conference in *Public Papers of Governor Thomas E. Dewey—1948* (Albany, N.Y., 1949) pp. 526–529.

## CHAPTER 11

1. For Truman's homecoming, *New York Times*, November 5, 1948; *New York Herald-Tribune*, November 4, 1948; and *Time*, November 15, 1948.
2. *New York Herald-Tribune*, November 5, 1948.
3. *Ibid.*, November 4, 1948.
4. *New York Times*, November 4, 1948.
5. New York *Star*, November 4, 1948.
6. *The Nation*, September 11, 1948.
7. *New York Times*, November 7, 1948.
8. *Ibid.*, November 4, 1948.
9. *Time*, November 15, 1948.
10. Frederick Mosteller, *et al.*, *The Pre-election Polls of 1948*, (New York, 1949).
11. The findings were analyzed in Angus Campbell and Robert L. Kahn, *The People Elect a President* (Ann Arbor, Michigan, 1952).
12. Mosteller, *Polls*, p. 301.
13. Campbell and Kahn, *People Elect a President*, p. 8.
14. Mosteller, *Polls*, p. 302.
15. Samuel Lubell, *The Future of American Politics* (New York, 1952) pp. 210–213.

16. *Ibid.*, pp. 209–210.
17. Samuel Lubell, "Who Really Elected Truman?", *Saturday Evening Post*, January 22, 1949.
18. Campbell and Kahn, *People Elect a President*, p. 37; Bernard R. Berelson, Paul F. Lazarsfeld, and William N. McPhee, *Voting* (Chicago, 1954) pp. 55–56.
19. Lubell, *Future of American Politics*, pp. 207–208.
20. *Ibid.*, p. 34.
21. *New York Times*, November 4, 1948.
22. Arthur Holcombe, *Our More Perfect Union* (Cambridge, Mass., 1950) p. 117.
23. Copy in author's possession.
24. Lubell, *Future of American Politics*, p. 160.
25. *Ibid.*, p. 161.
26. Campbell and Kahn, *People Elect a President*, p. 49.
27. *New York Herald-Tribune*, November 21, 1948.
28. *Ibid.*
29. As quoted in the *New York Times*, November 4, 1948.
30. *New York Herald-Tribune*, November 21, 1948.
31. *Ibid.*, November 4, 1948.
32. Lubell, *Future of American Politics*, pp. 30–31.
33. *Ibid.*, p. 34.
34. Samuel J. Eldersveld, "The Influence of Metropolitan Party Pluralities in Presidential Elections Since 1920: A Study of Twelve Key Cities," in *American Political Science Review*, XLIII, No. 6 (December 1949).
35. *New York Herald-Tribune*, November 5, 1948.
36. Arnold, *CIO's Role in American Politics*, pp. 341 and 344.
37. *New York Times*, November 4, 1948.
38. Richard H. Rovere, *Senator Joe McCarthy* (New York, 1959) pp. 122–123.
39. Marquis Childs, *Eisenhower: Captive Hero* (New York, 1958) p. 141.
40. Louis Harris, *Is There a Republican Majority?* (New York, 1954) pp. 126, 141, 147.
41. Harold Faber, ed., *The Road to the White House* (New York, 1965) p. 75.
42. Ralph de Toledano, *The Winning Side: The Case for Goldwater Republicanism* (New York, 1963) p. 22.
43. Phyllis Schlafy, *A Choice Not an Echo* (Alton, Illinois, 1964).

# Index

79
81
83
85
88